BUTLER

The Arguments of
the Philosophers

EDITOR: TED HONDERICH

Professor of Philosophy, University College, London

The purpose of this series is to provide a contemporary assessment and history of the entire course of philosophical thought. Each book constitutes a detailed, critical introduction to the work of a philosopher of major influence and significance.

Already published in the series

BUTLER

Terence Penelhum

Routledge & Kegan Paul
London, Boston and Henley

To Edith

First published in 1985
by Routledge & Kegan Paul plc

14 Leicester Square, London WC2H 7PH, England

9 Park Street, Boston, Mass. 02108, USA

Broadway House, Newtown Road,
Henley on Thames, Oxon RG9 1EN, England

Set in Linotron Garamond 10 on 12 pt
by Input Typesetting Ltd, London
and printed in Great Britain
by Billings & Sons

Library of Congress Cataloging in Publication Data

Penelhum, Terence, 1929–
Butler.
(The Arguments of the philosophers)
Bibliography: p.
Includes index.
1. Butler, Joseph, 1692–1752. I. Title. II Series.
B1363 Z7P46 1985   192   85–1943

British Library CIP Data also available

ISBN 0–7102–0599–6

Contents

Preface

Butler's writings are not voluminous, and he does not offer us a philosophical system. But he is generally regarded as among the very finest English moralists, and although his reputation in this respect has declined, he was for a long time considered to be a great philosophical theologian. In the course of his work in these spheres, he also produces some classic arguments in the philosophy of mind and action.

I try in this book to present his major doctrines and arguments, omitting purely theological material, and passing over wholly pastoral work, such as the *Six Sermons Preached on Public Occasions*. I have also had to leave aside the many interesting things he has to say on topics that are of real philosophical interest, but secondary to his central objectives: such as resentment, forgiveness, self-deception, and even freedom, since his comments on it are at the same time parenthetical and intertwined with detail of other matters. The book gives more total space to his philosophy of religion than to his ethics, partly because the literature on his ethics is far more extensive in the twentieth century, and also because the rehabilitation of his philosophy of religion, which I myself rank second in English only to that of Hume, requires a more elaborate sifting of his arguments. The greater space given to philosophy of religion is also partly the result of the fact that his well-known discussion of personal identity forms a part of it, although it is usually read and judged with no reference to this.

It has taken me much longer than I expected to write this book, and I would like to thank the publisher, and the series editor, Ted Honderich, for their patience. My wife, who has had to put up with the results of a preoccupation that has gone on much longer than I predicted, deserves much more than thanks, as always.

Much of the writing was done in a half-year sabbatical leave, spent in Cambridge, and a period of released time on a Killam Resident Fellowship at the University of Calgary. I am grateful to the University; to the Social Sciences and Humanities Research Council of Canada, who awarded me a Leave Fellowship; to the President and Fellows of Clare Hall, and the members of the Divinity Faculty at Cambridge, for providing their visitors with such a friendly and stimulating environment.

I am grateful to Béla Szabados for important ideas and suggestions.

Finally, my warm thanks to Rosanne Sullivan and Corinne Hergert for their prompt and accurate typing of the manuscript.

References and Abbreviations

Notes and references are at the end of the book, and full publication details of works cited are to be found in the Bibliography. The latter also contains works I have found valuable, even though they are not cited in my text.

References to Butler himself presented a problem. There appears, at present, to be no edition of the *Analogy* in print at all, although the Rolls *Sermons* are fairly easy to come by. Even these, however, often appear only in selections. Such selections sometimes include one or both of the two Dissertations appended originally to the *Analogy*, and not fully intelligible apart from it. Any serious study must therefore make use of earlier editions of Butler's works available in libraries. There are a large number of these, but the two standard ones are those by Gladstone (1897) and Bernard (1900). Gladstone is said to be easier to find than Bernard, but presents a serious disadvantage for references, in that he changes Butler's paragraphing in the interests of a supposed improvement in clarity. Both Gladstone and Bernard number the paragraphs, but Bernard merely prefixes numbers in square brackets to the paragraphs that Butler left us. Bernard also collates the texts of Butler's first and second editions, and his notes are still of real value to the reader. Other editions of Butler stay with the original paragraphing, so that a reference to Bernard's text by paragraph number makes it fairly easy to find a passage in one of these other editions.

I have accordingly incorporated most references to Butler himself into the text, in the following form. First, an abbreviation for the work cited: S for the Rolls *Sermons*, *An* for the *Analogy*, Diss I for the Dissertation 'Of Personal Identity' and Diss II for the Dissertation 'Of the Nature of Virtue'. Next, a high Roman numeral for the part of the *Analogy*, and a low Roman numeral for the chapter in the *Analogy* or the number of the Sermon. Finally, the paragraph is indicated by two numbers, with a stroke between; the first number is Bernard's, the second Gladstone's. For example, the reference *An* II ii 6/7 is to the paragraph numbered 6 by Bernard and 7 by Gladstone in Chapter ii of Part II of the *Analogy*. The abbreviation Pr stands for the Preface to the *Sermons*; Int stands for the Introduction to the *Analogy*, and Concl for the Conclusion. This method is a little cumbersome, but I hope it makes references reasonably easy for readers with different editions, in a way that page-number references to one edition would not.

Introduction

Butler's Life, Personality, and Objectives[1]

Joseph Butler was born at Wantage on 18 May 1692, the youngest of eight children. His father, a fairly well-to-do draper, was a Presbyterian, and wished Joseph to become a minister. His early education was in the local grammar school, but he was then sent by his father to a dissenting academy run by Mr Samuel Jones, first at Gloucester and later at Tewkesbury. He was still at the academy when he began a philosophical correspondence with Samuel Clarke, the moralist and theologian. The peaceable and respectful tone of Butler's queries, combined with the intellectual rigour with which he pursued them, impressed Clarke; and the latter's friendly response was undoubtedly part of the cause of the high regard Butler shows in several places for the work of a thinker whose methods are very different from his own.

Butler made a decision to join the established church, and when his father saw this decision was firm, he entered him as a commoner at Oriel College, Oxford, in 1714. Butler did not form a high opinion of his new intellectual environment, saying in one of his letters to Clarke[2] that 'we are obliged to mis-spend so much time here in attending frivolous lectures and unintelligible disputations, that I am quite tired out with such a disagreeable way of trifling', and that 'our people here never had any doubt in their lives concerning a received opinion'. He thought of moving to Cambridge, and Clarke recommended a tutor there, but nothing came of this.

At Oxford Butler made a friend of Edward Talbot, son of the Bishop of Salisbury. The Bishop continued to befriend him after his son's death in 1720. After graduating from Oxford, Butler, on the recommendation of Clarke and Talbot, was appointed Preacher at the Rolls Chapel. This does not seem to have brought him much money, and he still depended on family support, but it was at the Rolls Chapel that he preached the Sermons by which he is now best known, sermons in which he pleads the cause of moral virtue to a smart and sophisticated congregation. His

1

Fifteen Sermons Preached at the Rolls Chapel was first published in 1726; the second edition, with the important new Preface, was published in 1729.

In 1722 Bishop Talbot, now Bishop of Durham, presented Butler to the living of Haughton, near Darlington, and transferred him to the richer living in Stanhope in 1725. The income at Stanhope enabled him to live without family money, and he also resigned his Rolls preachership in 1726. He then lived for seven years in his country parish, and it was during this time that he prepared the *Analogy of Religion*. In 1733, however, Thomas Secker, a friend of his from Tewkesbury days who was later to become Archbishop of Canterbury, persuaded Lord Chancellor Talbot, brother of the late Edward, to appoint Butler to be his chaplain, and Secker's recommendation also drew Butler to the notice of Queen Caroline, the accomplished consort of George II and friend of Leibniz. Queen Caroline appointed Butler her Clerk of the Closet in 1736. Her main interest in him seems to have been to have him take part in regular evening gatherings of learned men, to discuss philosophical and theological topics. His mental and spirtual qualities so impressed her, however, that she had him administer the sacrament to her on her deathbed in 1737, and asked the King to advance him.

The *Analogy* was published in 1736, and went into a second edition the same year. It was better known in Butler's own day than the *Sermons*, and indeed the preference given to the latter is relatively recent.

The King followed his wife's request by making Butler Bishop of Bristol in 1738. Butler accepted this appointment with some reluctance, since he saw that to sustain the costs of the position he would have to retain the chaplaincy and the living of Stanhope. He was enabled to resign the latter in 1740, when he was named Dean of St Paul's. In 1746 he was made Clerk of the Closet to the King. We do not know whether there is any real basis to the story that he declined the archbishopric of Canterbury in 1747.

In 1750 he was offered the see of Durham, of which he took possession in 1751. This occasioned a famous remark of Horace Walpole that 'the Bishop of Durham had been wafted to that see in a cloud of metaphysics, and remained absorbed in it'. To see how unfair this comment was, it is enough to read Butler's *Charge Delivered to the Clergy* at the Primary Visitation of the Diocese of Durham, in 1751. Only a person of Butler's intellectual attainments could have written it, but it demonstrates a deep and detailed concern with the pastoral and ceremonial duties of the priesthood, and shows, as all Butler's writings do, the subordination of his theoretical concerns to the spiritual objectives which were foremost in his thinking throughout his life.

Butler was not destined to preside over the see of Durham for long. His health soon declined, and he went to Clifton, and then to Bath, but no recovery followed. He appears to have endured digestive disorders, high fevers, and exhaustion, and to have been near to unconsciousness in his last days. He died on 16 June 1752, and was buried in Bristol Cathedral.

Apart from his published works and a few letters, we have virtually none of Butler's writings, for he directed that his remaining papers and sermons be destroyed after his death. The request was typical of a private and retiring person, who spent a great deal of time in solitude (he never married) and preferred to do his thinking alone. One has the impression of a thinker who disliked the gladiatorial aspects of debate, was deeply suspicious of quick theoretical victories, and felt that both morality and religion were at real risk from those whose main concern was to score points. Although a man of the greatest eminence in his own time, Butler felt himself at odds with it in key respects. The church was in a period of spiritual laxity and worldliness, and, indeed Butler's own preferment was due to patronage; but he was a priest of unusual conscientiousness, who disliked the practice of multiple livings, and hesitated over accepting each of the bishoprics he was offered, for moral reasons. In the case of Durham, he risked the loss of the position by explicitly refusing to make, or even imply, a prior commitment to appoint a protégé of the Duke of Newcastle to a Durham vacancy.[3] He lived simply, and tended to spend all his money on the improvement of church buildings, and on charity. He seems to have been an indifferent money manager, much prone to impulsive giving. In a letter preserved in Bartlett's biography, it is said that at Stanhope he 'lived very retired, was very kind, and could not resist the importunities of common beggars, who, knowing his infirmity, pursued him so earnestly, as sometimes to drive him back into his house, as his only escape'.[4] Since we know he did not approve of indiscriminate almsgiving, there was an obvious personal conflict behind the point he makes in the Dissertation on Virtue, that conscience must sometimes win out over benevolence.[5] There is another story that, when solicited for a charitable donation in London, he asked his steward how much money he then had; he was told five hundred pounds, and then said, 'Five hundred pounds! what a shame for a Bishop to have so much! Give it away – give it to this gentleman, who has a good use for it!' The steward's thoughts are not recorded.

Other passages quoted in Bartlett describe Butler in later years thus: 'He was of a most reverend aspect; his face, thin and pale; but there was a divine placidness in his countenance which inspired veneration, and expressed the most benevolent mind. His white hair hung gracefully from his shoulders, and his whole figure was patriarchal.' 'In advanced years, and on the episcopal throne, he retained the same genuine modesty, and native sweetness of disposition, which had distinguished him in youth, and in retirement. During the ministerial performance of the sacred office, a divine animation seemed to pervade his whole manner, and lighted up his pale wan countenance, already marked with the progress of disease, like a torch glimmering in its socket, yet bright and useful to the last.'[6] His religious devotion can be felt even in the driest and most theoretical passages in his writings. But, in common with so many in his age, he had a horror of 'enthusiasm', that is, of undisciplined evangelical fervour. On this, we have a famous story recorded in John Wesley's diary, and reprinted in full in Gladstone's edition of Butler's works. Wesley's preaching in the diocese of Bristol drew unfavourable attention from Butler, who said to him, 'Sir, the pretending to extraordinary revelations and gifts of the Holy Ghost is a horrid thing, a very horrid thing.' Although Butler's writing is directed to religious doubters, it is vital for understanding him to recall that he thinks religious doubts are often based upon too great a confidence in our intellectual powers. It is equally important to notice that this story shows that Butler disapproved even more strongly of those within the church whose humility was threatened by a surfeit of certainty.

Newman said in a letter that Butler was 'the greatest name in the Anglican Church'. This was, and is, true. But the high regard in which his church has held him has not been good for his standing among his fellow philosophers and theologians. The *Analogy* was, for a long time, required reading for generations of intending divines, and much of the extensive but uninteresting literature about it consists of 'cribs' designed for their use. The ultimate incorporation into the establishment probably came when he was edited and defended by Gladstone. The inevitable reaction set in, and the *Analogy* now ranks as the greatest unread classic in philosophical theology. The Rolls *Sermons*, much less influential in the past, have been more fortunate, and Butler has acquired a secure place in the esteem, and indeed the affection, of English-speaking moral philosophers, including many, like C. D. Broad and Duncan-Jones, who in no way share his religious persuasion. Even here, however, there has been a tendency to present Butler to undergraduate students as Kant without tears, which is a gross distortion.

In what follows I shall be discussing only those parts of Butler's work that can properly be classed as philosophical. But it is impossible to understand them without bearing in mind one or two key features of all his writings. First and foremost, Butler writes as a Christian priest who sees the social and intellectual life of his time as presenting dangerous challenges to the faith he represents. Although a theorist of the highest quality when he chooses, he is not interested in theory for itself; indeed, he thinks such a concern is spiritually and morally questionable.[7] His purpose is always a practical one: to bring his hearers and readers to the acceptance, and above all to the *practice*, of 'virtue and religion'. This phrase is frequent, and significant. He sees secular morality not as something to be contrasted with the requirements of religion, but as a necessary part of them: morally speaking, the specific demands of the Christian revelation merely add additional duties, such as those of worship and sacramental participation, to requirements that all of us, Christian or not, can recognise, through conscience. The contrast between secular duty and Christian love, of which some present-day theologians have made so much, is quite alien to Butler, as to all his contemporaries. He believes morality can stand on its own feet without explicitly religious support, but he also sees the religious life as incorporating the demands of morality as everyone knows them. Hence it is not surprising that his approach in the *Sermons* and the *Analogy*, even though the former were preached to congregations and the latter was not, is at bottom identical.

This approach, once again, is practical. So Butler disregards theoretical issues that have no practical import – such as the question of whether the intuitions of conscience should be called rational or quasi-sensory. The claims of conscience on our conduct are unaffected by the view we take on this question. But he is intensely concerned with those theoretical questions which affect the moral decisions of the man of the world even though he may not fully realise it – such as the credentials of the selfish theory of human nature, which Butler regards as a dangerous obstacle to the practice of benevolence and virtue. He is also quite willing to argue from the positions of his opponents, if in so doing he can elicit agreement from them on the wisdom of following conscience or satisfying the demands of religion. Hence he spends a whole chapter in the *Analogy* trying to show that a determinist is not barred from recognising the morality of God's governance of the world; and in the *Sermons* he is willing to commend the claims of conscience to egoists by arguing for a much closer congruence between the claims of conscience and self-love than he really should. His purpose is reconciliation of a practical sort, not philosophical triumph, which has no interest for him. His main motive is the ultimate spiritual welfare of his readers, and there is never any doubt what course of life he thinks will lead to this. He is an *apologist*: an apologist for virtue in an age of moral laxity, and an apologist for Christianity in an age of indifference and scepticism. And those to whom he addresses his apologetic are people he sees as endangered by frivolity and by muddled theory. His arguments are designed above all to reach them and persuade them to change, not to refute their contentions, though he often does this.

His style reflects a decision on how they are best to be reached. He does not try to charm them, but to remove confusions and put together a case that they cannot reasonably reject. The 'cloud of metaphysics' is nowhere to be seen. Instead, there is a constant obsession with saying no more, and no less, than the point at hand requires, and a recurrent appeal to the native common sense of his readers, who will not, he thinks, ever be so confused by fashionable doctrine that they cannot be reminded of the basic lessons life teaches. For obsession with clarity, the only philosophical writer in English who seems to me comparable is G. E. Moore. Both are very successful stylists when judged by their purposes: neither disdains repetition, dryness or qualification if clarity requires them, and each is quite prepared to sacrifice the elegance of a Hume or a Russell if the price of elegance is ambiguity. The belief in the inherent wisdom of the common consciousness is also present in both, and each is eager to appeal to it when trying to push aside the self-deceiving constructions of philosophy. In Butler's case, the result is a large number of trenchant sayings which serve to remind you of what you now realise you thought all along: 'Everything is what it is, and not another thing'; 'Though a man hath the best eyes in the world, he cannot see any way but that which he turns them'; 'Many a man would have died, had it not been for the gout or a fever; yet it would be thought madness to assert, that sickness is a better or more perfect state than health; though the like, with regard to the moral world, has been asserted'; 'If to acquire knowledge were our proper end, we should indeed be but poorly provided: but if somewhat else be our business and duty, we may, notwithstanding our ignorance, be well enough furnished for it; and the observation of our ignorance may be of assistance to us in the discharge of it.'

In what follows, I have not sought to provide much comment on the details of the relationship between Butler and other thinkers; I have confined myself to evaluating Butler's own position, and to doing this in a manner which is appropriate to readers of our own time, in keeping with the intent of this series. It has been necessary to describe or quote the positions of others in two sets of cirumstances: first, when Butler is claiming to refute the specific arguments of identifiable figures, in particular Hobbes and Locke – in such instances he has to be judged against the positions he is attacking; second, when it is necessary to deal with the question of how far his position has become obsolete at a time when no one holds the views he makes his target. This has required a considerable amount of attention to the fact that the *Analogy* is directed to the stance of the deists; it is commonly alleged that since there are no deists now[8], the neglect of Butler's work is justified. I hope to prove that this view is mistaken, but to do so I must separate the obsolete from the contemporary. This task is far less necessary with the ethics, where his position can hardly be said to have dated at all.

PART ONE

THE ADVOCATE FOR VIRTUE

I

Moral Conduct and Human Nature

Butler's *Sermons* present us with many closely-connected doctrines and arguments. But these are not presented in a continuous or systematic form. As he says himself, modestly:

> It may be proper just to advise the reader, that he is not to look for any particular reason for the choice of the greatest part of these discourses; their being taken from many others, preached in the same place, through a course of eight years, being in great measure accidental. (*S* Pr 45/39)

One result of this is that many of the doctrines and arguments are undeveloped. Since the *Analogy of Religion*, by contrast, is a much more systematic treatise, it is often helpful to turn to it for amplification of things Butler tells us in the *Sermons*. But the fact that they are indeed *sermons* should remind us that even when he is arguing quite abstruse points, it is practical and pastoral concerns that are always uppermost in Butler's mind. This practical emphasis dictates his method, as indeed it also does in his philosophical theology.

I shall begin this chapter with a few comments about his method. I shall then outline his main moral argument, which is a well-known one, and begin discussion of it by examining the fundamental notion of human nature on which it depends.

1

Butler's high reputation as a moral thinker is due to the fact that his readers find him to be a wise moral psychologist, who rests his case upon a perceptive understanding of how our nature actually is. In this he is often contrasted with those who prefer to deal with ethical matters by propounding dogmatic theses which fly in the face of common experience. This is a correct enough judgment, especially since Butler is

9

generally agreed to be successful in exposing the errors of doctrines like that of universal selfishness, which he rightly sees as morally dangerous as well as theoretically confused.

But it is very important to notice, at the outset, that when Butler tells us of his preference for a more empirical method, he does not say that no valuable results can be achieved through more abstract arguments. Just as in philosophical theology he does not reject *a priori* proof, but merely prefers to work in a different way himself, so in ethics his empirical stance is not intended to exclude *a priori* investigations. This is quite clear from his own words:

> There are two ways in which the subject of morals may be treated. One begins from inquiring into the abstract relations of things: the other from a matter of fact, namely what the particular nature of man is, its several parts, their economy or constitution; from whence it proceeds to determine what course of life it is, which is correspondent to this whole nature. In the former method the conclusion is expressed thus, that vice is contrary to the nature and reason of things: in the latter, that it is a violation or breaking in upon our own nature. Thus they both lead us to the same thing, our obligations to the practice of virtue; and thus they exceedingly strengthen and enforce each other. The first seems the most direct and formal proof, and in some respects the least liable to cavil and dispute: the latter is in a peculiar manner adapted to satisfy a fair mind: and is more easily applicable to the several particular relations and circumstances in life. (*S* Pr 12/7)

Here, as elsewhere, Butler is careful not to disavow the method he is not himself using; and his reason for preferring his own method is pragmatic. Butler is, above all else, a thinker who engages in philosophical reasoning for a practical purpose. The purpose in religious matters is the apologetic one of removing barriers to the acceptance of Christianity. The purpose in his moral *Sermons* is to encourage the practice of moral virtue. To do this, he wishes to meet his listeners and readers where they are, and to use arguments of a kind that they will heed. This gives an obvious reason for preferring arguments that depend on the analysis of the place of moral judgment in human personality; but there is more to it than this. He says more about the way his purposes determine his methods in an important passage near the close of the *Analogy*. He is responding there to possible criticisms of his method in that work, and insists that he has, throughout, 'argued upon the principles of others, not my own: and have omitted what I think true, and of the utmost importance, because by others thought unintelligible, or not true' (*An* II vii 11/23). He has, for the sake of argument, granted positions held by his opponents in order to show that, even if they were true, his conclusions would still have weight. He has also avoided appealing to principles which he thinks true himself, if appealing to them would not move his opponents because they do not share them. He gives as an example of a principle which he accepts but has not appealed to, 'the moral fitness and unfitness of actions, prior to all will whatever; which I apprehend as certainly to determine the Divine conduct, as speculative truth and falsehood necessarily determine the Divine judgment'.[1] This has not formed part of his argument in the *Analogy*, because he has deliberately confined himself there to considerations which the work's intended audience, namely the deists, would be sure to grant; so he has argued for a future judgment from observable evidences, rather than from the 'moral fitness' of vice being followed by punishment. While the purposes of the *Sermons* and the *Analogy* are not identical, we can still infer that his choice of method in the *Sermons* is not the result of any doubts of the possibility of arriving at the truth about morals by inquiring into the abstract relations of things. It is the result of a practical judgment about the nature of the audience he is trying to reach. For such an audience, an abstract appeal is out of place, because they will not be moved by it. They might fail to be moved by it for two reasons. One is that, even though, as he puts it in the same *Analogy* passage, the principle of moral fitness forces itself upon the mind, they resist it; Butler is very conscious that the most forceful general argument does not seem obvious to everybody. The other is that, even though they may see that some course of conduct is of itself right, and another of itself wrong, this may not seem to them a compelling reason for *doing* the right one and avoiding the wrong one. Butler wants to make his readers more likely to practise virtue, or follow conscience. An argument that convinced them of the rightness of certain actions and policies might not be enough for this. It might not be enough because they had, with the encouragement of other philosophers, come to feel that the only compelling reason for action is self-interest; or even that the only *possible* motive for action is self-interest. So he wants to support the claims of morality in a way that such an audience may be more willing to consider: by showing them that morality is 'correspondent to' their natures.

If this is correct, it should make us wary of two things. We should be wary of assuming that the premises of his arguments are always premises that he believes himself; and we should be wary of assuming that a doctrine he refrains from appealing to explicitly is one which he does not believe. The former assumption has been at work in those who have ascribed some form of egoism to Butler in spite of his efforts to refute it. The latter has recently led to doubts about the possibility of conscience having a distinctive role in human nature. For conscience is a principle in us, I think, which in Butler's system bases its judgments

11

upon its perception of the 'fitness' or 'unfitness' of certain classes of actions. Butler's arguments in the *Sermons* are supposed to show that we should follow conscience at all times because it is a law of our nature to do this, and (secondarily) because self-love dictates the same course. But it is a mistake to deduce from this that he thinks the needs of our natures, or the demands of self-love, must form the primary content of the judgments of conscience itself.

We shall have to return to these considerations when discussing some of the most common criticisms of Butler's moral psychology. For the moment, however, I shall proceed with an outline of what Butler does explicitly argue, leaving aside what he disbelieves and what he takes for granted.

2

Butler tells us that his moral *Sermons* are 'intended to explain what is meant by the nature of man, when it is said that virtue consists in following, and vice in deviating from it; and by explaining to show that the assertion is true' (*S* Pr 13/8). He recalls to us that the principle that virtue consists in following nature goes back to the 'ancient moralists' (particularly the Stoics), but he feels it necessary to 'lay it open in a more explicit manner' than has been done hitherto. In fact he lays it open in a way that emphasises its psychological, rather than its metaphysical, implications, though as a Christian he does not have any doubts about the existence of the latter and leans upon them from time to time in his argument.

We can fairly easily set out Butler's case as a consecutive argument in three parts, primarily located in four of his *Sermons*[2] and in the Dissertation 'Of the Nature of Virtue', which appears as the second of two appendices to the *Analogy*.

(i) Human nature contains within it a variety of 'internal principles', which are clearly distinguishable from one another in spite of the tendency of theorists to confuse them. In particular it is important to distinguish between the 'particular passions, appetites, and affections' and the 'general affection or principle of self-love'; and to distinguish both from the 'natural principle' of benevolence. In addition to these elements in our natures, there is 'a principle of reflection in men, by which they distinguish between, approve and disapprove their own actions'; this is *conscience*. A dispassionate recognition of the presence of all these 'principles' is sufficient to prove to us that we 'were made for' society, as well as for ourselves, and that we may just as well be capable of neglecting our own interests as of neglecting the needs of others. To put the same point in another form, it is as much in accordance with our natures to act for the good of others as it is to act for our own good. In maintaining these theses, Butler sees himself as defending obvious truths against the misleading claims of 'selfish' theories of human nature which fail to distinguish between self-love and particular passions and appetites, and which wilfully deny the presence of benevolence in our natures.

(ii) To prove the presence of all these principles in human nature may be enough to show that virtue is, in some sense, concordant with that nature. But, thus far, it does nothing to show that virtue is concordant with it in a manner in which vice is not. We must therefore distinguish between three ways in which we can follow nature. We can do this by acting according to some principle that is in us; we can do it by following the principle in us which happens to be the strongest; and we can do it by doing what is dictated by the whole constitution of our nature. Virtue is concordant with human nature in this last sense. We can only recognise the truth of the principle that virtue consists in following nature, and that vice violates nature, if we recognise that human nature has a structure, or 'constitution'. In that constitution conscience has *authority*. Authority must be distinguished from strength or power. We often act contrary to what conscience tells us, but in so doing we act against our natures, because we violate the authority that conscience has. The doctrine of the natural authority of conscience is Butler's best-known contribution to ethical theory, even if it is not his clearest contribution. He insists that the authority which conscience has is a sufficient reason, at all times, for following what conscience dictates. But he does not offer it as the only reason for following it. In addition, he maintains that conscience and self-love point in the same direction; that is, that, at least for the most part, virtue is in our best interests.

(iii) These arguments leave unanswered some serious questions about the relationships between the elements in our natures which Butler has distinguished. In particular, they leave unclear the extent to which the superiority of conscience could require the frustration of particular passions, could demand choices that might conflict with self-love, or could direct us to do things that benevolence would not independently suggest to us. The first two questions are alternate aspects of the traditional problem of the relation between virtue and happiness; the third is, roughly, the problem of how far one can give a Utilitarian account of our moral obligations. Butler tries to fill out his picture of human nature in Sermon xi and in the Dissertation, in order to deal with these questions. (a) He argues that the popular antithesis between benevolence and self-love is erroneous, and is mostly due to a failure to recognise that self-love, which is the general desire for our own happiness, requires us to satisfy particular passions, and that these latter include among them desires to do good to others. This mistake is compounded by the confused theses of psychological egoism (that all desires are selfish) and psychological hedonism (that all desires are desires for pleasure). Butler's arguments here are only slightly less famous than his doctrine of the authority of conscience. (b) Butler infers from the above that the pursuit of the good of others, and indeed the pursuit of 'virtue and moral rectitude', is fully coincident with the dictates of self-love. (c) This suggests that virtue and benevolence, or rather the life dominated by benevolence, are (contingently) one and the same – and also that both can get independent justification from an appeal to self-love, even though this is a principle distinct from them. The Dissertation is partly designed to rebut this natural reading of Butler's position. While still maintaining that prudence (or self-love in action) is itself virtuous, he subordinates both it and benevolence to conscience in an unambiguous way, rejecting in particular the Utilitarian view that benevolence and virtue are identical.

All aspects of this threefold argument have been subjected to criticism. In what follows I shall try as far as possible to keep separable issues separate, although some overlap is inevitable. I shall include a discussion of Butler's arguments about egoism and hedonism (that is, iii(a) above) in what I say about the first phase of Butler's case, since that phase is primarily devoted to an account of the elements actually present in human nature: the arguments in Sermon xi are intended to show that the theses he attacks misdescribe those elements. Accordingly, I shall proceed by examining, first, Butler's attempt to establish the presence in our natures of the various 'principles' he distinguishes. I shall follow this by examining the doctrine of the supremacy of conscience. I shall then discuss what Butler says about benevolence and its relation to morality.

Under the first heading, the most important questions to consider are these. First, what is the concept of 'human nature' with which Butler works? How far is it a normative notion, and how far a purely psychological one? (This will be discussed in sections 3 and 4 of the present chapter.) Second, what is the character of each of the principles or elements in human nature which Butler claims to uncover? What, that is, is involved in accepting or rejecting doctrines about the presence of each, and its distinctness from, or relationship to, the others? (This is the theme of sections 5–8.) Third, how successful is Butler in refuting egoistic and hedonistic accounts of human motives? (This question will occupy Chapter II.)

Under the second heading, we must consider the relation between the two basic doctrines of Butler's ethics: that virtue consists in following nature, and that conscience has supreme authority. (I discuss this in sections 1 and 2 of Chapter III.) Second, we must assess the case he makes for these doctrines. (This occupies section 3 of Chapter III.) Thirdly, we must address the vexed question of the relationship between conscience and self-love. (This concludes the same section.)

Under the third heading, the most important questions are these. First, what is the way in which Butler thinks benevolence, or the love of our neighbour, motivates us? Second, how good a case does he make for the claim that benevolence and self-love point the same way? Third, is he guilty of serious inconsistencies in what he tells us about the distinction between benevolence and virtue? (These questions are the topic of Chapter III, section 5.) I turn, first, to Butler's concept of human nature.

3

Butler contrasts his investigations into human nature with the abstract, or *a priori*, investigations of other moralists. The way he does this suggests that he thinks he is engaged in empirical psychology. If we accept this suggestion unreflectively, it is easy to feel we have caught him out when he makes obviously normative pronouncements. I do not think his procedure is as confused as this. But it is important to make a preliminary analysis of his concept of human nature before assessing his detailed arguments.

I have already emphasised that Butler's preference for the study of human nature over the abstract demonstration of moral principles does not imply any doubt on his part about the possibility of arriving at truths by the latter method. The two methods are complementary, not competitive. This implies that there is nothing in Butler's system to rule out the possibility that the morally supreme element in our nature, namely conscience, should be able to know moral truths *a priori* (just as reason can gain *a priori* knowledge of the practically valuable truths of mathematics). The authority of conscience may be something that can be shown to us by an examination of the place it has in our nature; but it might also be a consequence of its access to *a priori* moral knowledge. The two are not exclusive.

A similar consideration helps us to understand the way Butler compares his use of the concept of human nature with that of the Stoics. On the face of it, he seems to say that their metaphysical understanding of the principle that virtue consists in following nature expresses 'some inward feeling or other' about a truth which is actually purely psychological (*S* Pr 13/8). But his own analysis of human nature leans upon metaphysical assumptions he makes no attempt to conceal. These are the assumptions of a theistic teleology, which is at much at work in the *Sermons* as it is, later on, in the *Analogy*.[3]

Butler's ethic is not a theological ethic; it is central to it that we have the capacity to perceive moral truths independently of our recognition of the commands of God.[4] But there is still a theological underpinning to the account of human nature that Butler uses to reinforce the claims

15

of morality. It is important to be clear what role this theological under-pinning plays. We can be guided in this by two quotations:

> If the real nature of any creature leads him and is adapted to such and such purposes only, or more than to any other; this is a reason to believe the Author of that nature intended it for those purposes. Thus there is no doubt the eye was intended for us to see with. And the more complex any constitution is, and the greater variety of parts there are which thus tend to some one end, the stronger is the proof that such end was designed. (S ii 1/1)

> The due and proper use of any natural faculty or power, is to be judged of by the end and design for which it was given us. The chief purpose, for which the faculty of speech was given to man, is plainly that we might communicate our thoughts to each other, in order to carry on the affairs of the world. . . . The secondary use of speech is to please and be entertaining to each other in conversation. (S iv 7/8)

Butler takes it for granted, as he does in the *Analogy*, that his readers will share with him the assumption that we are created by God. He further assumes that this means that the salient features of our physical and moral makeup have specific purposes – so that our eyes do not merely enable us to see, but are part of our physiological constitution *in order that we should see*. Whatever doubts Butler is trying to combat, he takes it for granted that his readers will not be in any doubt about this, just as he takes this very same deistic premiss for granted when defending revelation in the *Analogy*. This is odd to modern readers, who suppose that to assume a theistic teleology is already to assume the morality Butler is defending; but in Butler's day, when atheism was an extreme rarity, this supposition would not have been made. While the public to whom the *Sermons* is addressed is no doubt wider than the audience of the *Analogy*, it would certainly have included deists, who accepted, for intellectual reasons, that the world had a creator, and might have gone on to concede that this entailed that the course of nature was providentially governed, but did not necessarily go further.[5] So Butler follows his standard practice of making whatever assumptions his audience would make, and assumes that we are creatures of a God, and that our natures are the way they are for a purpose. But he thinks he needs to argue for the view that the furtherance of virtue, or morality, is part of that purpose.

His argument[6] is one that avoids the *a priori* demonstrations, found in Clarke, that the sort of creator we can prove to have caused the world must be one who expects virtue from his creatures. Instead Butler proceeds from 'matter of fact' – from how we find man's nature to be.

This has to mean that he considers the observation of human nature makes it clear that certain kinds of action accord with the purposes for which we are created, and certain others not. Given this understanding of what he intends, he cannot simply identify what we find people doing with what they were intended to do; yet the inquiry he is engaged in has to be empirical in spite of this. His solution is to use the notion of man's *real* nature. This cannot be identified with man's nature as we see it in action all the time, or there would be no room for the vital insistence that we often act unnaturally; but neither can it be identified with an ideal or perfect nature which is untouched by temptation or evil.[7] Although the doctrine of the Fall is not one Butler appeals to in the moral *Sermons*, as a Christian theologian he is committed to it; so for him our nature, as it is, is damaged goods, and falls short of the Christian ideal. When I act viciously, or sin, I act in a way that is alien to my real self; yet my real self is something that I have, here and now, not something that would only be present if I were wholly virtuous.

The two quotations above tell us one way in which investigation can show us what our real nature is. The example of the eye indicates that those who have it are intended to see with it. Butler does not, in the *Sermons*, even allude to the problem of what we are to make of beings, in this case the blind, who do not have a power most of us have, though the doctrine of probation in the *Analogy* is no doubt an attempt to deal with its theological aspects. So he does not answer the question of whether the blind are in an unnatural condition; he merely says that the primary natural function of the eye, for those who have functional eyes, is to see. This would seem to mean that other uses of the eyes, such as charming the opposite sex, are secondary (indeed dependent on the primary use). It is clear, however, that Butler could not argue that the fact that we have eyes shows that we act in accordance with our real nature every time we use them to see, for that would prevent our saying that some spectator activities, like the contemplation of violence for amusement, are unnatural. The second example, that of the power of speech, brings out in a more explicit way the conditional nature of the claim that our real nature leads us to certain uses of our capacities. Butler thinks it quite obvious that our power of speech was 'given us' for the communication of useful thoughts in the first instance, and only secondarily for entertainment; the latter is permissible and harmless, so, though not part of what our real nature demands of us, it is not a violation of it. Let us use our own technical distinction here, and say that for Butler some activities are *concordant* with our real nature if they are what, in his words, our nature leads us to,[8] and that other activities are *consistent* with our real nature if we find ourselves commonly engaged in them as a result of having certain powers, but that they are not what these powers are primarily *for*. Not all communication of thoughts is

17

concordant with our real nature, and not all verbal entertainment is consistent with it. If Nero had not merely fiddled while Rome burned, but had planned and ordered the fire for his own amusement, this would certainly have been unnatural, even though he would still have been carrying on the affairs of the world as he gave the orders. Similarly, if he engaged in entertaining chit-chat, as well as in fiddling, while the fire raged, this was not natural either. These actions would not have been concordant with our real nature, nor would they have been consistent with it, if such notions are to have any normative function whatever. So while communication and vision are, in themselves and for the most part, concordant with our real nature, and attractive glances and conversational entertainment are, in themselves and for the most part, consistent with our real nature, sometimes they are not. When they are not, they violate it. Clearly a power or principle in us is part of a creature's real nature if its exercise is, in general, *for the creature's good.* The theistic teleology, or providence, that Butler assumes, and ascribes to his readers, does not yet include a divine ordinance of virtue and prohibition of vice; but it is taken already to include a general benevolence towards species, or towards individuals as members of species. It is this which enables Butler to present his investigation of our nature as an empirical one, since he and his readers would feel no difficulty in deciding which activities of a creature were, for the most part, conducive to its survival or health. It would be a matter of observing the most usual *effects* of those activities.

So it is a necessary condition of a creature's either following or violating its nature that it should be using some organ or power the exercise of which is generally for its good, and which has accordingly been given to it by divine providence. But it is not a sufficient condition. It turns out that only human beings can ever violate their nature, or act unnaturally; other beings can never do so. This is true, even though they may often exercise a power that they have and destroy themselves in the process. Butler gives the example (in S ii 10/13) of an animal lured into a snare by a bait. The appetite which drives it into this disastrous course is one which is in general beneficial to it, and when it follows it it does so because it is the strongest inclination within it at the time. In the case of animals we cannot raise questions about the morality or the prudence of what they do. If we ask whether the animal has followed 'the bent of nature', however, the answer has to be that is has. For in the animal's nature we find a number of powers and appetites that are simply ordered according to their relative strengths at any given time. It follows from this that, for non-human creatures, all the actions they actually perform are natural, since they always follow the strongest current appetite or inclination. It also follows that, for non-human creatures, some natural acts are not for the creature's good, even though it does not seem possible to suppose that the *majority* should not be. (The destructiveness of

animal nature is a theme which seems mildly to worry Butler theologi-
cally, but which he treats as an impenetrable mystery.[9])

Although animal natures are assemblages of powers and inclinations
which are exercised according to their relative strengths, human nature
is systematic in another way; and only beings like ourselves whose
natures are systematic in this latter way can act both naturally and
unnaturally. Human nature contains within it certain principles which
have a superiority over other factors which is distinct from the superiority
that comes from mere strength. When we act contrary to our natures,
we follow an inclination that one of these principles would, on this
occasion, require us not to follow. Butler introduces this point by reference to self-love: if a man, 'foreseeing the same danger of certain ruin',
which the animal entering the snare could not foresee, should still follow
the strongest desire, his action would be 'disproportionate' to his total
nature. The point is not that the inclination does not form part of his
nature, but that to yield to it on this occasion runs counter to the
principle of 'reasonable and cool self-love'. To say this is not to say that
self-love was weaker than the inclination, although obviously it was; it
is to say that self-love is a *superior* principle to any of the inclinations.
It has *authority* over them. It is, of course, Butler's fundamental contention that conscience has *supreme* authority, being superior both to the
inclinations and to self-love – although he gives his readers more than
one occasion to doubt his firmness on the latter point.

I think Butler's wavering on this last issue is something we can already
understand, if not fully excuse. A human being who follows an inclination, contrary to self-love or to conscience, will violate his or her
nature, even though an animal doing the same thing would be following
its nature. So unnaturalness is a consequence of a natural element within
us being followed in a way that flouts a superior principle. The presence
of the superior principles, then, enables us to avoid the predicament of
sub-rational creatures: that of following their nature to their own detri-
ment. So whenever *we* act naturally, in accordance with the superior
principle within us, we shall presumably be acting for our good. If he
holds, as he does, that it is *always* the one and only natural course to
follow conscience, or at least not to do what it forbids, then he is
committed to the view that following conscience is *always* for our good.
There is no doubt at all that this is what he believes, though he expresses
it in many unfortunate ways. He puts it the right way when he says:

> Conscience and self-love, if we understand our true happiness,
> always lead us the same way. Duty and interest are perfectly
> coincident; for the most part in this world, but entirely and in every
> instance if we take in the future, and the whole; this being implied

in the notion of a good and perfect administration of things. (S iii 9/13)

But he is writing, it will be remembered, for some readers who are *to be persuaded* that the providence they nominally admit to exist really does favour virtue. So they will not be persuaded by the mere assertion that providence always does favour it, because the evidence sometimes seems to show the opposite. Yet in order to show that our *nature* requires us to be virtuous, he is committed to showing that virtue is in our interest. So he writes, from time to time, as though a purely secular appeal to self-love can justify the practice of virtue – even, on occasion, as though conscience were answerable to self-love rather than the other way around. He believes neither of these things, but in the specifically Christian doctrines of the justice and love of God. He does not assume these in his argument here, even though, as he speaks from a pulpit, he acknowledges them. He attempts to deal with this problem in the *Analogy* when he tries, in Chapters ii – v of Part I, to establish for deistic readers that the world is morally governed, and that the tribulations of the virtuous are for their ultimate good. I think his argument there fails; but at least it is explicitly theological. In the *Sermons* the appeal to human nature is an ostensibly non-theological one, and to maintain this Butler has to make verbal concessions to the very egoism which he wants his audience to overcome. He has, that is, to forget the importance, in the passage just quoted, of the qualifying phrase, 'if we understand our true happiness'.

So far, then, we can say that the concept of human nature with which Butler works in the *Sermons* is that of a system of inclinations, passions, and principles, each of which is, in itself, placed there by divine providence for a purpose which can be assumed to be beneficent. The system of which these elements form a part is one in which, in addition to the relative strengths that they have, the rational principles of self-love and conscience have a built-in authority or superiority to all the other elements, conscience being the highest authority of all. If we always follow the authority of conscience, therefore, we shall always act in ways that are concordant with our natures, and hence in our ultimate interest. If we act against conscience because our inclinations are too strong for us, we shall act unnaturally, and hence (barring special divine interposition) against our interests. So conscience and self-love cannot really conflict, though they may appear to do so. Butler can never *contrast* conscience and self-love. He in fact holds, though it is not required in logic for him to hold, that prudence, or the informed pursuit of one's interests, is a moral virtue.[10]

Before proceeding to a further examination of each of the elements in our 'real human nature', a few more comments are needed to complete the conceptual picture. Butler assumes, first, that human nature, as he describes it, is universal – that the morally relevant aspects of human personality are constant and uniform. While he could no doubt accommodate, somehow, the fact that some people lack certain perceptual powers, such as sight, and others do not have certain inclinations, such as ambition or curiosity, he does not contemplate the possibility of there being humans who lack conscience, self-love, and the bulk of common human wants and fears. Second, the nature that we all share is not perfect, even though the best course of action will always consist in following it rather than violating it. He makes this clear in another connection in the *Analogy* when he gives an account of 'how it comes to pass, that creatures made upright fall' (*An* I v 14/26). He seems to hold that even if vice is not necessary to the human condition, temptation is a necessary consequence of it. Even if all our inclinations are suitably subservient to conscience, all this means is that conscience sees to it that they are not indulged when this indulgence would be morally forbidden. This does not mean that the inclinations are not *felt*: 'they must be conceived to have some tendency in how low a degree soever, yet some tendency, to induce persons to such forbidden gratification'. So our real nature is always subject to some degree of temptation, and would be whenever we found ourselves in circumstances that aroused inclinations that it would be wrong to satisfy, even if we never yielded. I do not think that Butler would concede that this means our real nature contains desires that are in themselves bad – any more than the desire for food which the animal seeks to satisfy by entering the snare is in itself bad. But we are constantly in circumstances where it would be morally inopportune to indulge desires, in spite of this. So the Fall of man, in which of course Butler believes, did not have the effect of eliminating any components of our moral constitution; it disrupted their relationships, so that strength rather than natural authority commonly determines whether we follow an inclination or not, and we become set in bad habits of choice. If this is what the Fall has done to us, then it has not changed 'real human nature', for it has not taken away the inbuilt *authority* of conscience, but introduced a situation in which authority and strength no longer coincide. Since depravity and corruption consist in knowingly doing what we ought not to do, then we can manifest them while still retaining our real human nature – indeed, we cannot manifest them otherwise. So 'real human nature' is not a perfect ideal, but a constant reality, though someone who always acted concordantly with his real nature would be a wholly virtuous human being.[11]

A final point, to which I shall have to return. To act naturally is to follow conscience, or self-love, or both, and to accede to our inclinations if and only if these higher principles approve them. In the *Sermons* Butler urges the life of conscience upon his readers on the ground that it is

21

natural in this way. It does not follow, however, that he is committed by this to the opinion that either conscience or self-love enjoins or vetoes actions on the ground that they fit or violate our natures in this way. This is clear, at least, in the case of conscience. I might well act naturally by doing what conscience tells me to do, and act unnaturally by doing what conscience tells me not to do; but this does not show that conscience tells me to do things because they are natural, or not to do them because they are unnatural. On the face of it, it tells me to do them because they are *right*, and not to do them because they are *wrong*. In view of a recent criticism of Butler, this is of great importance.[12] In the case of self-love, the position is not as clear. If my account of Butler's concept of human nature is correct, then it is conceptually true that actions that are consonant with my nature are in my interest; but it does not follow from this that when those natural actions are dictated by self-love, I will be seeking to do what is natural, *per se*. I will be pursuing what I think to be *in my interest*. On the other hand, in calculating what is in my interest, I may well ask what will best serve the needs of my whole nature, as distinct from the promptings of this or that desire, so the naturalness of the proposed action may well enter indirectly. Put another way, the concepts of my happiness and my nature are not as clearly distinct as are those of my nature and my duty. There is little risk for Butler's main argument in finding that self-love requires the appeal to our nature, however. There would be a real risk, on the other hand, in finding that conscience necessarily made use of the concept of what is natural. For what value could there be in showing that it is natural to do what our highest principle tells us nature requires?

4

With this brief survey of Butler's understanding of 'human nature' behind us, it is appropriate to make a few general comments about the character of arguments that make use of it.

Butler's central contention is that we should follow conscience because in doing so we conform to our real nature, whereas in not doing so we violate it. He regards this contention as a way of leading us to 'our obligations to the practice of virtue' (*S Pr* 12/7), that is distinct from the inquiry into the abstract relations of things. While I shall attempt to argue this further in my discussion of conscience, I infer from this that Butler considers that the naturalness of following conscience, which his method is intended to prove, is a reason for following it that is additional to, and distinct from, the rightness of what conscience commands and the wrongness of what conscience forbids – and a reason, in fact, that may be more successful than the abstract ones in getting us to do what conscience tells us. How persuasive can such an argument be?

It faces a twofold difficulty. There is a problem in showing that we can judge actions to be natural or unnatural in some way that is distinct from judging them right or wrong. There is also the problem of why such weight should attach to the fact of an action's naturalness or unnaturalness.

Butler certainly seems to think we can all see that we have some sense of naturalness and unnaturalness that is above and beyond our sense of right and wrong. When he writes of the animal entering the snare and the human being knowingly choosing a ruinous course, he assumes we can all readily see that the former behaviour is natural and the latter unnatural 'from comparison with the nature of the agent' (S ii 10/14). He contrasts this recognition with the consideration of the action itself, and with consideration of its consequences. Later in the same sermon he instances blasphemy and parricide as self-evidently unnatural in a similar way (S ii 17/22). The judgment he appeals to here looks like the one made in common speech when certain classes of act (parricide, suicide, sodomy, cruelty to children) are selected for special condemnation as unnatural. As I have just interpreted the judgment that an action is unnatural, for Butler and for his audience as he judges it, such a verdict would imply that the acts condemned involve the wilful misuse of powers given us by God for quite opposite purposes. (In so far as this type of moral condemnation is still common, it would still be likely to carry with it a residually theological judgment that the powers used in such action are being used in a way that contradicts what they are 'for'.) If used for their intended purposes, that is, naturally, they would serve our good.

That Butler's concept of naturalness has this theological content must never be disregarded. But he wants to argue that all acts that violate the edicts of conscience are unnatural in this way, not just those of a specially self-destructive or unlawful kind. Telling lies has to be unnatural too. He also wishes, in the *Sermons*, to argue his case in a way that does not depend upon the righteousness of God's providence, even though there is no pretence that he does not believe in this, and no attempt to do without the existence of some kind of theistic teleology or other. Since Butler is always emphatic that judgments of right and wrong are *not* theological in content, his core argument for the naturalness of virtue is one that leans on discernible features of those judgments themselves, and is therefore not theological in character. Although the conclusion that virtue is natural has theological implications, it is not reached by appealing to theological commitments. It is reached by appealing to alleged features of our *experience* of conscience and its judgments.

Once again, it is important to point out that he makes an independent case in the *Analogy*, for holding that the Author of nature favours virtue,[13] but he does not appeal to that claim here. He wants, here, to

23

argue for virtue's naturalness in a way that can reach those who might well part company with him on theology at the very point where he made that appeal.

He thinks he can do this because their hesitations about virtue are not due to a denial that conscience can tell right from wrong. They are due to an indecision about whether this is enough to justify doing what conscience says. His argument is that the very moral consciousness they do not deny having, carries clear signs of its own authority in their natures. His task, as a moral psychologist, is to activate their self-knowledge sufficiently to enable them to see this.

I think this argument has two aspects, though they do not separate readily. The first is a claim that we all have an inbuilt capacity to recognise that the judgments of right and wrong that conscience makes are stronger reasons for choice than the judgments of other principles, or the presence of contrary desires. This is an appeal to a form of knowledge that he thinks we all have. The second is an argument that there is an intrinsic absurdity in questioning the authority of conscience, when its verdicts are known; that the notion of having a sufficient reason to do what conscience forbids is in some way incoherent. I think both claims are embodied in the following passage:

> Thus that principle, by which we survey, and either approve or disapprove our own heart, temper, and actions, is not only to be considered as what is in its turn to have some influence; which may be said of every passion, of the lowest appetites: but likewise as being superior; as from its very nature manifestly claiming superiority over all others: insomuch that you cannot form a notion of this faculty, conscience, without taking in judgment, direction, superintendency. This is a constituent part of the idea, that is, of the faculty itself; and to preside and govern, from the very economy and constitution of man, belongs to it. (S ii 14/19)

The doctrine that virtue consists in following nature, and the doctrine that conscience has supreme authority, have always been treated as inseparable by Butler's commentators, until very recently. While it is now necessary to defend it, and I shall attempt to do this in Chapter III, I shall proceed for the present as though this obvious principle of interpretation is true. My more detailed reading of the connection between the two doctrines is that the doctrine of the supremacy of conscience functions as the ground for the assertion of the naturalness of virtue.

I suggested earlier that the theological underpinnings of Butler's conception of human nature make it easier to understand his determination to argue that conscience and self-love point the same way. If following conscience is natural, then it will have to be, somehow, for our good. This claim has embarrassed Butler's admirers. Some of his critics have sought to create embarrassment over the 'nature' argument I have just outlined. Surely Butler is merely doing here in an obscure way what he does when he claims virtue meets the needs of self-love: arguing that morality is to our advantage? Why do we need to be told this? Surely, when we know what our duty is, we *already* know that we should not disregard it?

In a way, Butler is on the side of such moralists; but in another way he is not. He is on their side in that his argument for the supremacy of conscience amounts largely to an appeal to the very knowledge they emphasise. But he begins from the fact that, for some, this knowledge is not enough to motivate virtuous action, and that some of them still raise questions. He is not content to rest on the fact that, by rights, what they know already should be enough. It might be of service to point out that the knowledge of duty that they have is a sign of the authority conscience has in their nature, especially if his hearers are hesitant because of the theoretical blandishments of egoism. To get more moral practice, Butler is happy to pay the price of theoretical over-determination.

Of course, some moralists, influenced by Kant, or perhaps Prichard, would say at this point that such theoretical over-determination is not morally productive, but morally corrupting. All Butler is doing, they would say, is offering *inducements* to moral behaviour, just as Plato did in the *Republic*; and even if these inducements produce acts done in conformity with conscience, they still cannot produce genuinely conscientious, or genuinely moral, action. Genuinely moral action would be motivated only by the rightness, and never by the naturalness or advantageousness, of what is done. In spite of the common tendency to do Butler the dubious honour of thinking of him as the poor man's Kant, we must stress that this line of reasoning runs directly counter to the way he approaches morals, as well as to the way he approaches religious faith. Butler is a compassionate thinker, whose primary motive is to lead men to follow the demands of morality, and the demands of faith, because he believes they harm themselves utterly if they do not. He thinks that if there is no other way to get them to meet those demands, he will show them that they will indeed harm themselves by refusing to do so. Here, as elsewhere, the *Analogy* clarifies the *Sermons*. In Chapter v of Part I, he is arguing that the trials and sufferings of the virtuous can be seen as a kind of probation, which God imposes on us to fit us for a higher future, and which trains us by entrenching the habit of resisting temptations. He then makes the following comments:

> Against this whole notion of moral discipline, it may be objected, in another way; that so far as a course of behaviour, materially virtuous, proceeds from hope and fear, so far it is only a discipline

and strengthening of self-love. But doing what God commands, because He commands it, is obedience, though it proceeds from hope or fear. And a course of such obedience will form habits of it. . . . Nor is there any foundation for this great nicety, with which some affect to distinguish in this case, in order to depreciate all Religion proceeding from hope or fear. For, veracity, justice, and charity, regard to God's authority, and to our own chief interest, are not only all three coincident; but each of them is, in itself, a just and natural motive or principle of action. And he who begins a good life from any one of them, and perseveres in it, as he is already in some degree, so he cannot fail of becoming more and more, of that character, which is correspondent to the constitution of Nature as moral. (*An* I v 19/36)

So if there are several motives conspiring to make us do what conscience tells us, this is not bad, but good; and if only one of these will work for me, and not the others, the philosopher who gets it to do so is doing me a service. The rest we can leave to providence.

5

I turn now to Butler's account of the major constituents of human nature. This account makes no pretence of being a systematic one. Butler mistrusts systems; and since his major arguments have to do with the interrelationships between conscience, self-love, benevolence, and other motives, he tells us only enough about the detailed character of each to support what he says about their connections with each other.

Butler tells us that man has 'various instincts and principles of action, as brute creatures have' and 'several which brutes have not' (*S* Pr 18–19/15). The term 'principle' is his commonest general name for all the motives he discusses, and there does not seem to be any implied contrast between 'principle' and 'instinct', since animals, in this passage, have both and not just one. The term 'principle', then, appears to be used indifferently for any conscious inner source of human action.[14]

Butler's terminology is at its most imprecise when he writes of those elements in our natures other than conscience, self-love, and benevolence. The three words used most commonly to talk of these are 'appetites', 'passions', and 'affections', though both of the latter are used on occasion to refer to self-love and to benevolence also.[15] Before examining the differences that he does indicate, it is necessary to notice some claims he makes about all of them together.

First, he tells us that they are necessary parts of our natures, and that reason alone, with which he contrasts them, would not be enough to motivate us:

26

Reason alone, whatever anyone may wish, is not in reality a sufficient motive of virtue in such a creature as man; but this reason joined with those affections which God has impressed upon his heart. (S v 3/4)

Although it is tempting to compare this with Hume's famous dictum that reason is, and ought only to be, the slave of the passions, Butler does not go this far. On the contrary, he tells us in the same passage that these affections have to exercise themselves 'under strict government and direction of reason', which implies that reason can at times rule us in a way contrary to the affections; and he introduces conscience to us in Sermon i as the source of a moral motive that is *additional* to that of natural affection. But he flatly rejects the Stoic ideal of passionless virtue as alien to man's nature as God has created it. Conscience, as the rational faculty, may have vital supervisory power, but one cannot run a constitution like that of mankind using a supervisory power alone.

The second thing that he holds about our appetites, passions, and affections, is that they are all, in a clear sense, good. This is a consequence of his understanding of what human nature is, and requires a special interpretation of evil motives. They have to be understood as inappropriate or inopportune exercises of motives that are present in us for a good purpose. 'Our appetites, passions, senses, no way imply disease' (S v 3/6). Not only are they present in us for a good purpose, but none of them involves the pursuit of evil for itself. One passion he discusses at length, in Sermon viii, is resentment, which he subjects to detailed examination because it looks like a motive that is in itself bad; but he breaks it down, roughly, into instinctive anger at injury, which we need for physical survival, and indignation against moral wrongdoing against ourselves, which we need for social integration; in the following Sermon he argues that neither, properly understood and controlled, is inconsistent with the Christian obligations to forgiveness and love of neighbour. Another interesting example is shame, which sometimes leads men to compound their villainies through a desire to avoid the humiliation of discovery, but is clearly present in us to prevent our doing evil (S i 12/12). The satisfaction of an appetite or affection at the wrong time he describes as *disproportionate*: he tells us that 'every affection, as distinct from a principle of reason, may rise too high, and be beyond its just proportion' (S vi 9/10). Any passion that is satisfied against the veto of conscience is disproportionate, so although 'just proportion' suggests moderation, disproportion is to be recognised by collision with the higher principle of conscience.[16]

The third thing Butler tells us about all these principles is that they have *objects*. This notion is a notorious source of difficulty in the philosophy of motivation. The best-known arguments of Butler that make use

27

of it are those designed to undermine egoistic and hedonistic theories of human nature. He insists that such theories confuse the objects of 'particular passions' with that of self-love, or confuse the object of a passion with a state of mind resulting from the attainment of it. I shall examine these arguments shortly. But there are three assertions about appetites, passions, affections, and their objects which need immediate comment.

The first is the statement that 'the very nature of an affection consists in tending towards, and resting in, its objects as an end' (S xiii 5/4).[17] The second is the statement that there is a 'prior suitableness between the object and the passion' (S xi 6/3). Thirdly, we are told that 'passion or appetite implies a direct simple tendency towards such and such objects, without distinction of the means by which they are to be obtained' (S ii 13/17). These are all somewhat dark sayings; but taken together they seem to tell us the following. The notion of the object of an affection or passion has its use primarily in those cases where the state in question has an aim or objective.[18] The paradigm cases will be desires or wants, of which appetites will be special cases; other examples will be anger, resentment, or compassion, where the state in question is logically connected with a desire to do something, good or bad, to or for someone. In the case of desires, these dicta amount to saying that every desire is a desire *for* something, and that one knows what desire it is when one knows what it is the desire *for*; hence it is satisfied when that which it is for is obtained. The 'prior suitableness' is the logical connection between the desire and its object, in this sense, and it is this connection which entails that the desire has been fulfilled when the object has been gained. And even though I cannot pursue the object of my desire without first pursuing the means to it, I can identify the object without having any idea what those means are. This lack of connection between object and means is a major source of temptation: although wanting some object may well be, in itself, innocent, we often find there are no morally acceptable means of obtaining it, and conscience must then exercise its veto.

If this is correct, then passions and affections that are not desires will be related to their objects analogously. If anger has an object, it will be the person who has injured me who is the object of my anger, not the injury he has done me: it will be the person I am angry *at*, not the injury I am angry *about*. But this raises two difficulties. The first is that it seems natural to say that it is the injury, if anything, that creates the 'prior suitableness' of the emotion here. And the *objective* that the angry person has will presumably be that of doing something (bad) *to* the person he is angry at. It is not worth pursuing these questions in detail; whether their resolution is easy or difficult, most of the contexts where the objects of affections need careful identification in Butler's arguments are cases where a desire is clearly involved, or, as in the case of self-love, where there is a clearly distinguishable *objective* (such as my happiness) even if this is not something we would readily call an object in ordinary speech, or in contemporary philosophy.

The fourth general fact about appetites, passions, and affections is that although they are controllable by reason, in that conscience can approve or veto them, and although the language of due proportion, and the views Butler expresses in the *Analogy*[19] about the development of good or bad habits, suggest that their intensity is also subject to indirect control, they are all mental occurrences which are aroused in us from time to time, and are not in themselves directly subject to the will. We are 'so constituted, as to feel certain affections upon the sight or contemplation of certain objects' (*S* xiii 3/3). There is an essential *passivity* about them, even though it is critically important for the virtuous life that we should be endowed with them.

With these common features now stated, we can indicate briefly the differences between the three classes of mental state. Appetites are primarily the desires that relate to physical survival or well-being, such as hunger, thirst, or sexual desire. Passions are states which, even if themselves good, are very commonly indulged in disproportionate ways that merit disapproval. (So resentment is a passion which, though not evil itself, is frequently perverted into hatred and vengefulness.[20]) Affections are more positively regarded, and although they can be disproportionate too, conscience does not have to veto them so often. Love and compassion are prominent examples.

6

We can now turn to the three principles of self-love, benevolence, and conscience. All three are apparently contrasted with the appetites, passions, and affections; but the nature of the contrast, if it is indeed a real one, varies from the one to the other. Butler makes it harder for us to be sure of the nature of the contrast by speaking both of benevolence and of self-love as affections, and even by referring to self-love, on one occasion, as 'the favourite passion' (*S* xi 3/2).

To begin with self-love. If it were not indeed an affection, it would be odd for Butler to have called it self-*love*; yet it is introduced in ways that seem to contrast it with the affections. In fact the contrast is not with affection *per se* but with '*particular* passions, appetites, and affections' (*S* i 7/6n). Self-love is a general, rather than a particular, affection. Its generality comes from the character of the *object* which it has. Its object is happiness – the long-term good, or interest, of the subject. 'It is an affection to ourselves; a regard to our own interest, happiness and private good: and in the proportion a man hath this, he is interested, or a lover of himself' (*S* xi 8/5). Butler does not say very much about happiness, and this is no doubt partly because his very point about the generality of self-love excludes too precise an understanding of it. Self-love is the desire to seek whatever it is that makes me happy – a desire that most people have without being able, notoriously, to say exactly what would satisfy it. This desire is the one that Hume later called 'the general appetite to good and aversion to evil, considered merely as such'.[21] Butler does, however, tell us that 'happiness or satisfaction consists only in the enjoyment of those objects, which are by nature suited to our particular appetites, passions, and affections' (*S* xi 9/6); he believes, in other words, that whatever particular choices lead to happiness, the happy person is one whose life largely fulfils the particular appetites, passions, and affections that are implanted in him. The universal character of human nature, as he outlines it, does not preclude each of us having a different optimal balance of satisfaction. But no one can be happy, on this account, if the majority of his particular wants are frustrated in the long term. Given this, admittedly partial, understanding of happiness, self-love is, as commentators have emphasised, a *second-order* affection – a desire that other desires should be satisfied to this or that extent in the long term, and that certain objects of aversion should be avoided in the long term. The due exercise of self-love will, of course, require self-knowledge – knowledge that this or that mode of life will be a happy one for a being like myself.

So it follows from the things Butler tells us about self-love that it has to be classed *both* as an affection, in this case a desire that *I* should attain happiness, *and* as a rational principle. It is a rational principle in the sense that it requires a rational being's capacity to distinguish between such a general and second-order object as happiness and other objects of want, and in the sense that it is an affection that can only be exercised through judgments that particular objectives will, or will not, contribute to this general one. He brings out this necessary element of calculation by calling it 'cool self-love' and 'reasonable self-love'. Sometimes when speaking of conscience, he talks of it as though it alone is to be equated with the 'reflective' capacity we have to assess and evaluate our desires and objectives; but unless we are prepared to make self-love a special application of conscience, we have to recognise that self-love, as well as conscience, does this. This is easy to see from the fact that when he first tells us how human beings, uniquely, are able to act in ways that violate their natures, he illustrates this by speaking of acts which involve gratifying desires 'against the principle of cool and reasonable self-love' (*S* ii 10–11/13–15).

But, since self-love *is* an affection, two things follow. One is that self-love can be immoderate. Though, on the whole, Butler takes the view that we are too imprudent, and that self-love does not guide us enough, he does also think that self-love can dominate too much, just as immoderate desires can, and that we may rein ourselves in too much for our own good, even while seeking that very thing.[22] The second thing that follows is that self-love will have to have a feeling-tone of its own as he thinks all affections have, and will be *aroused* in us when it guides us. The fact that self-love is 'cool' in Butler's view shows the oddity of insisting on this, and the over-accommodatingness of the notion of an affection. Most of us would probably think that someone whose concern for his own welfare always had a discernible feeling-tone was someone whose self-love had become chronic anxiety, and was, in Butler's terms, disproportionate to his nature. What makes us exercise our self-love is the intellectual perception that perhaps something we want to do is not as good for us as we think; so what arouses self-love into action will be a judgment of the sort that Butler's restricted conceptual apparatus has to represent as the *outcome* of self-love, rather than something that stimulates it. This is one place where Butler's human understanding is subtler than the linguistic resources he allows himself to use.

When making his case against psychological hedonism, Butler says that the object of self-love differs from the objects of the particular affections in being internal when they are external. Duncan-Jones has pointed out that this is unsatisfactory as it stands, although the argument can be recast.[23] We will return to this below, but Butler's point is easy enough to illustrate. If I am hungry and want food, my desire is for *food*, not for my own well-being, or even for my own pleasure. Both the well-being and the pleasure may follow, but the object which has the 'prior suitableness' to my desire is the food. Self-love is a desire for my happiness, which is a desire for an internal state of myself. Duncan-Jones points out that we do, often, desire internal states, such as the thrill of the switchback or the cessation of pain. So the distinction Butler wants to make, and seems intuitively correct in making, cannot be expressed in this way.

7

The status of benevolence in Butler's moral psychology has divided the commentators, and there is no doubt that his references to it point in different directions. The fundamental dispute about it has been over whether it is a rational principle like self-love, which has some kind of general role distinct from that of the particular appetites, passions, and affections, or whether the word 'benevolence' is merely a general name encompassing all those particular desires which are desires for the good of other people. The problem about this is easy to illustrate from the first Sermon, where Butler argues that there is 'a natural principle of *benevolence* in man; which is in some degree to *society*, what *self-love*

31

is to the individual' (S i 6/4). The use of the phrase 'natural principle' is merely an indication that Butler is emphasising its presence in our nature, and tells us nothing about the sort of principle it is. But the understanding of 'benevolence' as a generic term covering all other-regarding affections is supported by the next sentence, in which Butler lists a number of motives which are proofs that we are capable of benevolence: the 'disposition of friendship', compassion (which he calls 'momentary love'). paternal and filial affection, and 'any affection . . . the object and end of which is the good of another'. The presence of any of these is enough to prove the existence of benevolence. In the next paragraph he goes on to distinguish between those passions and affections which, under providence, work for the good of others, but which do not have 'the security and good of society' as their 'primary use and intention', and benevolence, which does. Examples of the former are love of esteem and reputation, which is a 'public passion' in the sense that satisfying it involves gaining a certain relationship to others, 'love of society as distinct from affection to the good of it', and 'indignation against successful vice'. These will probably generate socially valuable behaviour, but that is not their intrinsic object. Towards the close of this Sermon (12/11) he equates benevolence with 'good-will'; and insists that it has no opposing principle in our natures – 'neither is there any such thing as ill-will in one man towards another, emulation and resentment being away'.[24] Our passions lead 'only secondarily and accidentally to what is evil'.

There is nothing in this introduction of the idea of benevolence to make us think it is more than the generic name for all affections which have the good of other persons as their objects. This view is reinforced when we turn to the next two Sermons, which argue for the hierarchical structure of our nature and the supremacy of conscience. In the final paragraph of Sermon iii we have the blunt statement that 'reasonable self-love and conscience are the chief or superior principles in the nature of man'; benevolence is conspicuous by its absence.

In places where benevolence comes in for more specific attention, however, Butler treats it in ways that support a different understanding of it. The most explicit occurs in the first of the two Sermons 'Upon Compassion'. Compassion, it will be recalled, is one of the affections into which the notion of benevolence is unpacked in Sermon i. In Sermon v he asks:

Is it possible any can in earnest think, that a public spirit, i.e. a settled and reasonable principle of benevolence to mankind, is so prevalent and strong in the species, as that we may venture to throw off the under affections, which are its assistants, carry it forward and mark out particular courses for it; family, friends, neighbourhood, the distressed, our country? (*S* v 10/10)

This passage, with its talk of one principle being an assistant to another, clearly implies that it is not a form of the other, but something distinct. This suggests that compassion is a particular affection which has as its object the furtherance of the good (or, more accurately, the reduction of harm) of another individual known to us, and which is more effective in getting us to do good to others than the independently existing but motivationally weak general principle of doing good to mankind. This does not indicate that the more general principle is not an affection, any more than the parallel fact that I am more likely to feed myself from hunger than from self-love shows that self-love is not an affection. Butler has, indeed, another name for this general affection of benevolence: the love of our neighbour. Sermons xi and xii are based on the New Testament commandments to love our neighbour as ourselves, which is interpreted (plausibly or not) as telling us something about the proper relationship between benevolence and self-love. In Sermon xii, towards the conclusion, Butler discusses the question (to which he returns more forcibly in the Dissertation on Virtue) of whether benevolence is the whole of virtue. Those who suppose this, he says, do not speak of benevolence 'as a blind propension, but as a principle in reasonable creatures, and so to be directed by their reason' (*S* xii 27/19). This still does not indicate that Butler does not think of benevolence as an affection, for he goes on to say that what makes benevolence such a plausible candidate for identification with virtue is the fact that reason 'must come in as its guide and mentor', to prevent our ignoring consequences and circumstances in our wish to do good. I think this means that the general kind of benevolence which is distinguished from such particular affections as compassion is still an affection, which reason has to direct and rein in, in order to avoid undiscriminating good will. Benevolence, thus interpreted, is capable of disproportionate exercise, just as self-love is. Reason has to be used to determine what is or is not for the good of others, and to help us recognise where such good needs to be done, and where harm may befall others if we do not act.

In spite of this, T. A. Roberts is not *quite* correct when he says that the general affection of benevolence stands in the same relation to particular affections like paternal and filial affection as self-love does towards that group of affections having as their end the good of the self.[25] The parallel holds well enough if we compare the two in one mode. I might eat because I am hungry, with no thought at all of my good. On the other hand, I might eat because, even though I am more inclined to continue some absorbing activity than interrupt it for supper, I know it is good for my delicate digestion to eat at regular intervals. The latter motive is a particular affection, that has as its end the good of the self. The general affection of self-love, or the general desire for my own welfare, has a slightly different relation to each. It can reinforce both, but of the two only the desire for a sound digestion is a desire that specifies or particularises the desire for my good. In the case of benevolence, the situation is more complex. A mother giving her child a snack may do so simply out of a desire that the child should have the pleasure of eating it. If she gives it to the child in order to provide it with needed energy, she is probably seeking this object for the child's *good*. The *general* desire for the child's good, while it may *reinforce* the desire to please the child, has a closer relationship to the desire for it to have the energy it needs. Thus far, benevolence and self-love are parallel. But there is another dimension to the generality of benevolence that cannot be present in the case of self-love. Parental affection is a desire for the good *of my children*; friendship is, or entails, the desire for the good *of my friends*. Benevolence *per se* (the settled principle) is the general desire for the good *of all those with whom I may have to do*. It is the desire for the good of my fellow-creatures, or my *neighbours*. In Sermon xii (3/2) Butler points out that in God, whose benevolence is perfect, the whole universe is the object of it; for us, the requirement is to love our neighbour, since we are incapable of 'absolutely universal' goodwill, although the scope will vary with the station of the individual concerned. The object of benevolence for most of us has to be 'that part of mankind, that part of our country, which comes under our immediate notice, acquaintance, and influence, and with which we have to do'. So although he is not very clear about this, I think Butler considers benevolence in its most general aspect as the desire for the good of other persons *as our neighbours*, or as fellow-humans with whom we have to do. The affection of compassion will be a particularisation of this, in that compassion is felt for any *distressed* person with whom I have to do. This is, then, the application to a special group of the general desire for the neighbour's good. But it is at least odd to treat parental affections as specifications of the love of neighbour, since it is odd to talk of my children as my neighbours.

With this emendation, I think Roberts is correct to argue that what Butler says about benevolence, though not fully consistent, does, on the whole, require us to say that he thinks of it as a general affection for the neighbour's good, which is also a rational principle in the way that self-love is. It is cool, in that it is less likely to determine our actions on its own than in conjunction with particular affections like compassion which assist it. It is reasonable, in that it requires the capacity to distinguish, in others, the difference between short-term satisfactions and long-term good that self-love requires us to distinguish in ourselves, and it will be aroused, or brought into play, by circumstances which bring the needs of others, as distinct from their short-term wants, to our attention. And

just as self-love can control us too much, so benevolence may need to
be frustrated or reined in by our reason (in this case our conscience),
since the very desire for the good of others may now and then lead us
into acts which do not, in the long term, serve their interests, even
though that is what we intend.

In spite of this, there is no doubt that Butler treats benevolence as
inferior, in the hierarchy of human nature, to self-love, as well as to
conscience. I think that this is, in the end, a simple judgment that it is
weaker than self-love is. Given Butler's emphatic distinction between the
strength and the power of the inner principles that motivate us, this has
to mean that *God intends* it to be weaker; that he has made us with a
capacity to care for our neighbour's good, but that he has not made us
with a capacity to care for it more than for our own.[26] The teleology he
assumes is to this extent an egoistic one. It is because of this that he
takes the command to love one's neighbour as oneself to be in need of
philosophical elucidation, and assumes that such an elucidation has to
consist in a demonstration that benevolence is not contrary to self-love,
but 'contributes to private interest' (*S* xi 19/20).

8

Self-love and benevolence are affections which involve reason.
Conscience, however, is not an affection at all. However vital it is for
us, as human beings, to have a nature in which our affective makeup
prompts us to act in desirable ways, there is no doubt that to Butler,
when conscience motivates us, its contribution is a rational one. He
introduces conscience to us as 'a principle of reflection in men, by which
they distinguish between, approve and disapprove their own actions' (*S* i
8/7). The language of this introduction suggests that conscience is the
only reflective principle, the only faculty by which we 'reflect upon our
own nature' and on the motives and actions proper to it. While he often
talks in this way[27], it is clear that self-love, and, if the preceding section
is sound, benevolence also, require reflection upon our motives and
actions, and cannot function without it, since each necessarily involves
a consciousness of my own nature, or that of others, and its needs. If
conscience is to have a distinctive character, it has to be found in the
special manner in which it exercises its reflective power. He makes it
clear enough in the same Sermon, and emphasises it more than once in
the Dissertation on Virtue, that its judgments are distinctive in the form
they take: that of *approval or disapproval*. (In Sermon i he adds indifference, or moral neutrality, to these.)

Conscience, then, is our 'approving and disapproving faculty' (Diss II
2/2). It judges its objects as 'virtuous and of good desert' or 'vicious and
of ill desert', as 'right and wrong, odious and amiable, base and worthy,

35

with many others of like signification in all languages' (Diss II 1/1. It makes such judgments upon 'actions, comprehending under that name active or practical principles: those principles from which men would act, if occasions and circumstances gave them power; and which, when fixed and habitual in any person, we call his character' (Diss II 2/2). In other words, conscience is our capacity for making moral judgments, these judgments being applied to people's actions and their motives, on the understanding that they are free to do or not to do those actions, and to follow or not to follow those motives. This latter is important, for it implies that even when I act from a motive that is stronger than my conscience is, I am able to refrain from acting on that motive, and the authority which conscience has is unaffected by its strength. If this were not true, I could not be judged morally.[28]

This notion of conscience is wider than the popular one in one respect. We do not, in common speech, talk of my conscience as judging anyone's actions but my own.[29] In ordinary speech you cannot violate my conscience, or be troubled by promptings of anyone's conscience but your own. Yet, as Kant was later to remind us so powerfully, it is integral to my moral judgments of my own actions, if I make them sincerely, that I apply the same standards to them that I would apply to those of other agents. So conscience, in the narrower sense, is a special application to oneself of a power that we can and do exercise in relation to others. But in spite of this, Butler's wider use of the term leads to some unfortunate ambiguities in what he says about the role of conscience, and he would have been wiser to keep to the narrower use, on which his arguments often depend in any case. (This point will concern us particularly in Chapter III.)

Even though Butler does not classify conscience as an affection,[30] this does not mean that he thinks it has no emotional aspects. In the Dissertation he says that our common language presupposes that we have such a faculty, 'whether considered as a sentiment of the understanding, or as a perception of the heart; or, which seems the truth, as including both' (Diss II 1/1). This clause is intended, no doubt, to evade involvement in contemporary controversies over whether virtue is a matter of reason or sentiment, but it certainly is also intended to recognise that the judgments of conscience have emotional overtones and consequences: guilt, indignation, and the like. As twentieth-century arguments about emotivist theories of ethics have reminded us, the concept of approval is complex, involving both commendatory judgment and positive attitude. However we judge these matters, I do not think it alters the fact that conscience is something that Butler deliberately and habitually *contrasts* with affections, indeed with all other motives, however classified, and that the concept of conscience is primarily that of a faculty which makes *judgments* that are (or should be) practically effective. If its doing this entails that it includes emotional elements, this does not make it an affection, any more than the fact that self-love is rational shows self-love not to be one. Conscience can, and does, co-operate with affections in motivating actions. Butler gives the example of the parent who cares for his children from affection, but whose good behaviour towards them is reinforced by the fact that it is also 'his proper business' as a parent to do this (*S* i 8/8).

While this will have to be developed later, there is a fundamental feature of the judgments of conscience that should be stressed now. Butler makes it clear in Sermon ii (8/10). Conscience, he tells us, 'pronounces determinately some actions to be in themselves just, right, good; others to be in themselves evil, wrong, unjust'. The key words are 'in themselves'; conscience, in judging actions to be right or wrong, judges them as actions of a certain kind, not as leading to this or that result. In the Dissertation he makes the point more generally, applying it to motives as well as to actions:

Acting, conduct, behaviour, abstracted from all regard to what is, in fact and event, the consequence of it, is itself the natural object of the moral discernment; as speculative truth and falsehood is of speculative reason. Intention of such consequences, indeed, is always included; for it is part of the action itself: but though the intended good or bad consequences do not follow, we have exactly the same sense of the action as if they did. (Diss II 2/2)

It is not what we achieve, but what we intend to do, that is the object of moral judgment. Butler is clearly deontological, not utilitarian, in his view of what moral judgment is, however we assess his view of human nature as a whole. It is striking that in the part of the Dissertation where he argues that prudence is a moral virtue, he goes out of his way to say that when our conscience approves prudent actions (which he insists it does) it is prudent actions as such, and not their consequences, that it judges (7/7). Conscience has another unique feature. Butler says that it

. . . without being consulted, without being advised with, magisterially exerts itself, and approves or condemns. . . . accordingly: and . . . if not forcibly stopped, naturally and always of course goes on to anticipate a higher and more effectual sentence, which shall hereafter second and confirm its own. (S ii 8/10)

Conscience makes its judgments whether we seek them or not; it *intrudes itself* on our thoughts, unasked. Butler thinks that in doing this conscience is acting in a special way that God has implanted in our nature to prepare us for the final judgment. In the *Analogy* he tells us that 'the dictates of this moral faculty, which are by Nature a rule to us, are moreover the laws of God' (*An* I vi 11/14). No doubt Butler thinks of the 'magisterial' aspect of conscience as a sign of its being the vehicle of God's laws. But it is vital to remember that this does not mean that when conscience pronounces an action to be right or wrong, this in itself is a judgment of a theological sort. This is shown both by his saying that the dictates of conscience are 'by Nature a rule to us', and only *additionally* laws of God, and by his clear commitment to the view that what God commands he commands as being morally fit or unfit, 'prior to all will whatever' (*An* II viii 11/24). Conscience is that faculty in us which discerns the moral rightness or wrongness of actions which God also commands or forbids on the basis of a superior but essentially similar recognition.

Finally, the fact that prudence is, to Butler, a virtue, implies that conscience will approve of actions that are motivated by a proper understanding of our nature and its needs (that is, by self-love). But the fact that conscience approves or disapproves of actions in themselves, and not for their consequences, shows that the relation of those acts to our nature is not itself the content of the moral judgments conscience makes. Following conscience is, no doubt, for my good; God has placed conscience in my nature for that reason; but that does not mean that my nature and its needs are the object of the judgments of conscience, any more than the fact that I have the appetite of hunger for the good of my nature means that I am pursuing the good of my nature when I eat my lunch.

II

The Reality of Benevolence

Whatever the theological underpinnings of Butler's thought, his moral psychology is, in one key respect, as wholly empirical as it appears. He claims that observation of our own thoughts and actions, and of the behaviour of others, is itself enough to show us that the 'principles' he discusses in his arguments are indeed *present* in human nature. In this he is surely right, at least to the extent that anyone who denies the presence of one or other of them has to offer special arguments. It does *look* as though we act from self-love, from benevolence, and from conscience, at least sometimes, and if a thinker denies that one of these is really to be found among our motives, he has the special duty of explaining apparent examples of their presence in some other way. If he fails, he can reasonably be accused of espousing *a priori* theories in the face of the evidence. Butler claims that both the psychological egoist and the psychological hedonist are guilty of this. The former holds that all our motives are selfish, and the latter holds that all our motives reduce to a desire for our own pleasure.

Butler contends that both theories are due to elementary mistakes. He also thinks them morally dangerous, since they have perennial appeal to the wordly-wise, and encourage them to mistrust the genuineness of their better aspirations. Each implies the unreality of conscience, as well as that of benevolence, but his arguments against them deal with their denial of benevolence only; and, even here, there are limits on what they show.

1

Butler's historical target is Thomas Hobbes, who viewed social morality as an alien way of life imposed by sheer power on beings whose natural inclinations are wholly self-centred. Butler is on record as rejecting the view that moral rightness derives from commands, even divine ones;[1]

but his arguments against Hobbes in the *Sermons* are all designed to show that his cynical estimate of human motives is a baseless 'general hypothesis', and to defend the common-sense alternative to it.

Butler's arguments are telling, but vary a great deal in quality, partly because his outrage occasionally gets the better of him. It is best to begin with two sets of arguments directed against specific Hobbesian claims: those relating to 'good will or charity' (what Butler calls benevolence) and his comments on pity (or compassion).

The first set of arguments is better known, and appears in a long footnote to paragraph 6/4 in Sermon i, where Butler first asserts that there is a 'natural principle of benevolence in man'. In the note, he specifically refers us to a passage in Hobbes's discourse *Human Nature*. I quote the offending sentences from that passage:

> There is yet another passion sometimes called *love*, but more properly *good will* or *charity*. There can be no greater argument to a man, of his own power, than to find himself able not only to accomplish his own desires, but also to *assist* other men in theirs: and this is that conception wherein consisteth *charity*. In which, first, is contained that *natural affection* of parents to their children, which the Greeks call *storge*, as also, that affection wherewith men seek to *assist* those that adhere unto them. But the affection wherewith men many times bestow their benefits on *strangers*, is not to be called charity, but either *contract*, whereby they seek to purchase friendship; or *fear*, which maketh them to purchase peace.[2]

To a present-day reader, there is a problem in deciding whether Hobbes in this passage is engaged in conceptual analysis or psychology. If he is engaged in conceptual analysis, then he is maintaining that the concepts of charity and love of power are the same. If he is practising psychology, then he is maintaining a thesis whose coherence and shock-value require the assumption that these two concepts are *not* the same: the thesis that those actions which appear to be motivated by charity are in fact not so motivated, but are due instead to the love of power – that benevolence is never to be found among our motives. While Hobbes's language lends itself naturally to the former reading (especially the clause 'and this is that conception wherein consisteth charity'), it is more plausible to read him as maintaining the psychological thesis. This is how Butler reads him; but he begins with a conceptual point. Surely, he says, someone offering a theory like that of Hobbes would cause his readers to think that he had made 'a mistake of one word for another', and was talking about some behaviour other than that of apparent benevolence? There is a faint hint here of what has been called the Paradigm Case Argument – that we learn general terms through observation of actual examples of the qualities they name, so that someone who denies that ostensibly benevolent behaviour ever *is* really benevolent, has failed to learn the appropriate language when confronted with activities to which it applies: that a correct use of language precludes the denial that there are *any* benevolent motives. But if this is what Butler intends, he does not develop it, and proceeds immediately with criticisms that assume Hobbes to be arguing the psychological thesis that apparently benevolent acts are really done from love of power. Such a view, he says, can only be persuasive to someone who has 'a general hypothesis, to which the appearance of good-will could no otherwise be reconciled'.

He offers four arguments in refutation. (i) No doubt 'delight in superiority' often mingles with benevolence, so that there is more plausibility to the suggestion that acts of apparent benevolence are really exercises of love of power than to a suggestion that they are due to some appetite, like hunger, that does not mix with it. But the explanation still does not fit the appearances it is designed to account for. People often appear to rejoice when someone they themselves are not able to help is helped by a third party. Good will explains this very well, but if the alleged motive is the love of power, the rejoicing is unaccountable. (ii) People select some, rather than others, as recipients of their good deeds, in ways that love of power cannot explain. If love of power motivates us when good will appears to, this would imply, according to Butler, that the objects of our ostensive beneficence would be selected because doing good to them involved greater exercise of power than would be involved in doing good to others. This is a weaker argument, and is not helped by the total absence of examples. If we assume that good will is our motive on all those occasions when it appears to be, this does not force us to hold that the selection of persons to receive our beneficence is itself an exercise of good will: if I give money to a charity that benefits members of my own community, rather than to one that benefits those in a far-off country, my choice does not have to be due to good will merely because giving to a charity itself is benevolent. The choice can be due to quite independent factors. Similarly, if I choose to display my power over my own children by getting them to perform pointless tasks, rather than to do the same to the schoolchildren I teach, my choice of victims will probably be due to a factor like the risk of legal repercussions, not to the fact that I display more power by harassing the group I select. (iii) Delight in the exercise of power can as readily take the form of inflicting pain and evil on others, as in doing good to them. In the absence of restraints, cruelty would be as likely a manifestation of it as charity. If charity is nothing more than love of power, therefore, cruelty 'would be exactly the same in the mind of a man as good-will', since the two would only differ in their consequences, not in themselves. The point is not well-expressed, but I take Butler to be saying that if, when we perform acts that produce good for others, what motivates us is the love

41

of exercising power, many acts that produce good will have just the same motive as acts that cause others suffering; since, however, in calling them charitable rather than cruel, we refer not only to their consequences but also to their motive (charitable acts being acts in which we *deliberately* do good, and cruel acts being acts in which we *deliberately* do harm), we would not make use of the distinction in the way that we do if Hobbes were correct. The argument is not compelling, since it would be easy enough for Hobbes to reply that we use the distinction in the way that we do because we mistakenly *think* that the acts we call charitable are done from good will; they are in fact done from a love of power, which happens to manifest itself in acts that are good to others because of secondary considerations such as a wish for a good reputation. This retort would be enough to make the facts Butler mentions consistent with Hobbes's theory. They would, however, run us immediately into Butler's main argument, which follows.

(iv) A theory of human motives that runs counter to common opinion in the way that Hobbes's does, needs to be well-supported. How, asks Butler, are we to establish whether man's 'inward frame' includes good will or not? It is a 'question of fact or natural history, not provable immediately by reason'. Hence it has to be decided like other matters of natural history in one of three ways. Butler claims that each of these ways establishes the presence of some degree of benevolence in human beings. (a) The first way is that of external or internal observation. He does not elaborate, and he is perhaps open to the charge that external observation can only show us what *seem* to be benevolent actions; this is a charge which he tries to meet, I think, in his comments on the second way of proof. When he speaks of 'inward perceptions' he presumably means introspective awareness of one's own motives. Here, of course, we run into the difficulty, of which much was made by Kant, that we are not good judges of the purity of our own intentions, so that what we tell ourselves is intended benevolently may well be done from some selfish motive that we are concealing from ourselves – even if it is not the particular selfish motive that Hobbes says it is. Self-deception is a fact of human psychology of which Butler is well aware, and on which he even has a separate Sermon; in the present context he deals with this difficulty at the end of the footnote, where he makes it clear that he knows that benevolence is often mixed with lesser motives, and needs to be cultivated. All he claims is that the evidence of our own self-knowledge establishes *some degree* of it in us. 'It is sufficient', he says, 'that the seeds of it be implanted in our nature by God.'³

(b) The second way in which the presence of benevolence can be proved is 'by arguing from acknowledged facts and actions; for a great number of actions in the same kind, in different circumstances, and respecting different objects, will prove, to a certainty what principles they do not, and to the greatest probability, what principles they do, proceed from'. This point is rather abstractly put, but Duncan-Jones seems right to interpret it as a generalisation from arguments like (ii) and (iii) above: if we find a large number of cases in which people seem to act benevolently, and where another motive like that of the love of power would lead us to expect them *not* to behave in the way they do, then we have an accumulation of evidence that augments the judgments we are inclined to make from individual observations. (c) The third way in which the presence of benevolence can be proved is from testimony. Here I take Butler to be making the familiar point that our knowledge of human nature is not based on our own observations and generalisations alone, but upon those of others, whose experience is as greatly at variance with theories like those of Hobbes as our own is.

Butler's case, though not free of detailed flaws, is compelling because of its simplicity, and is one of the best-known confrontations of common sense and ordinary experience with a dogmatic cynicism that masquerades as worldly wisdom. That egoisms like that of Hobbes still flourish does nothing to suggest Butler has not proved his case.

He argues a similar case against Hobbes with regard to pity, or compassion, which he treats in Sermon v as a psychological counterpart to benevolence – as distress at the misfortune of others, and the wish to lessen it. His arguments are once more found in a long footnote to the first paragraph of that Sermon, and refer again to a particular passage in Hobbes. The first three sentences of that passage are these:

> *Pity* is *imagination* or *fiction* of *future* calamity to *ourselves*, proceeding from the sense of *another* man's calamity. But when it lighteth on such as we think have not deserved the same, the compassion is greater, because then there appeareth more probability that the same may happen to us: for, the evil that happeneth to an innocent man, may happen to every man. But when we see a man suffer for great crimes, which we cannot easily think will fall upon ourselves, the pity is the less.[4]

This very implausible interpretation of compassion distresses Butler even more than the corresponding attack on benevolence, and his criticisms are more heated.

They are also more conceptual than the arguments he uses about Hobbes's treatment of love. (i) He begins by accusing Hobbes of sustaining a system which excludes concern for others by defining pity in terms that manifestly describe something else. If pity were indeed a sense of future danger to ourselves, it would be identical with fear; but everyone sees that the two ideas are different. If this could be doubted, the doubt would be dispelled by the fact that a habitually compassionate man is the object of admiration and concern, whereas the habitually fearful, or cowardly, man is not; it is the brave man we admire. (ii) He proceeds to expose alleged absurdities in Hobbes's thesis by saying that if it were true, we could substitute Hobbes's *definiens* for his *definiendum* without change of meaning. Where Hobbes gives a reason why we pity our friends more than others, we could regard this as a reason why we *fear* our friends more than others. In addition, if his definition of pity were accepted, it would imply the obvious falsehood that the object of pity is not some other person, but oneself, which is palpably false. Hobbes may deserve these arguments, but they are neither fair nor compelling if one reads him as offering a psychological argument, however badly expressed. His claim is, surely, that when we say we pity another person, we may indeed mean that we are distressed at his sufferings, but on all the occasions when we claim this we are deceiving ourselves. What in fact is taking place is that the sight of the other's distress arouses in us anxieties about our own future. So the object of our concern and distress may *appear* (even to us) to be the other person in his trouble, but in fact it is ourselves. Such a doctrine, misanthropic though it may be, is not obviously incoherent; to show it to be incoherent one would have to demonstrate some such thesis as the one Butler hints at in his discussion of benevolence: that we could not acquire the concept of pity that we have unless some of the occasions when we use it were real cases of its occurrence. It is certainly not enough to point out that the verbal substitutions Butler ridicules are impossible. Arguments of that sort only refute the explicit claims that the words 'pity' and 'fear for ourselves' have the same meaning. Although Hobbes is open to this reading, it misrepresents his obvious intent. What is needed to refute Hobbes's psychology is better psychology. Fortunately, it is this that Butler goes on to give us.

(iii) He begins by saying that everyone would agree that the sight of the innocent, or of our friends, in distress, moves us more than the sight of others, such as criminals, in distress. If Hobbes were correct in saying that when we think we feel compassion we are really anxious about ourselves, then we would be more fearful for ourselves when we see the distress of the innocent, or of our friends, than when we see the distress of others. But it is not at all obvious that we *do* feel more anxiety about ourselves in the one case than in the other. Since whatever emotion we are feeling is indeed more strong when it is our friends' distress we see than when it is not, it is quite implausible to interpret it as selfish anxiety rather than the compassion we suppose it to be.[5]

(iv) He next says that if we forget we are in danger, and some event reminds us of it, Hobbes's theory would suggest that the things or persons involved in that event would be called objects of compassion whatever sort of event it was; but in fact we only use this language when speaking of persons involved in *distressful* events. Hence compassion cannot be a mask for anxiety about ourselves. This is a very bad argument. Hobbes is not committed to the view that *every* occasion of anxiety for oneself is one that masquerades as compassion, but only to the view that our anxieties are disguised in *this* way when they are aroused by the sight of the distress of others. His theory would allow other disguises on other occasions.

(v) Butler is at his best, however, when he attempts to do justice to the psychological truths on which Hobbes is trying to capitalise. There are, he says, three 'inward feelings' that we may have when we notice the distress of others. The first is sorrow for the victim. The second is relief that we ourselves are spared the suffering that the victim is enduring. The third is the recognition that we are also liable to the same misfortunes. While the second and third often accompany the first, only the first is properly called compassion, and it is quite distinct from the others. Hobbes gains a hearing by confusing them. In particular, he seeks to identify the emotion we have on such occasions with the third. This is not an emotion at all; it is a 'reflection of reason'. Even if there were some affective state corresponding to it, it would be some form of mutual sympathy or fellow-feeling, and this would be a counter-example to a selfish theory of human nature, not a confirmation of it.

2

These attacks on Hobbes's selfish analyses of charity and compassion are only part of the case Butler feels obliged to mount in order to defend his view of the role of benevolence in our nature. In addition, there are the more famous and systematic arguments designed to refute psychological egoism and psychological hedonism, and to demonstrate the falsity of the popular view that self-love and benevolence are antithetical principles. I shall only consider the former here, since they are, in effect, part of his case for the *reality* of benevolence, as distinct from his particular estimate of its proper place in the moral life; but it is not possible to separate them altogether.

The arguments I shall examine are to be found in the Preface to the *Sermons* (paragraphs 35–42/29–37) and in Sermon xi (especially paragraphs 5–18/3–18), though they depend on the accounts of self-love, benevolence, and happiness that Butler gives us elsewhere. There are two positions that Butler is trying to refute. The first, which I shall call E, is the thesis of psychological egoism, that all our actions are done from selfish motives. Butler interprets this in two related ways. The first, expressed in the language of his own moral psychology is (E^1) that all actions are done from self-love. The second, expressed with a term from common speech, which he tries to define, is (E^2) that all our actions are interested, or that there are no disinterested actions. The second thesis

45

that Butler tries to refute is the thesis of psychological hedonism, which I shall refer to as H. This is the thesis that all actions are done for the sake of the agent's own pleasure. It is a special version of E, but raises particular problems of its own, which require separate attention.

Butler's refutation of E[1] can be summarised as follows. E[1] rests on a failure to distinguish between self-love and the particular passions and affections. When the distinction is properly observed, we can readily see four things. (i) Not all actions could, in logic, be due to self-love, even if they were all to serve the objective that self-love has. (ii) In fact, we all act, quite frequently, *against* self-love, and most of us could do with a greater measure of it. (iii) Unselfish, or benevolent, actions may well conform to the dictates of self-love. (iv) The objective of self-love, namely our happiness, is more likely to be attained if we do not always act *from* self-love.

The refutation of E[2] can be summarised like this. The distinction between an interested and a disinterested action is easy to misinterpret. The proper definition of an interested action is that it is one done from self-love. Once this is understood and observed, we can see two things. (i) Many actions which serve self-love, in that they contribute to our happiness, are still disinterested, since they are not done *from* self-love. (ii) Benevolent actions, though indeed disinterested, share this characteristic with many others, including many vicious actions. The question of whether benevolent actions serve self-love, by leading to our happiness, remains open when their disinterestedness is admitted.

Butler's refutation of H proceeds as follows. It depends, he says, upon two confused inferences. (i) The first is the inference from the fact that all my motives are my own, and not another's, to the conclusion that I must always aim at some internal state of my own being. (ii) The second is the inference from the fact that I usually find pleasure in satisfying my desires, to the conclusion that my desires are always desires for my own pleasure.

Butler appears to take it for granted that E and H between them exhaust all possible versions of selfish theories of human motives. He assumes, that is, that if such theories do not claim that all our acts are due to the search for our own happiness, then they must ascribe the remainder to the pursuit of pleasure. In our own day we have many more egoistic accounts of human action than this, such as those of Freudianism, Marxism, and Sociobiology. Butler's arguments are not intended to respond to theories that invoke motives of which the agent himself is not aware, or able to discern through conscientious introspection. But even here, arguments like his are, minimally, a necessary propaedeutic to the evaluation of such theories.

The refutation of E[1] depends, of course, on Butler's theory of self-love, which I have already attempted to outline. To act from self-love is to follow the desire for my own good, or for happiness. To follow this desire, however, I have to have made the rational judgment that the course before me is one that will further that objective. Since Butler holds that happiness requires the satisfaction of particular desires or aversions, the role of self-love cannot be to *replace* these. He appears to suppose its normal function to be that of saying Yes or No to particular desires, depending on whether or not they are judged to contribute to happiness. It is clear that this account of how self-love can, and should, function, provides ready refutations of E^1 and E^2. (i) In the first place, it requires a clear distinction to be made between self-love and other, particular, desires. So even on those occasions when the two coincide, and self-love says Yes to some particular desire, there is a motive operating in addition to self-love, which self-love encourages or permits to be satisfied. So even when we do what we want to do, and judge it to be for our own good, our own good is not the whole of our motive. (ii) On those occasions when we do something we do not want to do, or refrain from doing something that we do want to do, because we judge it to be against our interests, Butler would presumably hold self-love to be our only motive. But these occasions are matched by those on which we act *against* the dictates of self-love, often fully conscious that what we are doing is ruinous to us. There is no neo-Socratic nonsense about Butler, who holds that we frequently act, knowingly, against our interests, and that it is obvious that we do. When this happens, we follow some particular desire because it is stronger in us than self-love is, even though the latter has authority, that is, *should* be able to override the desire and stop us. So little is it the case that all our actions are due to self-love, that Butler is moved to say that most people have too little self-love for their own good:

> they have not cool and reasonable concern enough for themselves to consider wherein their chief happiness in the present life consists;
> or else, if they do consider it, . . . they will not act conformably to what is the result of that consideration. (S i 14/15)

(iii) The distinction between self-love and particular desires can be partially made by saying that they have distinct objects. The object of self-love is my own happiness, whereas the object of particular desires is the particular thing or event wanted, such as my lunch, a house, a holiday, or a nap. I leave aside for the moment Butler's unfortunate characterisation of this difference as one between internal and external objects, since his point can be expressed readily enough without using this language. He holds that although I may be unable to pursue happiness without judging whether particular desires contribute to it, I can, and do, act from particular desires without considering whether they contribute to happiness or not. Once this is accepted in all its generality, it can be seen that among the desires that motivate me there may well be desires that contribute to the good of others – even desires *for* the good of others. Whether or not such desires contribute to my own happiness is a question I have to decide by exercising self-love. The answer may be No, but it may also, for all we can tell *a priori*, be Yes. So benevolence, at least in the sense of particular other-directed desires, is something that is no more contrary to self-love in principle than any other particular desires may be. I might well serve the objective that self-love exists to protect, by following my benevolent impulses. Butler's crucial point here is that even if, contrary to fact, we were always to follow self-love, this might well lead us to indulge, not to curb, our desires to do good to others. The only way the psychological egoist can prove the non-existence of benevolence (at least in this particular sense) is by denying the broader distinction between self-love and particular desires, or by adopting the special thesis of psychological hedonism that all particular desires are in fact desires for my own pleasure, which Butler considers separately.

(iv) Butler adds the important observation that we sometimes further our happiness better by *not* considering whether what we want to do contributes to it, since calculating what is to our advantage can prevent the enjoyment of these very activities that happiness requires. '*Disengagement*', he says, 'is absolutely necessary to enjoyment; and a person may have so steady and fixed an eye upon his own interest, whatever he places it in, as may hinder him from *attending* to many gratifications within his reach, which others have their minds free and open to' (*S* xi 9/7). He sees here that enjoyment is a form of attention, and that the reflections of self-love can be distracting. This is his explanation of the fact that selfish persons (those over-endowed with self-love) are often less happy than others. Duncan-Jones finds a problem with the suggestion that self-love can be over-dominant in a personality, presumably on the ground that the authority given by Butler to self-love requires us to say that we are not acting from it when we do not follow our real interests.[6] But although Butler is inclined, both with self-love and with conscience, to assume too readily that due care and objectivity are enough to ensure the right answers, and therefore to talk about 'supposed self-love' when self-love gives the wrong ones, I do not think he falls into the trap of treating self-love as immune to error. When he tells us, in the Preface, that it is normally too weak, he says that its judgments are 'constant and habitual' and 'cannot but be', and our most common problem is that the desire for happiness, which prompts these judgments, is not strong enough to override the harmful passions of the moment. This does imply that for most people the problem is not that they do not judge their self-interest correctly, but that they do not enforce these judgments on themselves. But he modifies this position in Sermon xi in two ways. He says that the selfish person, who is on guard against his benevolent impulses, is making an error of *judgment* about which desires will lead to happiness and which will not. He also says we can make our lives miserable by having so strong a general desire for our own good that we raise over-anxious questions about every desire that arises, to discover what profit is in it. I think the phrase 'immoderate self-love' is intended to cover both failings, though only the latter involves too strong a desire for happiness. There is a minor inconsistency here. Someone inordinately endowed with the desire for his own good presumably has to learn when *not* to ask whether a desire leads to it. If he asks it constantly, he should not. So Butler must be wrong to say that the judgments of self-love cannot but be constant, even if we can allow that they are habitual. Similarly, while some of those in whom self-love is too weak ask the questions but do not heed the answers, surely some do not even ask them. It is clear from Sermon i itself, however, that Butler interprets the weakness of self-love in both ways, so that the ascription of constancy to its judgments must be a lapse.

I turn, next, to Butler's refutation of E^2, the thesis that there are no disinterested actions. His case rests upon his definition of the word 'interested'. He begins by accusing a number of writers, including Hobbes, of a confusion: 'the confusion of calling actions interested which are done in contradiction to the most manifest known interest, merely for the gratification of a present passion' (S Pr 35/29). He claims that the 'most natural way of speaking plainly' is to confine the word 'interested' to actions done from self-love. If we accept this, it follows that actions done to gratify a present passion, but in known opposition to the agent's interest, are not interested actions. Given this, we can say two things. (i) The purpose of self-love, namely the satisfaction of an adequate number of the particular desires that make up our nature, is often met by actions that are not done *from* self-love, but from the simple occurrence of those desires themselves. These are, therefore, disinterested actions. (See S Pr 37/31.) (ii) More importantly, we can agree that benevolent actions are disinterested, but see that the same thing can be said of many other actions also, including the most vicious ones: 'disinterestedness is so far from being in itself commendable, that the utmost possible depravity which we can in imagination conceive, is that of disinterested cruelty' (S Pr 39/34).

Unfortunately, Butler's account of our usage seems deficient. He is right, of course, to say that the mere fact that an act I do is done from a motive of my own, is not enough to make it interested, since all my motives are motives of my own. But someone who claims they are all interested is not bound to such vacuous argument. He is making a claim about the sort of motives we have; and it is not the obviously false contention that every time I act, I am pursuing what I consider to be in my overall interest. Many of the actions we call interested are so called because we surmise that the agent is trying to gain pleasure for himself, or to acquire property for himself, or to avoid pain or embarrassment or insecurity for himself, and these are, indeed, objects that we often pursue, as Butler himself emphasises, without considering whether in attaining them we are serving our own good. When the roué showers gifts on the innocent girl, his actions are certainly not disinterested; but they are much more likely to be due to what Butler calls a particular passion, than to the cool pursuit of his long-term good. When the politician earnestly advises me to vote for him so that I can find a job, his advice is undoubtedly interested; but it does not follow from this that the power which he wants is something that he has coolly judged to be in his long-term interest, since he may know it to be a sure path to the next coronary. Duncan-Jones is probably correct when he says[7] that Butler is led astray here by his opinion that particular passions always have 'external' objectives, but this is a matter we must turn to below. For the present, it is enough to note that Hobbes and others are right to use the term 'interested' to include many actions that are not done from what Butler calls self-love. To refute them we are better advised to rely on Butler's wise appeals to the evidence, which does not suggest that all the desires we act from are desires for things we ourselves hope to enjoy, or for possessions we ourselves hope to have, or to avoid pain that we ourselves otherwise expect to endure, though it does suggest that we have motives like this more often than we care to admit. The egoist has to do more than point this out, however, when he claims that all the acts that seem to flow from desires for the good of others are in this contaminated category.

3

Butler's refutations of psychological hedonism are rightly celebrated, not least because the sophistries he exposes are so widespread. His particular target, once more is Hobbes,[8] but the points he makes have much wider application – to John Stuart Mill, for example.[9] What Butler shows, once more, is that the view he attacks is a gross over-simplification, due to confusions. Unfortunately, in the course of showing this, he over-simplifies a little himself.

(i) His first argument is too intertwined with his assaults on E^1 and E^2 to be stated clearly without some element of interpretation, but I think it comes to this. The distinction between self-love and particular affections, especially desires, is a distinction between motives which are all, necessarily, the agent's own. Just as the desire which I follow (whether it is for my happiness, or for some particular object) is my own, of necessity, so the pleasure I may get from satisfying it is my own also. But neither fact shows that all my motives are selfish, since only those actions done from self-love are done for my own good. When the object I have pursued, and achieved, is not pursued from self-love, then the pleasure I take in attaining it will be pleasure at attaining something that I have pursued for *it*self, rather than for *my*self. And for all we know to the contrary, the object so pursued and attained may be some benefit to another person. Then I have taken pleasure in doing good to another person; a state of mind it is a sheer misuse of words to call 'selfish'.

The now-familiar distinction between self-love and particular affections is aptly applied here. The only qualification it is necessary to make is that Butler seems, throughout Sermon xi, to assume too readily that our common notion of selfishness can be wholly defined in terms of self-love in his technical sense. Someone over-motivated by self-love is indeed selfish in our common idiom; but he narrows the notion too much, just as he narrows the notion of interest too much, when he overlooks the fact that an agent may pursue something in order to make money, or impress a neighbour, or gain more power, rather than for the thing itself, and so act selfishly, even though he or she ignores all consideration of long-term good while doing so. The recognition of this fact does nothing for the egoist, however, since we need evidence to show that apparently benevolent actions are really selfish in this sense, and it is only forthcoming some of the time.

A more serious defect in Butler's argument is the fact that he feels it necessary to claim that particular affections 'rest in' *external* objects. He seems to think that his distinction between particular affections and self-love requires him to say this; but, as Duncan-Jones says, this is untrue. When an agent does something for the sake of his own happiness, then his objective is reasonably called internal, because it is a long-term condition we ascribe to that same agent. It is also true that when an agent seeks some particular object, such as a higher salary, the pleasure he derives from getting it, if he is successful, is also internal, in that it is a state we ascribe to the same agent. Butler seems to think that in order to maintain the vital distinction between the objects of our particular desires on the one hand, and *either* the object of self-love *or* the pleasures of satisfied particular desires on the other, he has to view the objects of particular desires as external to the agent. But there is no interesting sense in which this is true. All he needs to insist upon is that the objects of particular desires are things we want for, or in, themselves, without any necessary regard to the happiness they contribute to, or to the pleasure we derive from attaining them. Once this distinction is grasped, it can be seen that the objects of particular desires may be as internal as happiness is, or as the pleasure they lead to is. It is hard to see what is external about the object of my desire when I want to be rid of a headache, or to taste a new wine, or to get a sun-tan.

(ii) With these clarifications behind us, we can consider Butler's important, but brief, second argument against psychological hedonism. I shall first quote it in full.

> That all particular appetites and passions are towards *external things themselves*, distinct from the *pleasure arising from them*, is manifested from hence; that there could not be this pleasure, were it not for that prior suitableness between the object and the passion: there could be no enjoyment or delight from one thing more than another, from eating food more than from swallowing a stone, if there were not an affection or appetite to one thing more than another. (*S* xi 6/3)

We can now ignore the claim that the appetites or passions are for *external* things, since Butler's point is not affected by the admission that we sometimes desire objects that are *in*ternal. He claims that what we want is not the pleasure we have when we get what we want, but whatever it is that we want, itself. He gives a reason for this: that there is a 'prior suitableness' between desires and their objects, and that if this were not so, there would be no enjoyment of one thing more than another. In this over-compressed argument, he clarifies some fundamental facts about the logic of human motives, but supports this in unsatisfactory ways.

The notion of prior suitableness is one I have already tried to unpack[10]. It is Butler's way of emphasising the connection between a desire and what makes it the desire it is. To know what desire is the cause of my inattention at work (whether it is the desire to take a walk, or the desire to eat my lunch, or the desire to phone my wife) is necessarily to know what the desire is *for*, what its object is. Butler seems to argue that the fact that I get pleasure from taking the walk, or eating my lunch, or phoning my wife, does not show it was this pleasure, rather than one of these actions, that was the object of the desire that caused my restlessness. This is in a way true. But the reason he gives for it is certainly false. He says I could never get 'enjoyment or delight from one thing more than another' unless the object I enjoyed or took delight in were the object of the desire which led to its attainment. While there is undoubtedly an important connection between the fact that no one reports enjoying swallowing stones and the fact that no one reports wanting to swallow stones either, we can certainly enjoy or take delight in many things we have not previously wanted. I might well enjoy a television show I have had no prior desire to watch, but which is just 'on'. I might take great delight in some event which happens to me quite unexpectedly and has therefore not come about because I have wanted it, such as a chance encounter with an interesting stranger. It is not even true that we do not take pleasure in events unless they are the sorts of events that we *would* desire if we had reason to anticipate them; for we are often surprised by how pleased we are at events we have previously wished would not happen: the births of infants are often like this.

So Butler seems to be placing far too much weight on the logical connection between desires and their objects. But his purpose is merely to refute the view that pleasure is our only motive, and for this he only needs to attend to those pleasures that arise from the attainment of desired objects, not to those which come about without prior desire. Here his thesis looks much better: that when we desire some object and attain it, our pleasure in doing so can only be rendered intelligible if we presuppose that it was the object itself that was desired, not the pleasure it subsequently gave us. This suggests that the psychological hedonist, who tells us that what we want is always the anticipated pleasure, is claiming something incoherent. How good is Butler's argument, thus interpreted?

To assess it, I must first develop the distinction implied in Butler's disjunction of 'enjoyment or delight'. There is an important difference between those pleasure-concepts and idioms associated with *enjoyment*, and those associated with satisfaction, or *being pleased*[11]. Briefly, enjoyment seems to be a special form of attention or absorption which is necessarily contemporaneous with its object and excludes more than peripheral attention to other objects – hence Butler's wise remark in paragraph 9/7 of Sermon xi that enjoyment requires 'disengagement'. To enjoy something, I have to be present at it when it occurs, even though it may not be anything I myself am doing or anything that is happening specifically to me. Being pleased, on the other hand, is an emotional state akin to, and involved in, such conditions as joy, delight, or relief; it is a positive response, commonly one that includes a positive evaluation, of facts, or of events that may already have taken place, and which I do not have to have been present at but may merely have learned about. Sometimes the two can have one and the same object, as when I enjoy my daughter's wedding as it occurs and am pleased by the success of the arrangements afterwards. But they may well *not* have the same object: I may enjoy the very cigarette I am displeased about having smoked, and I may well be pleased at having given up smoking without finding the experience enjoyable at any stage.

Psychological hedonism is most naturally interpreted as a thesis about enjoyment: that we are always motivated by the anticipation of it. But it is common for those tempted by this thesis to deal with apparent counter-examples, such as actions done from moral duty, by saying that the dutiful person gets pleasure from following his conscience, and displeasure from violating it. The best-known example of this type of reasoning is J.S. Mill's notorious account of conscience as an internal sanction[12]. But although we may be *pleased* when we have followed our conscience, and *displeased* when we have not, it is far less obvious that this can be construed as *enjoying* duty and disliking its violation. This, however, is aside from our present purpose. Butler's argument against psychological hedonism seems to be that, whichever way we understand the notion of pleasure, when we get pleasure from what we have previously wanted, it cannot, in logic, be that what we previously wanted was the pleasure.

If we take 'pleasure' to be 'being pleased', then it is not only true that I can be pleased about many things, including my own actions, without previously having wanted those things; it is also true that I can want something, get it, and then not be pleased by it, and not even have expected to be pleased by it. (Think of the craving for the cigarette.) I can also get something I want, fail to be pleased at having done so, but find that some other, unanticipated aspect of it pleases me – as when I unexpectedly get the school prize for writing an essay I wanted to write but was not pleased with when it was finished. But there is a truth in Butler's claim: if I am pleased at having done something I wanted to do, then the object of my pleasure is the fact that I have done what I wanted to do; and this requires that what I wanted was to do that action, *simpliciter*. This is enough to refute any possible universal thesis that we always do things in order to be pleased at them. On the other hand, it does not seem to me absurd to say that our being pleased at having done certain actions contributes, in a substantial way, to our motives, and helps make us want to engage in some activities. Almost all of us some of the time, and some of us a great deal of the time, are motivated by the prospect of achievement. The mountaineer who wants to climb the unconquered peak, or the executive who wants to balance the company's budget, may not enjoy the process, but may get great satisfaction afterwards at having succeeded. It is well known that this sense of satisfaction decreases as similar achievements are repeated, and this reduces the degree to which such persons want to continue performing such actions; they look instead, as we say, for new challenges. So there does seem to be a familiar way in which the anticipation of being pleased at succeeding in some undertaking *contributes* to the desire to enter into it. So although Butler's logical point is unaffected, the thesis of psychological hedonism, if it is a thesis about satisfaction, as distinct from enjoyment, at all, is still partially correct. But it must be added immediately that recognising this does nothing to show that there are no genuinely benevolent actions, for one of the things that we seem to be pleased about having done, and to want to do, is furthering the good of others.

The psychological hedonist is much more likely to be telling us, however, that we are always motivated by the hope of enjoyment. How does Butler's argument fare against this claim? Again, we may disregard the fact that we often enjoy actions or events that we have not wanted beforehand. If we *have* wanted them beforehand, this may contribute to our enjoyment of them; if I enjoy visiting a famous resort, my enjoyment may be increased by the reflection that I have always wanted to go there. It is this aspect of enjoyment that Professor Anscombe calls 'enjoyment of fact'[13]. (It is noteworthy, however, that the very same reflections may dampen enjoyment, by making me feel that the place's actual charms, though real, are less than would justify such a long-standing desire.) Even though our enjoyment may be augmented in this way by the fact that the action was previously desired, this seems to imply, like the parallel point about being pleased, that our desire was, necessarily, the desire to do the action, not for the enjoyment consequent upon the fact that the action is what we previously wanted.

But this does not seem to take us far in dealing with psychological hedonism. For the psychological hedonist does not have to deny that these special features of enjoyment exist. It is at least pedantic, also, to suggest that he cannot admit that we want to perform certain actions, or to have certain experiences, as we say, for themselves. He is trying to offer an account of why we do. He is aware of the oft-mentioned fact, which some appear to think refutes him, that one cannot have, or, therefore, seek to have, enjoyment on its own, without the enjoyed activity or experience – a fact which follows from enjoyment's being a form of contemporary attention.[14] He claims that we only want those things which we believe we will enjoy when we get them. And in his favour we can point out that even though we may well not enjoy what we have wanted when we get it, this does make us less likely to want the same thing again, and that if we do enjoy it when we get it, we are more likely to want it another time. I am not convinced that there is any logical absurdity in the thesis that we always want things because we expect to enjoy them; and I am afraid that Butler's argument, which only holds for those special cases where the satisfaction of the prior desire is a consciously contributing element in the enjoyment we have, does nothing to refute the hedonist's theory of desire. On the other hand, there is abundant evidence that we want to do things we do not expect to enjoy (such as paying our bills even when we could evade them), and to experience things we do not expect to like (such as learning what it feels like to go without food for a week). And, more to Butler's main point, there is ample evidence that one of the things many people enjoy most is doing good to others. Unselfish pleasures, in this sense, are indeed a fact of life; so also is the desire for them.

Butler's case against egoism and hedonism may not live up to its reputation, but it is still a strong one. He does succeed in showing that there
is no good reason to follow those who deny we have benevolent motives.
But this does not quite add up to a demonstration that we are capable
of benevolence in his wider sense. We may well act from a desire for
the good of particular individuals, from friendship, compassion, or filial
affection. But this is not self-evidently the same as acting from a general
desire for the public good. Refuting psychological egoism does not establish that we do *that*. Do we have such an affection?

Hume later denied that we do:

> In general, it may be affirmed, that there is no such passion in human
> minds, as the love of mankind, merely as such, independent of
> personal qualities, of services, or of relation to ourself[15].

In consequence of this, he held that we need the artificial virtue of
justice to ensure the impartial distribution of good to others that society
requires. Benevolence, as it exists, is *confined* to those who are connected
with us by family ties or common social life, and a generalised benevolence would be 'too remote and too sublime to affect the generality of
mankind'. It would take us too far afield to inquire whether Hume's
doctrine of extensive or general sympathy modifies this stance, but it is
clear that he is denying something that Butler wants to affirm. It is also
clear that the primary reason for this is that Butler is a Christian thinker
and Hume is not. For Butler equates benevolence, in the more general
sense, with love of one's neighbour.

He tries to deal with the limited scope of human emotions by treating
love of one's neighbour as the desire to further the good of anyone with
whom one has to do. Since most of us have to do with a relatively small
number of other persons, this gives the benevolence required in the
demand to love our neighbour a 'less general and nearer object' than
mankind as a whole, or even one's country. But this does not take away
from the love of others the impartiality that is demanded in the New
Testament commandment. For in that commandment the concept of the
neighbour is deliberately widened to become that of any other human
being I may meet. Even though Butler is, as always, anxious to show
throughout his two Sermons on the love of our neighbour that it has no
ultimate inconsistency with self-love, he nowhere suggests that we can
only have this affection towards those whose character or actions can be
seen to be good for us. And even though he makes it clear that the
benevolent person, who has benevolence as a settled and dominant principle in his personality, will be guided by reason into doing good particularly to those, like his family, whom providence has placed in his special

care, he does not suggest that benevolence is, or could be, confined to such persons. In both these ways, his moral psychology is different from that of Hume, whom he would certainly have judged, from this quotation, to be a psychological egoist.

The intricate discussions of the relation of benevolence, in this sense, to self-love, in Sermon xii do not concern us at present. What is important is that they all presuppose the reality of benevolence, and are not intended to prove it. Butler is clearly worried that if we think benevolence and self-love are at odds, the motive of benevolence will be too weak to activate our conduct. But he takes it for granted that we have it. This is true even in the infamous 'cool hour' passage.[16] It is fair to say that he nowhere defends explicitly his belief that the wish to do good to another, as my neighbour and fellow-human, is a real feature of human nature. No doubt he would take it for granted that the Christian command to do this would not exist if we could not obey it. There are Christian theologians who deny that love, in this sense, is a possibility for us in our present state, and say that it can only come about through special divine grace.[17] Butler, with his manifest belief in the continuity of human virtue and religion, is firmly in the opposite camp, and would no doubt say that such views can only be held by those who disregard the evidence of our actions and attend only to the requirements of a theological system 'to which the appearance of good-will could not otherwise be reconciled'. For the proponents of these views are forced to construe apparent examples of selfless love much in the manner of the psychological egoist.

III

The Case for Virtue

The two central contentions of Butler's ethics are that virtue consists in following nature, and that conscience is supreme. It is important to understand the nature of these doctrines, and of their relationship, before judging the criticisms that have been made of his position. I begin by stating briefly some of the relevant points of interpretation that have emerged so far.

1

The claim that virtue consists in following nature, and vice in deviating from it, is not offered by Butler as a criterion for determining what we ought to do. He has no doubt that most of us almost always know this, because our consciences make clear enough to us what duty requires:

> In all common ordinary cases we see intuitively at first view what is our duty, what is the honest part. . . . That which is called considering what is our duty in a particular case, is very often nothing but endeavouring to explain it away. (S vii 14/14)

A priori ethical arguments may reinforce our recognition that virtue requires acts of this or that kind, but Butler does not see this reinforcement as meeting the major practical need that concerns him. For he wishes to answer waverers who do not deny what virtue requires, but wonder whether to *practise* it or not. They do not seek to avoid their duty by contesting what it is that conscience tells them; they wonder whether what it tells them is what they should do. Rightly or wrongly, Butler feels he has to respond to this doubt. Those who feel it may perhaps feel they have been slaves to moral custom, or too ready to sacrifice happiness to conformity. So when he says that virtue consists in following nature, he is offering them a reason for virtuous action that is *additional* to its sheer virtuousness. Butler sees no moral oddity in the presence of more than one reason for good conduct. On the contrary, the reason he offers us here is not merely additional to the rightness of the actions that conscience identifies; it is also, very probably, additional to the motives of self-love or benevolence or particular desire which may also be present, and which conscience does not displace.

If we ask what sort of additional reason the naturalness of virtue is, the answer seems to be this. Virtuous action is action done from motives which are implanted in us by providence, and which have a hierarchical relationship. This relationship is one in which the rational principle of self-love has superiority over particular passions and affections, and in which conscience has superiority over both. So to act virtuously is to act as we are intended to act and are constituted to act, by providence. The kind of superiority that a principle higher in the hierarchy has over lower principles or affections is, in the last resort, that which comes from the fact that the dictates of the higher principle are better reasons for action than those of the lower principle or affection – and (I think Butler would say) that we know they are better reasons. Since acting for better rather than worse reasons, or, for that matter, acting for worse rather than better reasons, is always free action, subject to praise or blame, it is always possible for us not to follow the higher principle, but, unnaturally, to follow the lower. When this happens, it is because the lower has a strength which overwhelms that of the higher, even though we know quite well that it does not have the requisite superiority. This superiority Butler calls *authority*.

If a reflective agent asks on some occasion why he or she *should* follow a higher principle rather than a lower principle or desire and thus tread the path of virtue, Butler's answer, 'because in so doing you will be following nature', does not amount, therefore, to the claim that the agent is so constituted by providence that he or she can only do what virtue demands, for that is obviously false, and its falsity is implied by the question. It amounts, instead, to the claim that every agent is so constituted by providence that, barring special circumstances, he or she will make the judgments that the principle prompts, and will recognise them to be better reasons for action than the presence of lower principles or inclinations with which they conflict.

This might not seem like much of an answer. For it tells someone who questions whether the dictate of a higher principle really is a better reason for acting than the urgings of a lower one, that he is so made by providence that he knows quite well that it *is* a better reason. I shall attempt to deal with this obvious objection throughout, but for now three comments. First, just as bad choices can so strengthen our desires that they win out over higher judgments, so prolonged bad choices can make us indolent or careless in the exercise of our ability to make such judgments; sometimes (especially in the case of conscience) providence sees to it that these judgments intrude themselves regardless of this, but to a large extent the remedy for this prudential and moral indolence lies with us. Butler sees himself as helping to provide such a remedy by drawing his hearers' attention to their own unused capacities. Second, the fact that Butler considers it important to answer the reflective sceptic's question does not mean that he thinks it a proper or unconfused one; only that it is vital to the practice of virtue that it be answered. The answer, however, can consist in reminding the questioner that he is so made that he can see he really knows better than to ask it. Third, the question might be the result of the sceptic's having been confused or demoralised by bad theories like those of psychological egoism or hedonism.

Butler's 'nature' answer, then, consists ultimately of a reminder of an ability and a knowledge that he thinks we all have.[1] If I am right about this, it does not require that *any* superior principle in human nature is infallible, though in the case of conscience Butler does not seem to see this.

All it requires is that each of us knows that once the judgment of a superior principle is made, it gives the agent a stronger reason for acting than the principles or affections lower in the hierarchy. *This* is a sort of infallibility, no doubt; and it is one which we can, on his clear statements, conceal from ourselves through indolence or bad theory.

I have tried to expound Butler's appeal to the naturalness of virtue without touching on the special features of conscience itself. This is because Butler introduces the idea of superior principles by using self-love as his example, and clearly feels he needs to argue more for the superiority of conscience over inferior principles than for the superiority of self-love to particular affections. There is no doubt that the appeal to nature is an easy, and effective, one to make with regard to self-love. Few would argue with the claim that our natures are such that when we judge one of our desires to be inconsistent with our interests, we thereby know that we have a better reason for rejecting it than for yielding to it, even though we may still yield. Nor would there be much argument against the view that repeated imprudence, or bad company, or laziness, could reduce the frequency with which we make the necessary judgments. Butler's position here looks virtually self-evident.[2]

As we have seen, Butler is unclear about the status of benevolence, and omits it from his clearest statement about the superior principles within us (S iii 9/13). But it is not absurd to hold that it too is a principle with natural superiority: so that the fact that some action is for the good of my neighbour is a stronger reason for choosing it than the fact that I want to do something incompatible with it, and we all know it is a stronger reason. I incline to think that Butler does think this, or at least would have accepted it as the most appropriate development of his insistence that there is a natural principle of benevolence in us. It does not tell us, of course, how to resolve potential conflicts between benevolence, so interpreted, and self-love, though it is depressingly clear from his treatment of the love commandment in Sermon xii that he would give self-love priority.

In the case of conscience, which is not merely superior but supreme, the appeal to nature entails the claim that each of us is so made that we recognise the precedence of its judgments over *all other* considerations. The sceptic's hesitations are most likely to be based upon questioning the superiority of conscience to self-love. Butler does not rely upon the appeal to nature alone here, but adds two other arguments. The first is the argument that the judgments of conscience themselves bear intrinsic marks of its special status, a claim he does not make for self-love[3]. The second is the argument that has troubled so many of his commentators, that we have an additional reason for following conscience in the fact that conscience and self-love point the same way; so that, even if we were to concede that self-love had priority, it would still tell us to do whatever conscience enjoins. I have suggested that this has to be understood in the light of Butler's teleological reading of human nature, and of his later theological arguments in the *Analogy*, although I do not think this makes his view more persuasive. I shall return to these ancillary arguments of Butler's below.

2

The above account treats the doctrine that virtue consists in following nature, and the doctrine of the supremacy of conscience, as very closely connected. All Butler's commentators to date have assumed this, with one exception. In a recent essay, Nicholas Sturgeon subjects these doctrines to a searching study, and suggests that, as Butler develops them, they are even incompatible. He says that Butler should abandon the doctrine of the supremacy of conscience, even though he and his readers continually say it is the core of his theory.[4] He argues his case in such careful detail, that it requires some response before a more traditional reading like my own can hope to stand.

I have said that Butler's claim that virtue consists in following nature is not intended to help identify what virtue requires, but to help ensure its practice. It is also not a conceptual thesis about what the word 'virtue' means, though in developing it Butler makes comments about our ethical vocabulary. Butler claims that those who practise virtue are acting in the way that is consonant with the makeup given them by providence, and that this is one which includes the recognition of the supremacy of conscience. In the Dissertation 'Of the Nature of Virtue', appended to the *Analogy*, he uses the word 'conscience' less prominently, but describes virtue as that mode of life and character which consists in the performance of actions which are approved by our 'moral approving and disapproving faculty' of which 'conscience' is one of the common names. He says moral approval and disapproval are expressed in terms like '*right* and *wrong*, *odious* and *amiable*, *base* and *worthy*, with many others of like signification' (Diss II 1/2). Actions and their motives, when so characterised, are said to be virtuous or vicious. The central argument of the *Analogy* is that God's providence rewards virtue and punishes vice. The main purpose of the Dissertation is to make clear that even though this is so, the judgments of conscience do not extend to the consequences of actions and their motives, so that utilitarian understandings of virtue are false. Consequences are only relevant to the judgments of conscience through the fact that 'intention of such and such consequences . . . is part of the action itself'. This conforms to the earlier statement in Sermon ii, paragraph 8/10, that conscience judges actions as *in themselves* just, right, good, or the opposite.

Whatever may follow from this, two things do *not* follow. It does not follow, first, that virtue consists in *conscientiousness*, in acting always and only from conscience, or from a sense of duty. It does consist in doing that of which conscience approves, in the sense that it is conscience which determines whether the virtuous person would do this or that action. But in approving such an action, conscience is more likely than not to be approving some action for which a motive, such as desire or benevolence or self-love, already exists. It has its own motivating force to add – 'that this faculty tends to restrain men from doing mischief to each other, and leads them to do good, is too manifest to need being insisted upon' (S i 8/8). Butler says in this same paragraph that the natural desire of parents to care for their children is consolidated by the reflection of conscience that it is also the right and proper thing to do[5]; and it is clear that if conscience is ever to win out over contrary desires, it must motivate us by itself if it has to. So Butler is committed to the reality of actions done from duty alone, but not to the view that virtuous action consists in acting from duty. The virtuous man will normally want to do those things conscience approves and will not have to fight within himself to do them, so that conscience will usually give its blessing, and add its ancillary motivation, to the other principles within us. It will not displace them. Butler would undoubtedly reject Kant's doctrine that the good will is the will motivated solely by duty, however Kantian he may seem in other respects.

The second thing that does not follow is that the content of the judgments of conscience make any necessary reference to the naturalness of the actions conscience approves, or the unnaturalness of those it rejects. We might well see this from one of Butler's remarks in Sermon ii. Here he is showing that acting in accordance with our nature does not consist in following the strongest principle, and he says that the man who follows a desire and brings ruin on himself is acting disproportionately to his nature, or unnaturally. He says this disproportion arises 'not from considering the action singly in *itself*, or in its *consequences*; but from the comparison of it with the nature of the agent' (*S* ii 10/14). This implies that a judgment of an action's naturalness is *not* a judgment of that action in itself; yet the judgment of conscience is said, earlier in the same Sermon, and in the Dissertation, to be of actions *in themselves*. This seems to confirm my suggestion that the thesis that virtue consists in following nature is being offered as a reason for virtuous conduct that is *additional* to the promptings of conscience. It also confirms that when conscience makes its judgments, it judges actions to be right or wrong, base or worthy, and does not assert their naturalness or unnaturalness. For a judgment of naturalness or unnaturalness is based upon a recognition of the special place occupied in our nature by the judgments of the superior principles, conscience included; so it must require these judgments, including those of conscience, to have been identified independently.

There might seem to be a difficulty in the fact that the vocabulary of conscience includes the terms 'virtuous' and 'vicious', and is applied to character as well as actions in the Dissertation. The use of this language appears to involve conscience in the judgment of our natures. But this need not be so. To say an action is virtuous is to say that it is, of itself, the sort of action a virtuous person would do, and to call it vicious is to say that it is of itself the sort of action vetoed for the virtuous person; both without other implications about what sort of nature the virtuous person has. And to call a person virtuous is to say that he is the sort of person who regularly wants to act in certain approved ways. It is not to say, in addition, that the actions are the ones that would be done, or avoided, or the character is one that would be manifested, by someone whose personality corresponded closely to the hierarchical pattern of choice described by Butler – even though all these things are, in Butler's opinion, true. The naturalness of the virtuous person's mode of life is something we find on examination of the person we recognise as virtuous; it does not follow from this that it is something we have to have discerned before recognising it, or something we have stated when ascribing virtue to him. If this is sound, there is, thus far, no reason to ascribe to Butler what Sturgeon calls the Full Naturalistic Thesis: 'that conscience never favours or opposes any action, except on grounds which include its naturalness or unnaturalness'.[6] He ascribes it to Butler partly because he thinks it follows from the propositions that virtue consists in following nature, and that the judgments of conscience are based on the virtuousness or viciousness of actions.[7] If what I have argued is sound, it follows from neither. This is not Sturgeon's main argument for the

Full Naturalistic Thesis, however. Before considering that, I must fill out my account of the role Butler gives to conscience, and indicate why the Full Naturalistic Thesis would indeed be as devastating to his ethical system as Sturgeon says it is.

One problem that Butler's language gives us is his repeated equation of conscience and 'reflection'. This suggests that whenever we 'reflect upon our own nature' (S i 8/8), it is conscience that is at work. As I have already suggested, my nature and its needs have to be the object of attention for self-love also, or I could not ask myself whether or not an action I want to perform is for my good.[8] We have rather to interpret Butler as holding that conscience conducts the sort of reflection on our own natures that does *not* issue in judgments of what is good for us, but in other sorts of judgments. These are the judgments of moral approval or disapproval. So even though self-love has also to be classed as 'reflective', it is not occupied with our 'heart, temper, and actions' in the same manner. It considers them, not in themselves, but as having certain specific consequences – as contributing to, or detracting from, our happiness. It has to be admitted that Butler's language suggests that *all* 'reflective' thought is an activity of conscience, but his more detailed statements about self-love and conscience imply the sort of distinction within reflective activities that I have outlined.

One problem that Butler's method does not lead him to raise explicitly, however, is that of the status within human nature of the assertions he himself, as a philosophical psychologist, is making about us, and of the questions about virtue and our reasons for practising it that he takes his readers to be asking. In our own era of self-consciousness about philosophical method, such questions come to mind much more readily than they would have done for his readers. These are the sorts of general questions about our life and conduct that we think about in a 'cool hour'. Although a cool hour is presumably one in which we are free from the heated demands of urgent decisions, Butler certainly believes that what we determine during it is likely to have fundamental effects on our lives. This is why he takes even confused philosophical questions and theories very seriously.

I shall call the questions and judgments that we ask and answer in the cool hour, questions and judgments of practical philosophy. When we ask and answer them do we exercise self-love, or benevolence, or conscience? There seems no obvious reason why they have all to be of one sort, or another, and we could even suppose that they are a special class of questions and judgments requiring the postulation of another principle in our nature. Given Butler's psychology, however, it seems more plausible to suggest that they may be exercises of any of these principles. So when Butler says, as a reason for practising virtue, that conscience and self-love point the same way, I incline to interpret this

64

as an attempt to get us to make a judgment of self-love in favour of virtue. But what of his main arguments that virtue consists in following nature, and that conscience is supreme? Those, like Prichard, who see Butler as offering an inducement to morality, would no doubt class his 'nature' argument as being as much of an appeal to self-love as his claim that conscience and self-love point the same way, denying even that these arguments can be clearly distinguished; for they see Butler's appeal to human nature as like Plato's in the *Republic*. If, on the other hand, I am right to read him as reminding us of our supposed knowledge that rightness is an overriding reason for choice, perhaps it is an appeal to conscience. Perhaps it cannot be pigeon-holed either way. But, however we judge this, it does not affect one fact. If Butler is trying to respond to those who, in a cool hour, wonder whether the approval and disapproval of conscience really justifies actions that have other counts against them, then the 'nature' argument, just as much as the self-love argument, requires the primary role of conscience to be already identified. Even if the judgment that some actions are consonant with nature, or are unnatural, can be called a judgment of conscience, it is a judgment that conscience can only make if *most* judgments of conscience are of a different sort: that is, if the approval or disapproval that conscience generates, and which the question presupposes, is assumed to be made, already, on other grounds. At most the judgment of naturalness or unnaturalness is a supplementary, or additional, consideration.

I am here only saying in a different tone of voice what Sturgeon says in criticism of Butler. For if Sturgeon's Full Naturalistic Thesis is true, and a judgment of naturalness is a necessary component of *all* positive judgments of conscience and a judgment of unnaturalness is a necessary component of *all* negative judgments of conscience, then indeed the principle of the supremacy of conscience is quite empty. For conscience can then only approve of what it judges to be *natural*, and can only disapprove of what it judges to be *unnatural*; and since these judgments require us to establish that the actions in question are done from, or in the face of, a superior principle, then it is that superior principle, which must here be the highest principle other than conscience itself, which determines the proper action for us. Conscience has no independent selective role to play; so it will favour whatever the highest principle other than itself will favour, it will have no other grounds for its favour beyond the fact that this other principle favours the action, and can only conflict with this other principle if that principle conflicts with itself. If all this is true, then indeed Sturgeon is right to say that the support of conscience does not contribute to the naturalness of the acts which it favours. The claim of its supremacy is morally vacuous.

So if Butler is committed to the Full Naturalistic Thesis, he is indeed in all the trouble that Sturgeon says he is in. I have already tried to suggest that a principle with such consequences is one we have no need to ascribe to him, and that the doctrine of the supremacy of conscience is one that cannot be faulted on these grounds. (That does not mean, of course, that it is true.) But although I cannot discuss all Sturgeon's detailed arguments, there is still one important passage in the second Sermon in which Sturgeon thinks Butler commits himself to the Full Naturalistic Thesis unequivocally, and I must examine his comments on it.

The passage comes at the close of the Sermon. In it Butler is defending the claim that conscience has supremacy, and that this must be distinguished from its strength. He defends it with a *reductio* argument, based on the assumption that 'there was no distinction to be made between one inward principle and another, but only that of strength'. If this were true, he says, then an action like parricide, being done as it is from the principle which is currently strongest in the agent, would 'correspond to the whole nature of the man', and there would be no disproportion or unsuitableness between it and that nature any more than there is between an act of filial duty and that nature. He then concludes:

> If there be no difference between inward principles, but only that of strength; we can make no distinction between these two actions, considered as actions of such a creature; but in our coolest hours must approve or disapprove them equally: than which nothing can be reduced to a greater absurdity. (S ii 17/22)

I am not concerned to defend this argument, but only to see how far it requires us to ascribe the Full Naturalistic Thesis to Butler. Even if it did so, I would incline to dismiss it as an aberration, since the thesis is so radically at odds with the main drift of Butler's thinking. But I do not think we are required to infer the Full Naturalistic Thesis from it. After quoting it, Sturgeon comments as follows:

> Now, distinguishing between actions in a cool hour, and approving or disapproving them, is a function of conscience (S i 8/7–8). Stated generally, therefore, Butler's crowning conclusion is this: that if no principle of human action has a natural superiority to any other, conscience must approve or disapprove equally of *any* two actions whatever. And there is a problem, I submit, in seeing why this should be thought to follow. If no principle is superior to any other, conscience will be on a par with any passion or appetite; but why should its lack of superiority prevent it, in Butler's view, from distinguishing actions, approving one and disapproving another?
>
> The only reasonable answer, I believe, is that it is not the lack of the supremacy of conscience which is supposed, in these imagined

circumstances, to disable it. Its problem is explained, rather, by the principle I have called the Naturalistic Thesis: that conscience always *bases* its approval or disapproval of actions, in some essential way, on their naturalness or unnaturalness.[9]

It is true that the paragraph in Sermon i which Sturgeon cites does tell us that conscience is that principle which approves and disapproves our actions; and also that it gives, as an example, a case where someone who has done a kindness to one person, and has also injured another in a fit of anger, reflects on these acts 'coolly' afterwards and approves only of the first. Taking this as a precedent makes it very natural to say that the approval or disapproval in our coolest hours, of which Butler speaks in the quotation we are now considering, must also be an activity of conscience. I will not dispute this, except to point out again that the more famous 'cool hour' reflections of Sermon xi (20/21), in which we are said only to judge virtue compelling if it leads to happiness, seem equally obviously to be reflections of self-love. More important than this, however, is the fact that Butler nowhere says in the Sermon ii argument now before us that, in a world where no principle in our nature had superiority over others, conscience would thereby be 'disabled'. His point is one which, if it has any weight, can go through whether conscience is disabled or not. For what he says is that 'these two actions, *considered as actions of such a creature*' must be approved and disapproved equally. Now I would consider the judgment Butler is appealing to here to be one of what I have called practical philosophy; though I would incline to agree that *this* judgment of practical philosophy is also a judgment of conscience, in view of the use of the terms 'approve' and 'disapprove'.[10] Be this as it may, it is clearly a judgment that parricide and filial duty are equally natural, and it is this which Butler says is absurd. If this is a judgment of conscience, then in this case conscience makes a judgment of naturalness. But this does not prove the Full Naturalistic Thesis, which alleges that *all* the judgments of conscience are judgments of naturalness. The present judgment is in fact compatible with conscience not being disabled by the act of parricide, but *continuing to disapprove*; Butler's point would then be that even though conscience went on disapproving, the act of parricide could still not be faulted as unnatural, because the disapproval of conscience would be no stronger reason against it than the urgings of youthful rebellion which prompted it. Many admittedly wrong actions would be natural, if this were our situation. That many wrong actions *are* natural in some such sense as this, is a common enough view, and one which Butler is contesting.[11] It needs to be demonstrated that there is a problem for him in the fact (if it is one) that the original moral disapproval of parricide, and the supposed judgment that it is not unnatural, would be judgments passed by the same faculty.

I have offered an alternative interpretation. It may be that Butler does think that an assumption of equality of status between inward principles would disable conscience, and is therefore closer in this passage to committing himself to the Full Naturalistic Thesis than I suggest. But the consequences of that thesis are so destructive for him that he would surely have drawn back from an argument that implied it. His doctrines do not prevent him, at least, from recasting this argument in a form that does not imply it.[12]

The alternative interpretation I have offered is one which distinguishes between judgments of right and wrong on the one hand, and judgments of naturalness and unnaturalness on the other. When Butler tells us that these judgments of conscience override other motives, the judgments of which he says this are the judgments of right and wrong. The judgments of naturalness and unnaturalness that Butler urges upon us require the independent existence of the judgments of right and wrong. Butler's moral psychology is devastated if this independence cannot be maintained. I do not think it need be compromised by the mere fact that we have reason to ascribe the two kinds of judgment to the same faculty, any more than the ascription of all theoretical and practical judgments to reason would necessarily imply any confusion between the judgments of science, self-love, or speculative philosophy. There is no doubt, however, that Butler does express himself carelessly, and that there are, in consequence, texts which lend themselves to the reading that Sturgeon maintains. I think this carelessness, or tendency to confuse the one sort of judgment with the other, is traceable to the fact that Butler uses the term 'conscience' in a wider sense than normal. He introduces it, in Sermon i and in the Dissertation, in a way that gives it no less than three functions. The first function is that of making judgments of right and wrong about my own actions, past and future; this is the primary function, and the one to which the term 'conscience' is now confined. The second function is that of reflection upon one's whole nature; here, even though this reflection is assumed to be evaluative, Butler seems to be using the older and more general sense of 'conscience' as 'inward knowledge or consciousness'[13]. The third function is more general than either, in a critical respect: it is the function of passing evaluative judgments on the acts and the characters of other people. In an obvious way, if I can pass judgment on myself and apply common moral standards in the process, I can do the same to others; but it does not follow from this that I must use the same name for each activity, and we confine the term 'conscience' by now to judgments passed on oneself. I have already indicated that the second sense Butler uses would imply that some of the judgments of self-love are discharged by conscience. We can see that he is forced by his own wide use of the term to attempt to comprehend many different aspects of human behaviour under one rubric, when he makes the awkward statement that 'the object of this faculty is actions, comprehending under that name active or practical principles: those principles from which men would act if occasions and circumstances gave them power; and which, when fixed and habitual in any person, we call his character' (Diss II 2/4).

Butler's motive in extending the term in this way is no doubt to enhance the authority of conscience by giving it the general superintendency over our natures as well as the power to judge acts as right or wrong. But this runs the risk of ignoring the fact that the question 'Should I follow conscience when other principles clash with it?' is a question about conscience in the primary and narrowest sense, as the faculty that judges acts right and wrong; and the question is one which, if we give conscience the two other functions he ascribes to it, is then addressed *to* conscience, which, again in the wider signification, answers it in terms of the naturalness of doing those things that are dictated by conscience in the narrowest sense.

These complexities do not much matter, as long as Butler is clear about the distinctness of the tasks conscience is assigned. We have already had occasion to interpret passages where he does not take enough trouble to do this. There is one further passage where this leads him to court disaster – also a passage, unsurprisingly, where Sturgeon holds that Butler commits himself to the Full Naturalistic Thesis.[14] In paragraph 5/7 of the Dissertation, he says that 'our perception of vice and ill-desert arises from, and is the result of, a comparison of actions with the nature and capacities of the agent', and concludes that this is what causes us to apply the epithets '*incongruous, unsuitable, disproportionate, unfit* to actions which our moral faculty determines to be vicious'. Here he is perilously close to suggesting that the primary judgments of conscience require a verdict of naturalness or unnaturalness. I think we can find grounds for holding that this is not his real intent. For one thing, the clause quoted seems to imply that the judgment of viciousness is distinct from those of incongruity or disproportion. For another, the paragraph as a whole deals primarily with the fact that we pass moral judgments only on beings who are capable of what Butler calls good or ill desert, and not, therefore, on animals, children, idiots, or madmen. This means that the 'comparison between the action and capacities of the agent' which Butler here says precedes our determining an action to be vicious, need be no more than a recognition that the agent we are judging is one endowed with the ability to tell right from wrong, and to act on this knowledge. This recognition may be due to conscience in the third sense, as a faculty that judges other people, but even though Butler comes close to saying it is also a judgment of naturalness of the sort required by his 'nature' argument, he has no need to do so.

3

I return to the question of how good Butler's argument from the naturalness of virtue is. I have tried to give reasons for rejecting the radical criticism that it is inconsistent with the thesis that conscience is supreme. Assuming that they are as close as they are commonly supposed to be, what is their exact relationship?

The virtuous person does what conscience requires. But such a person does not, usually, need to do these things solely *because* conscience requires them. He will have the sort of personality in which his desires, his self-love, and his benevolence will prompt the choice of these actions of themselves, and will only occasionally need to act from conscience alone. From his remark (in Sermon ii 8/8) about parental affection and conscience, it seems that Butler regards it as better that conscience should supply some of the motivation than that actions should be done from prior motives alone, but there is every reason to think he would regard the state of someone who had to depend on conscience as the sole motivation of his good actions as inferior to that of someone who wanted to do such actions already. Conscience's primary role, then, is to *identify* those actions which virtue requires; its secondary role is to motivate us to perform them in one of the two ways indicated.

So when Butler argues that virtue consists in following nature, and offers this as a reason for following conscience (and therefore practising virtue) when we may be disinclined to do so, he is not equating virtue with conscientiousness; but he is, in the context where an objector might be presumed *not* to have independent motivation to do what conscience tells him, offering a reason why the prompting of conscience should be enough by itself. And his view of the virtuous person is that this person acts both from desire or benevolence or self-love, *and* from the prompting of conscience, simultaneously, on the whole; but will act from conscience alone if other motives should fail him, or appear to be in conflict with his conscience. Such a person will not need Butler's extra reason, presumably, but as even he may waver, the case Butler makes can reinforce his virtue too. What, exactly, is the case he makes, and how good is it?

I have already indicated the different parts of Butler's argument, and can now expound and comment on each with reasonable brevity. I have distinguished (i) a main argument from the *naturalness* of virtue, (ii) an apparently distinct argument that conscience carries its own marks of authority, and (iii) the argument that self-love and conscience point the same way.

(i) Butler's main 'nature' argument is as follows. Each of us is so constituted by providence that, barring special circumstances such as protracted viciousness or the corruptions of bad theory, we will regularly judge possible actions to be right or wrong, virtuous or vicious, and will also know that this is a stronger reason for doing them, or for refraining from them, than the promptings of desires or aversions, or the judgments of other principles in the personality. When he sums up this case in Sermon iii 5/6, there are two key sentences:

> The question then carries its own answer along with it. Your
> obligation to obey this law, is its being the law of your nature.

So the question 'Why should I do what I have already judged to be right?' is to be answered, 'You already know, not only that this action would be right, but that if an action is the right one, you ought to do it, whatever *else* is the case about it' – whether it causes you, or someone you care for, suffering or inconvenience, for example. The question, though it has been taken with full seriousness, is ultimately said to be improper and confused, since the analysis of human nature Butler has given shows that each of us is the sort of creature who is endowed with a recognition of the fact that the judgment of rightness or wrongness embodies an overriding reason, and that we should disregard the resistance to obligation of which the question is a sophisticated expression.

I have argued that this does not imply that conscience's judgments of right and wrong are infallible. What has to be beyond question however, is the recognition that once this judgment is given, it overrides the competition. It is natural to object that this is question-begging. Surely all Butler is doing is telling us (or reminding us) that we *know* there can be no better reason than a moral reason? Even if we all, by nature, *think* this, could we not be wrong?

I think that Butler *is* just reminding us, and does think this is something we all know. But, typically, he does not leave it at that. There are, in the *Sermons* and the *Analogy*, two related arguments to bolster the appeal to supposed knowledge. The first is implied, rather than stated. It is the view that a feature that is part of our real nature in this way is implanted in us by providence, and must therefore be for our good.[15] But aside from being an appeal to self-love, it can be answered by the resolute sceptic in another way. The sceptic may ask, 'Why must we assume that the implantation of a favour towards virtue is a sign that we are wise to practice virtue? Is it not possible that providence has implanted this tendency in us for the overall good of the universe, but that we ourselves are losers? Could it not be that we are made with a tendency to judge things right that make us sacrifice our own interests to the march of history?' Butler has an answer here, in Chapters ii–v of Part I of the *Analogy*, where he argues that the whole scheme of providence declares for virtue and against vice, and that this is not against our interests. But here the arguments go far beyond the contentions of the *Sermons* For Butler's case in the *Sermons* to be self-contained in the way he clearly supposes it to be, he has to be appealing to an inbuilt knowledge that does not depend for its epistemic credentials on the natural theology he supplies for it elsewhere.

(ii) There are suggestions that Butler also wishes to offer, as a distinct argument, the claim that the judgments of conscience are not merely judgments that our natures enable us to recognise as superior to those of other principles, but contain within themselves marks of conscience's authority. We do not merely know that we should never do what it forbids; there is an absurdity in the very notion that one could have a sufficient reason to disobey it.

Butler says that the superiority of conscience 'is a constituent part of the idea, that is, of the faculty itself' (*S* ii 14/19). The same suggestion is implied in Butler's unsatisfactory characterisation of conscience as the one and only reflective faculty, which I have already criticised. Using these hints, I shall try to construct his argument in an explicit form. I have already suggested that most of us do find it self-evident, in cases where a conflict with duty is not in question, that if I face a clash between a desire, however strong, and self-love, and judge that following the desire is against my interests, I have a sufficient reason to reject the desire: that, duty apart, it would be absurd to suggest I could have a sufficient reason for yielding to it. I cannot rationally identify myself with the desire and distance myself from my self-interest. It is by reference to this kind of occasion that Butler introduces the idea of the authority of an inward principle to us; and I think he wishes to suggest that the same manifest absurdity attaches to the idea that any principle, self-love included, could give us sufficient reason to reject the dictates of conscience.

If this is what he means, it implies that if I ask whether or not I should do what conscience tells me, the only coherent thing I can mean by this question is, 'Has my conscience made an error about what it is I ought to do? Ought I, perhaps, to treat the urgings of desire or self-love in this case as though they had more *moral* weight than they seem to have? Am I underrating the moral value of my own wants this time?'[16] But this is not the question Butler is addressing when he tells us that conscience has supreme authority; he is addressing the question 'Even if my conscience has correctly judged an action to be morally obligatory, should I do it?' and he is telling us that we cannot use the word 'should', or its equivalents, here, in any way that permits a negative answer.

I have claimed that Butler's 'nature' argument ends in an appeal to a form of knowledge he thinks we all have: the knowledge that the judgments of conscience are more stringent reasons for action than any others; and that the only supporting arguments are theological. The argument I have now ascribed to him is not an appeal to a supposed form of knowledge, but to what is nowadays often called a linguistic intuition. The intuitions of philosophers differ, especially on *this* matter. There are many who think that the 'should' in 'Why should I be moral?' has a clear sense, or at least a clearly elucidable sense. They do not think that this sense reduces the question, on examination, to the vacuous 'Why ought I to do what I know to be right?' Butler holds that it does reduce to this. The only comment I can make here is that it is Butler who has first shown us that the onus is on those who think some other clear sense exists, to elucidate it, and that their success is not conspicuous.

This needs emendation. Butler does admit that there is one other sense to the question. This is the sense that turns it into 'Is being moral in my own interest?' He thinks that whatever the answer to this question is, it could not show we should *not* follow conscience. But in spite of this, he seems determined to answer it, and his determination to do it has exasperated his most sympathetic readers. I turn now to his answer, and its implications.

(iii) The most famous expression of Butler's opinion on this matter is to be found in the 'cool hour' passage in paragraph 20/21 of Sermon xi:

> It may be allowed, without any prejudice to the cause of virtue and religion, that our ideas of happiness and misery are of all our ideas the nearest and most important to us; that they will, nay, if you please that they ought to prevail over those of order, and beauty, and harmony, and proportion, if there ever should be, as it is impossible there ever should be, any inconsistence between them: though these last too, as expressing the fitness of actions, are as real as truth itself. Let it be allowed, though virtue or moral rectitude does indeed consist in affection to and pursuit of what is right and good, as such; yet, that when we sit down in a cool hour, we can neither justify to ourselves this or any other pursuit, till we are convinced that it will be for our happiness, or at least not contrary to it.

This passage is, above all others, the one which has caused some of Butler's readers to think that, in the last resort, Butler is an ethical egoist, who believes that even the authority of conscience has to be justified on the ground that following it is in our interest.w6.5[17] If this is indeed Butler's view, it is flatly inconsistent with the claim that conscience is superior to all other principles, including self-love, at least as I have interpreted this claim. I think the literature contains sufficient refutation of this reading of this passage. Broad, Taylor, and Duncan-Jones[18] have made it clear that Butler is arguing here from a premiss that others believe, though he does not: the premiss that no pursuit is justifiable unless it is in our interest. This is clear enough from the 'if you please' and the 'Let it be allowed'. The Sermon's main point is that there is no ground for the common assumption that benevolence and self-love conflict, so in this passage Butler is emphasising that even those who think self-interest is the only justification for choice have, in consequence, no good reason to reject their own benevolent inclinations. The point is here extended to cover virtue as a whole, which is not clearly distinguished from benevolence at this stage in his argument. It is clear that Butler does not place himself among the egoists merely because he says this. If confirmation is needed, it comes immediately in the next paragraph:

> Common reason and humanity will have some influence upon mankind, whatever becomes of speculations; but, so far as the interests of virtue depend upon the theory of it being secured from open scorn, so far its very being in the world depends upon its appearing to have no contrariety to private interest and self-love. (S xi 21/22)

Butler could hardly have made his intentions more clear. He is seeking, with his customary moral pragmatism, to win over to the practice of virtue those in his audience whose minds are stuffed with egoistical theories. If that is the way he has to reach them, he will do it, in the hope that the practice of what virtue requires will produce virtue itself.[19]

But this is not quite enough. We are still left with the insistence that not only is there no necessary clash between virtue and benevolence on the one hand, and self-love on the other, but that it is *impossible* there should be one. One wants to say that there is no point in having a hierarchy of principles in human nature at all if there can be no clash between them, ever. We can get a partial answer from noting that Butler clearly thinks that the judgments of self-love can be mistaken, and that following conscience safeguards us from its errors.

But, aside from the special problem of whether conscience itself has then to be immune from error, the core problem remains: Butler seems to take the demand for justification of virtue in terms of self-interest with a degree of seriousness that goes far beyond the requirements of an *ad hominem* argument. How is this to be explained, how far does it create a major geological fault in his ethical position?

Sturgeon points out that if we ascribe the Full Naturalistic Thesis to Butler, the answer is clear.[20] For if conscience approves actions as natural, and disapproves them as unnatural, and naturalness is a matter of congruence with a superior principle – then, if that principle is self-love, conscience and self-love indeed cannot conflict. I have rejected the ascription of the thesis to Butler, and must therefore attempt another explanation. I have already outlined it.[21] I quote again Butler's key statement:

Conscience and self-love, if we understand our true happiness, always lead us the same way. Duty and interest are perfectly coincident; for the most part in this world, but entirely and in every instance if we take in the future, and the whole; this being implied in the notion of a good and perfect administration of things. (*S* iii 9/13)

The explanation has to rest on the theological underpinnings of Butler's thought. He assumes, and takes for granted that his audience would assume, that the human nature he describes is the way it is for a purpose laid down by God. His audience would not necessarily have shared his view that God's providence favours virtue, but they would probably have accepted the view that a creature's natural endowments are, in general, for its good, or to its advantage. It follows from this assumption that if conscience has natural superiority for us, following it will be for our good. Hence, if self-love makes the right judgments, it will support conscience, since it is the business of self-love to seek our good. This is a simple consequence of the assumption that the superiority of conscience is providential.

But a position so structured suggests a counter-argument: since there are some occasions on which following conscience seems obviously *against* the agent's interests, because it leads to poverty, isolation, or danger, conscience *cannot* have the natural superiority Butler claims for it. If it did, such things would not happen. To prevent this conclusion, Butler has to hold that those occasions when virtue seems to be against our interests are, rightly understood, still times when a right understanding of our interests would lead us to practise it. But this requires a fuller theological argument than he can make in the *Sermons*. It requires him to say that God is a righteous judge, who ultimately rewards virtue and punishes vice. He makes an extended case for this in Chapters ii–v of Part I of the *Analogy*; but in the *Sermons* he cannot assume that all his hearers believe it. So he is only able to indicate that this is his view, and offer for their immediate acceptance the lesser claim that in this world duty and interest coincide *for the most part*. His optimism on this point is probably not shared by many readers in our own day (though it would, ironically, have made some appeal to those of his hearers who were inclined to give an egoistic explanation of why virtue is so widespread). In any case, to argue that God's providence favours virtue and rejects vice, he has, in the *Analogy* to begin from the supposed fact that virtue can be seen to pay in our present life *for the most part*. This is an essential element in his analogical argument for the view that the tribulations of the virtuous are consistent with God's goodness. He does present there some claims that could well have appeared in the *Sermons* – for example, that society rewards virtue as such, and punishes vice as such.[22] But the *Sermons* do not offer us such arguments, and the claim that virtue is in our own interest stays at the level of mere assertion there. Fortunately, if I have analysed the 'nature' argument correctly, even though our nature is understood in it as providentially ordered, it rests primarily upon an appeal to a supposed knowledge that providence has imparted. Either we have that knowledge, or we do not. Since we do not need to appeal to natural theology to decide this, the core 'nature' argument is logically distinct from the appeal to self-interest.

4

I wish to draw a few corollaries before proceeding. I have argued, first of all, that Butler's 'nature' argument is not reducible to his view that duty and interest coincide, even though his views of nature and providence explain the firmness with which he holds the second. It follows that Prichard, for example, is mistaken in bracketing Butler with Plato as a thinker who 'seeks at bottom to convince the individual that he ought to act in so-called moral ways by showing that to do so will really be for his happiness'.[23] Butler does believe this; but for him it is a secondary matter, to be brought in to reconcile those with a different view of human motives to the practice of morality. There is another respect in which Butler's argument from human nature is different from Plato's. There is no trace in the *Sermons*, and hardly any in the *Analogy*, of the 'mental health' argument from human nature – the argument that since our natures are so constructed that the virtuous life is the life that exercises the various parts of our moral constitution most healthily, vice will disrupt the inner harmony of the soul and make us miserable and disorientated.[24] The emphasis on the constitution of human nature in the *Sermons* is not there for this purpose, but to support the concept of conscience's authority; and although the argument for the morality of divine government in the *Analogy* makes reference to the 'uneasiness' that accompanies vice, this is mentioned as a sign that God is in favour of virtue, not as a reason for practising it ourselves. So for all his talk of human nature, Butler is not one of those who seek to 'ground ethics in psychology', if this phrase connotes the attempt to make virtue and mental health equivalent.

I have also said that Butler's view of the status of conscience does not require him to hold that conscience is infallible. He is undoubtedly far too confident that we all know what virtue requires:

> The inquiries which have been made by men of leisure, after some general rule, the conformity to, or disagreement from, which, should denominate our actions good or evil, are in many respects of great service. Yet let any plain honest man, before he engages in any

course of action, ask himself, Is this I am going about right, or is it wrong? Is it good, or is it evil? I do not in the least doubt, but that this question would be answered agreeably to truth and virtue, by almost any fair man in any circumstance. (S iii 4/4)

The only source of moral error about which he has much to say, apart from bad moral theory, is self-deception, which he interprets as that special kind of partiality which prevents our seeing that a rule we apply to others also applies to some course of action we are engaged upon ourselves.[25] There is a natural tendency for him to think of the dictates of conscience as clear and unambiguous: for one thing, his main concern is with those who do not claim ignorance of what virtue requires, but ask why they should do it; for another, it helps him to deal with clashes between virtue and self-love if he can say that they arise from self-love being in error when conscience is clear and definite. But although we do often prevaricate, and claim not to be sure what is right when we know it very well, his confidence about what conscience dictates is something no wide-awake reader in our day and age can share. I do not, however, think it is essential to his argument for the supremacy of conscience. For that is an argument which tells us that when we have decided what is right, we have reached a point where we have decided, and know we have decided, what we should do. To maintain this he does not have to deny, even if he *would* have denied, that there are many occasions when we find it honestly hard to decide what is right, and therefore do not yet know what we should do.

There remains the question of how Butler supposes conscience comes to make the judgments it does make. There is no question that Butler believes that conscience is a law implanted in us by God, and that the commands of conscience are God's commands. But this does not mean he holds that our recognition of right and wrong in any way depends on our recognition of God's authority over us. He clearly holds the opposite. It is the fact that moral judgment is independent of the recognition of divine commands that makes it possible for him to preach Sermons ii and iii from the text which says that the Gentiles, which have not the law, are a law unto themselves (Romans 2:14). He goes further: while he does not use this principle in either work, he holds that 'God cannot approve of anything but what is in itself Right, Fit, Just.'[26] At the close of the *Analogy* he tells us that he has 'omitted a thing of the utmost importance which I do believe, the moral fitness and unfitness of actions, prior to all will whatever; which I apprehend as certainly to determine the Divine conduct, as speculative truth and falsehood necessarily determine the Divine judgment' (*An* II viii 11/24).[27] In other words, not only do human beings discern right from wrong independently of any awareness they may or may not have of the commands of

God, but God himself judges actions to be right or wrong because they are so, independently of his judgment. So with regard to the ancient 'Euthyphro' dilemma (the problem of whether those acts God commands are right because he commands them or whether he commands them because they are right), Butler is unequivocally on the side of those who place the rightness of actions before the divine selection of them, and of those who place our discernment of the rightness of them before our recognition that God commands them. He clearly believes, then, that conscience has insight into the rightness or wrongness of actual or possible actions. The *Analogy* quotation echoes the opinions of Clarke, whose ethical method Butler says in the Preface to the Sermons that he will not follow, but of which he approves. Clarke, in the *Discourse Concerning the Unchangeable Obligations of Natural Religion*, published in 1706, argued that 'from the eternal and necessary differences of things, there naturally and necessarily arise certain moral obligations, which are of themselves incumbent on all rational creatures, antecedent to all positive institution, and to all expectation of reward or punishment'.[28] He likens the necessity of these moral obligations to that of the truths of mathematics, and says that all men have the power to discern these obligations within them, quoting the same passage from Romans that Butler preaches from.[29] Clarke makes repeated appeals to self-evidence, and repeated uses of the mathematical analogy. Examples of the moral obligations we all discern are the duty to worship God, the duty to treat our neighbours as ourselves, the duties of prudence and sobriety, and the prohibition of suicide. While he does not reach detailed rules, it is clear that he sees us as all endowed with the power to see that certain *classes* of act are in all circumstances enjoined or forbidden.

From his own statements, and from his approval of Clarke, we can reasonably infer that Butler thinks conscience does not just issue commands, but judges the actions it commands to be right or wrong because of the *kind* of actions they are. Duncan-Jones says that the passage from Sermon iii 4/4 quoted above shows that Butler did not think conscience operates by reference to general rules,[30] but I do not think this is quite what it says. It says rather that conscience, in plain honest men, does not refer to rules of the very high level of generality that philosophers look for. This point, which would count against something as general as the Greatest Happiness Principle, would not rule out prohibiting actions because they were examples of bad faith. When he says conscience judges actions in themselves, I think he does not only mean it ignores consequences, but that it judges actions as being of this or that *kind*. He inevitably supposes that such perceptions are more easily come by than any judgment based on the uncertainties of future consequences can be. As he makes clear when rejecting the equation of virtue and benevolence, to which I turn next, he thinks we must leave

78

it to providence to ensure that when we follow conscience, the results are not ultimately contrary to our good, or that of our neighbours. God, of course, not only knows what acts are right or wrong, but can so arrange the world that when right is done, those who do it prosper in the long run.

Butler's position, then, comes close to what used to be called Dogmatic Intuitionism. Although he could not admit conscience makes mistakes regularly, he does not have to claim it never makes any. His main ethical point is that if conscience has made its judgment, the agent has. If the agent then does not act accordingly, strength has won out over authority.

5

I turn finally, to our three original questions about the place of benevolence in Butler's ethical thought.[31] These were: how does Butler think benevolence motivates us? how good a case does he give for supposing that benevolence and self-love point the same way? and does he have a consistent position on the relation of benevolence to virtue?

On the first question, I can summarise what has already been said as follows. The term 'benevolence' is often used by Butler as the general name for all affections which prompt us to act in ways that we hope will benefit others. This comprehends quite unreflective impulses to give someone pleasure or relieve their pain, as well as the determination to do things that are for their general good. Even in this general sense, it entails rational consideration, most obviously in the determination of what is indeed for the good of the other. The affective side of benevolence, in all these instances, directs itself towards individuals or groups known to us. In addition, however, Butler believes there is a more general affection, namely the love of our neighbour. This is specific also, in that it is directed, as he puts it, towards those with whom we have to do; but it is directed towards them *as* neighbours or fellow-creatures and is not based upon other ties we have with them. He seems to equate this with the general desire for public good. The person in whom benevolence is a settled state of personality is someone who is regularly motivated by both of these. Butler's vigorous arguments against psychological egoism and hedonism show that there is no sound theoretical reason to deny the reality of benevolence in the more restricted senses, and it is possible to accept them while still being unsure, as Hume is, about the reality of the impartial love of one's neighbour. Butler, however, takes the Christian love commandment to assume its reality.

On the coincidence of self-love and benevolence, we can find a similar limitation in Butler's case. His arguments against psychological egoism are based upon the distinction between self-love and the particular passions and affections. He insists, rightly, that the particular affections include many that are desires for the pleasure or good of others, and that if we achieve happiness by satisfying our particular desires, and these include desires for the good of others, the happiness at which self-love aims will not exclude that of our fellows. No doubt he would also say that when he advises against too much self-love, and in favour of 'disengagement' in the enjoyment of desired activities, this includes the enjoyment of other-directed activities. These arguments all occur in Sermon xi, which is called 'Upon the Love of our Neighbour', but they really only deal with the lack of conflict between self-love and specific benevolent affections. The question of the relation between self-love and love of neighbour in the impartial sense is the main theme of Sermon xii, where Butler tries to interpret the command that we should love our neighbours *as ourselves*.

He makes heavy weather of it, and one can only bear in mind the reasons, pragmatic and theological, that Butler has for trying to show that self-love is never really displaced by virtue. His various interpretations of the love commandment all seem designed to ensure that the relative priority of self-love over benevolence is consistent with it. This is the one place where his philosophical predilections lead him into a manifest misreading of the New Testament.

The injunction to 'love thy neighbour as thyself' will admit, he says, of three senses: (i) that we have the same kind of affection for others that we have for ourselves; (ii) that the love we have for our neighbour should bear some certain proportion or other to self-love; or (iii) that it should be equal in degree to self-love. Butler's comments on (i) are not his clearest, but he seems to read it as an injunction that just as we want our own happiness, so we should want our neighbour's, or 'have a real share' in it. On (ii), after pointing out that the selfish or benevolent person is not so much the one who has self-love or benevolence present in strength, but the person who has it present in greater *relative* strength, Butler draws the following uninspiring conclusion:

> Love of our neighbour then must bear some proportion to self-love, and virtue to be sure consists in the due proportion. What this due proportion is . . . can be judged only from our nature and condition in this world. (*S* 12 13/9)

Aware, as he could hardly fail to be, of the fact that this is a very deflationary reading of the love commandment, he proceeds in his treatment of (iii) to say that even if it tells us that we ought to have equally as much love for our neighbour as for ourselves, this would not lead to neglect of ourselves; for in addition to self-love and benevolence, we have 'several other particular affections, passions, appetites which we cannot feel in common with others', and these occupy our attention as much as self-love does. He gives no example, but if what he means is that each of us has his or her own built-in desires regarding physical and mental needs, such as food, grooming, cessation of pain, or security, and that I can only feel these desires for myself and not others, then his own theory on the relation of self-love to particular affections would require him to say that these are, indirectly but necessarily, the concern of self-love. So if I am to show equal concern for my neighbour as for myself, then I must be as concerned that my neighbour's desires for these things, however private, are satisfied, as that my own are. Butler seems to want to exclude these desires from the scope of the love commandment, so that the pre-eminence of self-love is untouched by it, but this is manifestly impossible, even on his own interpretation of that principle.

After the acuity of many of the arguments in Sermon xi, it is disappointing to read Sermon xii. The best case one can make for Butler here is that he is perhaps still trying to reach a supposedly self-centred audience the best way he can, and is trying to persuade them that the love commandment is not alien even to their restricted aspirations. If this *is* what he is about, however, he does not give the overt signs of it that he does in Sermon xi, and the resulting analysis of the command he is commending to them is Procrustean.

The last, and most important, question is the relationship of benevolence to virtue in Butler's ethics. There is no doubt that he often writes as though they are identical, in practice if not conceptually. He certainly seems to think that his proofs that benevolence is not contrary to self-love are defences of virtue. He says early in Sermon xii that 'our Saviour places the principle of virtue in the love of our neighbour' (4/2). He says a little later (8/5) that the 'principle of benevolence', by which he seems here to mean the love of neighbour, is 'itself the temper of virtue'; and in 31/22 he says 'it is manifest that the common virtues, and the common vices of mankind, may be traced up to benevolence, or the want of it'. These all suggest that he equates virtue and benevolence in some way. Yet they raise the same questions about the relation of benevolence to conscience that exercise Butler's readers when they reflect on the relation between conscience and self-love. A possible solution in the case of benevolence might be to say that conscience and benevolence (at least in the wider sense of impartial love of neighbour) would always prompt the same actions, so that benevolence always urges us to do that which conscience in fact approves, and that conscience has to supply the motive of duty to such actions if the motive of benevolence is wanting. This view has independent attractions, since it offers a coherent, if oversimple, theory of the relation between love and moral obligation. But Butler clearly rejects it. The rejection is clear enough in Sermon xii itself, or at any rate in the long footnote to paragraph 31/22. There he adds 'cautions and restrictions' to an unsophisticated acceptance of the Pauline view that all other moral commandments are comprehended in the command to love our neighbour. God, Butler says, may have placed us under particular obligations, which we can discern as binding on us quite apart from our wish to seek the happiness of our fellow-creatures; and he may have done this because 'we are not competent judges, what is upon the whole for the good of the world'. He says we know this to be the case, since there are certain motives and actions which we approve of in themselves, quite apart from the good they do (such as fidelity, honour, and justice), and others which we disapprove of in themselves, without regard for the harm they do (such as treachery, indecency, and meanness). This is a clear enough rejection of the view that it is enough to be benevolent in order to be virtuous.

But it still seems to leave it as an open possibility that although conscience can issue its own commands without regard to benevolence, it will always approve those things which benevolence presents to it. In the Dissertation, however, Butler very firmly rejects this. No doubt the special context of the Dissertation, in the *Analogy*, explains this rejection, as McPherson says,[32] though I do not think this justifies treating the Sermons and the Dissertations as though they embodied two different ethical positions. The second Dissertation was originally to have formed part of Chapter iii of Part I of the *Analogy* ('Of the Moral Government of God'). There, and elsewhere, Butler is concerned to emphasise and balance two things: that we are largely ignorant of God's detailed intentions and purposes in creation, so that we cannot lay down *a priori* decisions about what providence would or would not do; and that, in spite of this, there are clear signs, available to us through observation, that God's government of the world is moral and just. What he infers from this in the Dissertation is that the deliverances of conscience are likely to be for our ultimate good, and that of our fellow-creatures, but that we ourselves are unlikely to be the best judges of the detailed consequences of each decision. We should, therefore, rely on God to see to it that when we follow conscience, we contribute to the welfare of his creatures, and not play God ourselves by attempting to reverse the priorities of our natures and subject the deliverances of conscience to supposedly higher standards deriving from benevolence. More briefly, if your conscience tells you to do it, do it, even if a vague rule like the Greatest Happiness Principle suggests otherwise. Butler here enlists the resources of his natural theology to make it clear that his ethics really is one in which conscience is supreme.

(It is worth remarking, parenthetically, that the Dissertation attempts to tidy the account of the relationship between conscience and self-love in a similar way. In 6/8–10, Butler argues that we are not morally at liberty to 'make ourselves miserable without reason', that is, to neglect our greater good because of strong desires. Hence prudence (in other

words, cool self-love) is a virtue, although popular morality is unenthusi-
astic about calling it one. Although this seems, at first sight, to reinforce
the claims of self-love as opposed to those of conscience, and to aid the
case of those who find moral egoism in Butler, it in fact does the reverse.
For it says that conscience requires us to follow self-love when it conflicts
with particular passions; and this implies an ultimate subordination of
self-love to conscience, which can displace it if a conflict should arise.)

To return to benevolence: Butler gives several reasons for refusing to
equate benevolence and virtue. (i) If benevolence were the sole basis of
right decisions, we would be morally indifferent about the distribution
of goods among persons; but in fact we judge it morally better that the
deserving (such as friends, or benefactors) should have priority. (It is
worth mentioning that the New Testament love commandment quite
clearly collides with this judgment. See, for example Matthew 20:1–16.)
(ii) We would condemn as vicious the theft of a man's earnings, even if
they were given to another in greater need. (iii) We are, in fact, so made
as to condemn lies, violence, and injustice, irrespective of the fact that
they might have beneficial results. He concludes that God might well be
a Utilitarian, for all we know; if he is, then he will have seen to it that
our consciences lead us to do those things which are for our ultimate
happiness. But he has not made us in such a way that we can give
ultimate moral priority to 'the overbalance of evil or good'. He returns
to the theme of human ignorance in paragraph 10/15, where he attacks
those who seem to say that 'the whole of virtue' consists 'in singly aiming,
according to the best of their judgment, at promoting the happiness of
mankind in the present state'. No mistake, he says, could be more
terrible. For many of the most shocking misdeeds may appear to be
justifiable on such a principle, since they can seem to lead, as far as we
can tell, to good results, or not to have bad ones.

This argument has more than one strand to it. In the first instance, it
is a special application of the basic 'nature' argument of the *Sermons*.
The virtuous person is one in whom conscience and other principles
harmonise, but in whom conscience is supreme, so that if he is prompted
by the love of his neighbour to do something, conscience is most likely
to judge it is the right action also, so that the two distinct motives co-
operate to produce a common result. If, however, conscience leads the
agent to decide that virtue and duty point in different directions, the call
of duty overrides that of good will. Butler is clearer here than he is in
the case of self-love, that a conflict with conscience can indeed arise, at
least as far as the good of man in this life is concerned. We often have
to do things from duty that are hard on those our benevolence would
lead us to benefit, as when (my example) we are obliged to advise a poor
man to pay his debts to a richer one.

Thus far, the argument is not one that requires any particular understanding of how conscience arrives at its verdicts. As just interpreted, the argument would allow conscience to take consequences into account – not in the sense that it would judge an action, once performed, in terms of the results it has actually achieved, but that it could judge it partly in terms of its *intended* results. But Butler is anxious to picture conscience and its verdicts in a different way. He wants to argue that the rational calculations to which benevolence, if left to itself, would lead us, are necessarily less reliable than the verdicts of conscience, because of the depth of our ignorance of the world and its future. This would eliminate the possibility of a utilitarian view of duty, whereby the calculation of consequences would form a standard part of conscience's deliberations. He has to picture conscience as delivering its verdicts in a way that is free from the pitfalls and ambiguities that attend any calculation of the balance of goods over evils. Hence he has to picture it as in large part *non*-deliberative; and he sees it as enjoining and vetoing actions simply on the ground of their being actions of certain kinds, like justice, treachery, or adultery. These judgments have to be quicker, easier, and more reliable than any consequential judgments can possibly be. Conscience is intuitive.

The doctrine of the natural superiority of conscience does not, of itself, entail a belief in the intuitive character of its judgments. But the particular reasons that Butler offers in the Dissertation on Virtue for insisting on its superiority to benevolence do entail this. It also seems required by the place of our moral natures in the scheme of providence that Butler argues for in the *Analogy* as a whole. And even though the main argument of the *Sermons* may not demand it, there is no reason to think that Butler does not hold it there too.

Butler's anti-utilitarian arguments have been the standard criticisms of utilitarian ethics ever since, and we cannot explore the many answers here. The most common and influential of them amount to a claim that the very moral judgments Butler interposes between us and the actions prompted by unrestricted benevolence, embody rules that only have the authority he claims for them if they can be given a utilitarian justification. Although the conservatism of the popular moral consciousness is in decline, Butler seems, on the whole, to have the plain honest man's vote, especially in view of the anxiety of Utilitarians like Mill to make sure that their justifications yield results that square with the plain honest man's intuitions. The common moral consciousness has always tended to view Utilitarianism as the ethic of the social engineer, who rides roughshod over the moral rights of individuals to achieve general social objectives, and defences of Utilitarianism have had to try to show that this is not the way it is. The problem with Butler's position is that it requires a view of the plain man's intuitions which may not need to make them infallible, but does have to repose a primary moral confidence in them – a confidence that is eroded by the sheer variety of moral opinion in our present society. The best to be said for him on this score is that the justifications to which Utilitarians appeal imply judgments of long-term good which are equally open to widespread rejection.

PART TWO

THE APOLOGIST

IV

The Nature of Butler's Apologetic

The most common judgment of the *Analogy*, even among those who still read it, is that since it was addressed to an audience that no longer exists, it is obsolete. As Mossner has put it, 'The *Analogy* is dead now chiefly because it was a Tract for the times.'[1] I think this judgment is quite mistaken. It is true that Butler's work *was* a Tract for the times, as any apologetic work is bound to be. Its arguments are directed against objections to Christianity that were current in Butler's own place and time, just as, for example, those left to us in Pascal's *Pensées*, to which it is sometimes compared, were directed against sceptical attitudes current in France in the previous century. This means that many of the arguments arise in a context that is not a live one now, and a full understanding of them requires us to recognise the nature of that context. But it does not mean that these arguments have no value or application when the transitory features of their original setting are removed. I hope to show that their permanent value is much greater than this: that it is instructive to ponder them now, just as it is instructive to ponder those of Pascal.

1

Butler makes his basic intentions clear in the rather melancholy Advertisement to the first edition:

It is come, I know not how, to be taken for granted, by many
persons, that Christianity is not so much as a subject of inquiry;
but that it is, now at length, discovered to be fictitious. And
accordingly they treat it, as if, in the present age, this were an agreed
point among all people of discernment; and nothing remained, but
to set it up as a principal subject of mirth and ridicule, as it were
by way of reprisals, for its having so long interrupted the pleasures
of the world. On the contrary, thus much, at least, will be here found,

89

not taken for granted, but proved, that any reasonable man, who will thoroughly consider the matter, may be as much assured, as he is of his own being, that it is not, however, so clear a case, that there is nothing in it. There is, I think, strong evidence of its truth; but it is certain no one can, upon principles of reason, be satisfied of the contrary. And the practical consequence to be drawn from this is not attended to by every one who is concerned in it.

This passage is the key to the whole work. Butler's arguments are intended as an antidote to the frivolity with which he thought his contemporaries chose to approach the claims of Christianity. He intends to attack it by showing it to be unreasonable and *imprudent*. To show it is imprudent, he does not have to prove that Christianity is true, or even prove that it is *likely* Christianity is true; he has only to show that *it is not so clear a case that there is nothing in it*. The choice of double negatives is typical and important. In the last resort, Butler will be satisfied with showing that the common and easy assumption that Christianity is too clearly absurd to merit serious consideration, is false; and with showing that it is therefore practical foolishness to dismiss its claims out of hand. He is strongly of the opinion that the case for Christianity is better than this: that there is 'strong evidence of its truth'. But it is not as important to him to show this, as it is to satisfy the lesser objective of proving that it should be considered seriously.

Why would he be satisfied with so little, if he thinks there could be more? The answer is that Butler's primary aim is once more a practical one – to persuade his readers to recognise how important it is for them in practice to attend to the claims of Christianity. His procedure, though not his language, is strongly reminiscent of that of Pascal, and justifies comparison between them.[2] Pascal's unfinished *Apology for the Christian Religion*, the notes for which comprise the greater part of what we now know as the *Pensées*, is best known among philosophers for its famous 'Wager' argument. This would probably have appeared close to the midpoint of Pascal's work,[3] and is addressed to someone who has been shaken from the delusive frivolity of trivial social pursuits by Pascal's mordant exposure of the evils of the human condition, but has not yet been brought to any conviction of the truth of Christianity's estimate of these evils and their cure. Pascal mounts a prudential argument for such a supposed reader, appealing to considerations that might move him at the gaming-table. Even though, it is assumed, we cannot tell whether Christianity is true or not, we would be foolish not to bet on its being true, because by doing so we stand to lose almost nothing, but to gain eternal happiness; whereas by betting against it (which is what we effectively do if we ignore it) we gain almost nothing and stand to lose eternity. Hence, if there are no decisive *dis*proofs of Christianity, the sheer *importance* of the claims it makes are enough to count decisively in its favour in practice. Butler's stance is similar. Even though he thinks there is strong evidence for the truth of Christian claims, he thinks that the mere fact that the case *against* them can be answered is enough to prove that it is foolish in practice to reject them without the most careful reflection. There is no doubt that Butler oscillates between this minimal position and the stronger one that the evidence clearly favours the choice of Christianity, prudence aside; he is aided in this by ambiguities in the way he uses the notions of analogy and probability, on which I shall comment below. But there is, equally, no doubt that the minimal position he urges throughout, is this twofold one: that, in the first place, the case against Christianity is much weaker than its critics in his day maintained, and the evidence for it significantly better; and that, in the second place, it is frivolous and imprudent not to give the most serious consideration to assenting to it in the light of these facts.

The second part of this is vaguer in Butler than it is in Pascal. There is a strong suggestion that Butler is urging more upon us than that we should review the evidence for Christianity carefully, but he does not say too precisely what else he is suggesting. Pascal, at least in the 'Wager' fragment, is quite explicit. He tells us that, once we decide the believer has better cosmic chances than the unbeliever, we should take whatever steps are necessary to become believers, even though the evidence leans no more towards Christianity than away from it. We should act as if Christianity were true, hoping that this will make us come to believe it is. Butler does not say this, though his position seems to me to imply it. For the moment, it is enough to say that he is shielded from considering the difficulties of such a view, by his unexamined conviction that the practical requirements of religion are identical with those of the secular conscience, which he has defended elsewhere.

2

The requirements of practical choice are central to the way Butler thinks about probability in the *Analogy*. One of the remarks for which he is famous is that 'to us, probability is the very guide of life' (*An* Int 3/4). This dictum is usually taken to mean that we have to be content with estimating likelihoods when making our decisions, since certainties are not available to us. Undoubtedly he does mean this. But he also wishes to stress the fact that circumstances often force us to act on assumptions which, though they have *some* likelihood of being true, are not necessarily the *most* likely assumptions we could make. There are occasions on which it is manifestly foolish not to take steps to anticipate an unlikely set of events, as long as they are not without *some degree* of likelihood. To take a modern example: if the control-tower receives a bomb threat by telephone before the plane takes off, it is most prudent to delay departure and search the aircraft, just because there is a slight chance that there really is a bomb on it, even though it is far more likely that there is not. Probability is as much a guide of life on these occasions as on those when we provide only for what is most probable. What determines our decision, of course, is the recognition that the risks attendant on the wrong choice are very great. If we apply this to the case of Christianity, it implies that perhaps we should act on the assumption that it is true, even if, apart from these practical concerns, we judge it less likely that it is true than that it is false; provided there is *some* non-negligible degree of probability in its favour. There is no general guidance on how great a degree this has to be, but in view of the practical stakes, it would presumably have to be very low indeed to be discounted altogether. If this is correct, then Butler's position is in one respect more radical than that of Pascal. In the 'Wager' fragment, Pascal assumes he is addressing a situation in which reason can tell us nothing about which of the two alternatives is the more likely; so he assumes their relative likelihoods to be equivalent. Butler is suggesting that the wise man would consider acting on the assumption that Christianity is true even if the likelihood of its being true is much less than the likelihood of its being false – although he himself does not assess its relative likelihood so pessimistically.

It is not always easy to decide whether Butler's judgment about a particular doctrine is that it is *more* likely to be true than not to be, or that it is *as* likely to be true as not to be, or merely that it possesses *some* non-negligible degree of likelihood. (He does not consider the fact that all three are compatible with a fourth possibility – that Christianity is more likely to be true than any single one of the positive alternatives to it, though obviously his argument could only gain, not lose, by considering this option.[4]) He is always able to fall back on the third, if the first and second fail. So his argument would collapse, in his own estimation, only if he could not establish the third. Of course, it is hard to decide under what conditions an attempt to show the third alternative *would* fail. But the greater the degree of independent likelihood a doctrine has, the greater the frivolity, indeed the wickedness, involved in disregarding it.[5]

Butler's thinking about probability is not at all systematic. But it is conducted against the background of an important metaphysical assumption: that probability 'is to be considered as relative only to beings of limited capacities' (*An* Int 3/4). Nothing, says Butler, can be probable to an infinite intelligence. It is only to *us* that probability is the guide of life. The overall understanding Butler has, therefore, is of a world in which there are laws which, if known completely, would enable us to understand the past, present, and future, with a systematic certainty that

God already possesses, but in which we are limited to making probable judgments of what these laws are, and what the events they govern will be. It does not, and could not, occur to Butler that the laws the universe follows might themselves be ultimately probabilistic. To him the fact that we are beings who must base our decisions on probabilities is a clear sign that God has chosen to limit our understanding to matters we need to know in order to conduct ourselves in the station in which he has placed us. This is a vital clue to his mind, and there are several striking consequences of his seeing our knowledge of this world, and of God's purposes in it, in this way.

(i) In the first instance, it leads Butler to take a very modest view of his role as a thinker: it is that of leading his hearers and readers to choose wisely, not that of making them more knowledgeable. He is even led, in the important sermon 'Upon the Ignorance of Man', to censure those who have a loftier view of the function of intellectual inquiry:

> Men of deep research and curious inquiry should just be put in mind, not to mistake what they are doing. If their discoveries serve the cause of virtue and religion, in the way of proof, motive to practice, or assistance in it; or if they tend to render life less unhappy, and promote its satisfactions; then they are most usefully employed: but bringing things to light, along and of itself, is of no manner of use, any otherwise than as an entertainment or diversion. Neither is this at all amiss, if it does not take up the time which should be employed in better work . . . the only knowledge which is of any avail to us, is that which teaches us our duty, or assists us in the discharge of it. The economy of the universe, the course of nature, almighty power exerted in the creation and government of the world, is out of our reach. (S xv 16/18)

(ii) A second result of Butler's conviction that we are largely confined to probable judgments by God's choice, is his repeated insistence, fundamental to the second half of the *Analogy*, that men are in no position to insist, *a priori*, that God would only make himself known to man in some ways and not in others – for example, that he would only reveal himself in ways that are universally accessible. If we are prepared to consider that God exists at all, and are prepared to recognise that our knowledge of the world is partial and fragmentary, it is inconsistent to pronounce in advance that God's purposes cannot be learned from the history of Israel or the experience of the Church.

(iii) The fact that Butler's view of the limitations of our knowledge is religious, rather than epistemological, in its motive, helps to explain his apparent ambivalence on the question of whether there can be *a priori*, or demonstrative, knowledge of God. He writes more than once as though the existence of God can be, and has indeed been, proved. He says it has been proved 'from abstract reasonings', that is *a priori* (*An Int* 8/10); this appears to represent an acceptance of the Cosmological Argument as presented by Samuel Clarke,[6] since he gives a brief and approving summary of this (in *An* I vi 3/4). He also says it has been shown from 'this argument of analogy and final causes' (*An* Int 8/10), that is, by the inference from adaptation that is usually called the Design Argument, much as we later find it put into the mouth of Cleanthes in Hume's *Dialogues*.[7] After the manner of his time, he speaks of the being of God as something too obvious to be sincerely disbelieved (*An* II Concl 1/2). Yet he refrains, at every point, from using such arguments himself. This makes it questionable whether he can *be* Cleanthes in the way Mossner has suggested.[8] If we look carefully at the way in which he dissociates himself from *a priori* theology, however, we find that what he is particularly anxious to contrast with his own procedure is not the attempt to use pure reason to prove the *existence* of God, but the attempt to use it to arrive at conclusions about the governance of the world that God exercises.

He does this in two ways. (i) He rejects the procedure of resorting to 'hypothesis', by which he seems to mean the groundless introduction of metaphysical principles into speculation about God's attributes or intentions. This involves assuming that principles which may well apply in some other sphere will apply to 'cases to which we have no ground to apply them'. He contrasts this with his own procedure of basing all principles and applications on the observed constitution of Nature (*An* Int 7/9). (ii) He rejects the 'train of folly and extravagance' into which he thinks we enter if we speculate on 'how the world might possibly have been framed otherwise than it is' and wonder whether it is the best world possible. It is here only that he injects a wholly sceptical note. He says we can give a 'full direct general answer' to any criticism of Christianity that results from such reflections. The answer is 'that we may see beforehand that we have no faculties for this kind of speculation' (*An* Int 10/12).

It is not as easy as one would like to discern a systematic position on method in these remarks. But it is clear enough that Butler has no temperamental inclination to *a priori* theology, yet takes up a stance which presupposes that it has certain fundamental successes to its credit. Indeed, in battling the deists of his time, he frequently appeals to these successes in order to reach them, for they were at least nominally committed to them also. But it is an integral part of his case against them that *a priori* argument has severe limits. Inevitably someone who argues in this way exposes himself to the criticism that the limitations he discerns in the power of human reason affect his own easy acceptance of those theological propositions he wishes to utilise. (Such criticism need not come only from opponents of Christianity: those fideists among its defenders who insist that its credentials come only from revelation will argue in a parallel fashion.[9]) But Butler needs, or thinks he needs, to presuppose that God is known to exist and to govern the world, while at the same time arguing that we are not in a position to discern *how* God's governance is exercised without basing our judgments on observation of the way the world is, or upon revelation. He sees no way of inducing his deistic opponents to heed revelation without persuading them that it contains no blemishes which are not paralleled in nature, which they already agree to be governed by God. For this argumentative package to work, he has to take a particular view of God's purposes: that God makes his intentions known to us, but only in limited ways. God, in other words, both reveals and hides himself, in nature as well as in the Scriptures. The metaphysical and epistemological model which Butler uses is that of a God whose laws, both within and beyond observed nature, are through and through intelligible, but only partially known *to us*.

I have already compared Butler to Pascal. We now see another likeness, for the theme of the hiddenness of God is fundamental in the *Pensées*:

> It is true then that everything teaches man his condition, but there must be no misunderstanding, for it is not true that everything reveals God, and it is not true that everything conceals God. But it is true at once that he hides from those who tempt him and that he reveals himself to those who seek him, because men are at once unworthy and capable of God: unworthy through their corruption, capable through their original nature.[10]

> What can be seen on earth indicates neither the total absence, nor the manifest presence of divinity, but the presence of a hidden God. Everything bears this stamp.[11]

While this likeness is a real one, it is important to bear in mind, once more, that Butler thinks of God's hiddenness in a less radical way than Pascal does, even though he partially shares Pascal's view that it is a test God imposes in the face of human corruption.[12] There is no trace in Butler of Pascal's espousal of a Pyrrhonian scepticism regarding our natural ability to learn truths about God.[13] Butler sees our ignorance of the details of God's providence as similar to our ignorance of undiscovered details of the system of nature, about which some real though limited knowledge is possible. (A striking illustration of this is his suggestion that although miracles may be unpredictable by natural law, they may be fully intelligible as manifestations of some higher law of which we are presently ignorant (*An* II iv 4/4).) He is as concerned to insist that we can, within our limits, acquire insights into God's plans for us, as he is to emphasise those limits themselves. These insights he says we can gain through *analogy*.

3

For all the frequency of this term's appearance in the book, Butler says very little to elucidate analogy. I shall confine myself here to some general remarks, noting that one has to attend carefully to the context to interpret sentences in which it appears – as one does with the related notion of probability. When Butler introduces the concept of analogy in the Introduction, he tells us that in all probable reasonings we depend upon likenesses: that we can predict the outcome of a series of events with a degree of assurance that will depend upon the observed likeness of this series to others we have experienced in the past. He is writing, of course, about the way in which our knowledge of natural laws depends on induction from observed instances. Let us call reasoning that depends on analogy in this familiar way *natural analogy*. The sort of analogy to which the title of the book makes reference is only partly like this – a fact which Hume was to make the basis of fundamental criticism of Butler's mode of natural theology in the *Dialogues*. The title of Butler's book is *The Analogy of Religion, Natural and Revealed, to the Constitution and Course of Nature*. It is vital to notice that the analogy of the title is not between natural religion and revealed religion, but between both natural religion *and* revealed religion on the one hand, and the constitution and course of nature on the other. Let us call this *religious analogy*. Butler wishes to say that just as we can infer with a significant degree of probability that some natural phenomena, which we only know partially, will resemble others, which we know more fully, because they already resemble them in those features familiar to us, so we can infer, with a degree of probability that is high enough to determine our choices, that the claims made about our universe in religion are true. We can do this because the features religion says our universe has are similar to features we have already determined as belonging to it by natural analogy. The reason that such argument is not a straightforward extension of natural analogy is that when one ascribes these religiously important features to our universe one implies that it contains within it a supernatural order as well as a natural one – most particularly, that there is an afterlife. So the major arguments of the work are arguments to the effect that this (observed) life *and* the (unobserved) afterlife, taken together, exhibit features which resemble known features of this life taken alone. For example, we can infer that this life is a training-ground for the next life from the way in which the early years of this life are a training-ground for the later ones.

Religious analogy is clearly a very debatable form of argument. While

Butler does not have the benefit of Hume's critique of it, he is quite aware that it is not the same as natural analogy. This awareness is part of his reason for being content in the last resort with persuading us that there is no compelling reason to reject the results of religious analogy, rather than feeling obliged to demonstrate (what he actually thinks) that its results are likely. Manifestly the results of religious analogy will have a lower degree of probability than those of natural analogy, since when one argues by religious analogy one performs non-deductive inferences from premisses which depend on natural analogy in the first place. What Butler insists on, however, is that the results of religious analogy are sufficiently well supported to show that it is not so obvious that there is nothing in the religious view of the world; indeed, that they are enough to show that we ought to *act* as though it were true.

To summarise: Butler's primary purpose is to show that the claims of Christianity, both those that belong to natural religion and those that belong to revealed religion, have a degree of probability which is sufficient to make it frivolous and imprudent not to live as though they are true. The core of his case for this judgment is his view that we can infer that the cosmos taken as a whole, including both that natural part of it that we observe in this life, and that supernatural part of it that religion tells us we enter in the next, has features which are analogous to some we can find by inductive investigation of the natural order alone. Since he uses the notion of analogy to speak both of inductive reasoning about this life and of inferences about this life and the next taken together, I have suggested we might distinguish them by speaking of natural analogy and religious analogy – recognising, however, that religious analogy is used to support the claims of what he calls 'natural religion' as well as those of what he calls 'revealed religion'. I shall comment on this distinction shortly.

Religious analogy has been dealt severe blows by Hume. In the *Dialogues Concerning Natural Religion*, Hume has Philo argue that the inference from regularities in the natural world to conclusions that transcend the natural order are unwarranted, essentially for the reason that the very observations that establish our knowledge of nature are unavailable to us when we consider what may lie beyond it. It is obvious that this difficulty is very great, but we must be careful not to take it for granted that Hume's criticisms of the natural theology presented by Cleanthes in that work will always apply to the actual arguments that *Butler* uses. For Cleanthes claims to prove the being, as well as the nature, of God. He claims to prove this by an analogical argument, that since we find in our world that mechanical order is the result of intelligent design, the mechanical order exhibited by the world as a whole must be due to a designing mind also. Philo objects that we have no right to assume that the world as a whole can be compared with selected parts of it, or that an external cause of the world must resemble known causes within the world. Now there is every reason to grant that Butler accepted something like Cleanthes's argument; but he does not *use* it. He is arguing against the deists, who believed there is a God who governs the world; hence he assumes this much of the conclusion of Cleanthes's argument at the outset. So religious analogy, as *Butler* uses it, is openly based upon God's authorship of the cosmos. The present-day reader is unlikely to agree that Butler has any right to assume this deistic premiss, and is likely to give Philo's reasons in support of this judgment; but at this stage it is important to be wary of assuming that Philo's critique will fit Butler because it fits Cleanthes.

A fair estimate of the lasting value of Butler's work will certainly depend in part on a decision about how much of what he says can survive if the deistic assumption is rejected. As Broad says, even if the deists should have been convinced by him, it does not follow that we should be.[14] For the moment, however, we should notice how the deistic assumption of God's authorship of nature supports the form of religious analogy that Butler employs.

First, and most importantly, it leads him to take it for granted not merely that the natural order has an intelligent cause, but also that those features which natural analogy shows us to be present in it are present in it for a *purpose*. The order of nature is assumed to be teleological.[15] Sometimes the purposes we can discern will be purposes that we can see to be satisfied within the natural order itself. For example, the fact that we can learn in childhood from the pleasures and pains that follow on our actions can be seen to have the purpose of equipping us to exercise our powers responsibly in adult life. Sometimes, however, the purposes we can discern will not be satisfied here, but it will be reasonable to expect their satisfaction in the supernatural realm. Here the main example of interest to Butler is the fact that the demands of virtue are only partially matched by happy consequences in this life; he interprets this as showing that God intends the practice of virtue to be a way in which we fit ourselves for the life to come. For all their differences, both arguments depend for any merit they have on the assumption that discernible regularities in nature are placed there by God for a purpose.

The second way in which the assumption of God's governance serves religious analogy is by permitting Butler to take it for granted that God's treatment of us in the natural and supernatural realms will be consistent. This does not mean that the supernatural realm will be just like the natural one, for if it were it could not provide the theatre for the resolution of problems that we have to contend with here. It does mean, however, that any differences there may be between God's treatment of us here and his treatment of us hereafter, will ultimately be intelligible in terms of an overall providential plan.

The third way in which Butler depends upon the deistic assumption emerges in the way he holds that our knowledge of this world and our knowledge of the next are both instances of knowledge of a *system*. Butler is always anxious to emphasise the extent of our ignorance, and the fragmentariness and probable character of our knowledge; but he assumes that just as we have every reason to suppose the material universe is a law-abiding system whose laws determine those facts we do not understand as much as those we do, so we can equally well suppose that the fragmentary glimpses we have of the supernatural order are glimpses of an *order* with laws of its own which we may not fathom now but can understand better later. Just as our knowledge of this world is enough to guide our conduct, so our lesser knowledge of the next world is enough to enable us to take wise decisions respecting it here and now.

These three guiding assumptions are all unargued, and all highly questionable. And while they are related, they do not follow from one another. Broad has pointed out that even if we assume two works are by the same author, this does not entitle us to look for a common plot or style in them.[16] There are religious difficulties in supposing that because God's creation is law-like in this world, it has to be so in another, especially if we do not take it for granted beforehand that everything God creates must be in space or time. But there is a more elemental problem than these. Why should we even suppose that the divine being who has created this world has produced another order at all? Why should he not have been satisfied with creating the world we inhabit?[17]

This question is one that Butler does partially address. He addresses it in his first chapter, where he argues for immortality. The striking fact about this chapter is that it is the one place in the *Analogy* where his arguments do not depend upon any appeal to the reality of divine governance, but only upon discerned natural regularities and their alleged philosophical implications. While the arguments are sometimes highly metaphysical in character, so that I would hesitate to call them all examples of natural analogy, they do not require the deistic assumption for any force they may have. Butler argues *after* Chapter I in a way which assumes God's governance, as he says he intends to do before he begins (*An* Int 8/10). But in the first chapter itself his arguments do not depend on assuming it. If they were successful, they would show that there is a probable case for expecting, or at least for not acting as though we do *not* expect, life to continue after physical death. This would imply that the creation in which he henceforth assumes God to have placed us is one which we should, for independent reasons, not suppose to be circumscribed by our mortality. I share the common view that Butler fails to give a future life the independent probability that he tries to give it, but it seems clear that he does not infer its probability from the supposed fact of divine governance

A further comment on Butler's actual procedure. Even if all its presuppositions are accepted, religious analogy must still depend upon natural analogy, since it proceeds from natural regularities which have to be real ones for its case to succeed. If nature should not be the way Butler says it is, or if it contains regularities that suggest quite different divine purposes, his argument will be open to charges of selectivity and arbitrariness, even if there is no general obstacle to a teleological reading of our world.

4

The doubts about Christianity which Butler tries to answer were not, as we have already seen, doubts expressed by atheists, since open atheism was not a significant intellectual force in his time, and did not become one for many years. The anti-Christian critics were deists. I cannot add, here, to the accounts of deism already available, but it is worth noting that in his 1706 *Discourse Concerning the Unchangeable Obligations of Natural Religion*, Samuel Clarke distinguishes four kinds of deist. The first kind 'pretend to believe the existence of an eternal, infinite, independent, intelligent being, and, to avoid the name of Epicurean atheists, teach also that this being made the world: though at the same time they agree with the Epicureans in this, that they fancy God does not at all concern himself in the government of the world'. The second kind believe not only that God made the world, but that he exercises providence over it; that is, directs everything by his intelligence. They do not, however, ascribe moral government to him, and consider moral good and evil to be the result of human laws. The third group accept that God is not only intelligent, but moral in his governance, but deny human immortality. The fourth kind accept that God is creator and moral governor of the world, and that his moral governance imposes obligations on mankind; they also accept that this moral governance entails a future life in which virtue is rewarded and vice punished. But they claim that these truths are discernible by reason, and that there are no good reasons for accepting the Christian claims of special divine revelation.[18]

Butler, addressing himself to the audience he judges himself to have, writes for all of the last three groups. He takes it for granted, openly, from the beginning, that God has created the world and exercises providential governance over it. While assuming that this is common ground between him and his opponents, he does not assume that God's governance is moral. So although some of his deistic readers would have agreed with him that it is, he spends much of Part I trying to argue for it. He has another motive in so doing, in addition to that of reaching as wide an audience as possible. Even though most of his audience would have been in the third and fourth groups of Clarke's list, Butler wants to clarify the *evidential status* of those beliefs which they share with him. For he thinks it is only by overlooking this evidential status that they can have been so confident in rejecting those specifically Christian claims about God's relationship to men which they do *not* share with him.[19] It is in this context that we have to understand the significance of his use of the traditional distinction between natural and revealed religion. The deist, in essence, was a thinker who agreed that there is such a thing as natural religion, but rejected revelation. Butler, throughout, has the purpose of showing that this attitude is inconsistent.

The distinction between the two sorts of 'religion' (in reality, of course, it is a distinction between two sets of *doctrines*) is one Butler does not invent, but inherits. The doctrines of natural religion are those truths about God and his relation to our world and ourselves that can be learned by reason; the doctrines of revealed religion are those that have been made available to us because God has taken a special initiative and told us of them, in words, deeds, or events. Those who apply this distinction usually agree that the two classes of doctrine overlap, since there is more than one possible reason for God to have chosen to reveal some doctrines by special initiative. They might be doctrines which it is simply beyond our intellectual powers to discover in any circumstances. They might, on the other hand, be doctrines which it is within our powers to discover in some circumstances, but not in others. If they are in the latter class, God might reveal them because, without this, only some people could come to learn of them. So it is part of the tradition attaching to our distinction that some revealed doctrines can be learned without the aid of revelation. It is also customary to think of these as strictly part of natural religion rather than revealed, however, since they are in principle within the reach of the unaided human intellect, whereas other revealed doctrines are not.

Butler inherits this tradition as I have summarised it, and in so doing stands in direct line from Aquinas and his followers. There is, however, an important respect in which he represents a departure from it. It lies in his more modest view of the epistemic status of the doctrines of natural religion. In the thought of Aquinas, the doctrines of natural theology are proved, and therefore known; those of revealed theology are not known, but held on faith. Faith and knowledge are exclusive, because faith is a virtue and therefore meritorious, but there is no merit in adhering to what one knows. The meritorious adherence characteristic of faith is as firm psychologically as that characteristic of knowledge, but differs in being optional. It can only be optional if the epistemic grounds we have for the doctrines revealed to us are less than conclusive. When the grounds for secular beliefs are less than conclusive, we do not adhere to them wholeheartedly; so the fact that the faithful are free from doubt about the religious doctrines they accept must be due to the fact that their wills are disposed towards acceptance by supernatural grace.[20] Any doctrine that is properly classifiable as part of the faith is a doctrine that we are in need of grace to accept; hence the doctrines of natural theology are not part of the faith, even though some persons only come to learn of them through revelation, and faith is needed for *them* to assent to them. But even though the epistemic grounds for the doctrines of the faith are necessarily inconclusive, Aquinas insists it is rational for us to assent to them, since there are positive evidences in their favour (such as the fulfilment of prophecies and the occurrence of miracles), and the authority that proclaims them to us, the Church, has strong credentials, both because of its historical connections with these evidences and because of the established truths of natural theology. The latter prove to us that there is a God who is one and perfect, and guides our world providentially, and this makes it rational to attend to the claim that he has spoken to us through his church.

The change Butler makes in this is in part of consequence of his being influenced by Locke, rather than Aquinas, in his epistemology. Instead of holding that the doctrines of natural religion are conclusively demonstrated, he emphasises that for us they are merely *probable*. I have already indicated the range of possible estimates of them that this term can express: all the way from 'highly likely' to 'having a practically nonnegligible degree of likelihood'. But however we read him at any point when he says a doctrine is probable, he makes it clear in the Introduction that the analogical reasoning he is using does not aspire to the certainty supposedly provided by the metaphysical speculations he intends to avoid. But epistemology is only part of the story. The rest of it is to be found in his anti-deistic strategy. In arguing for the *probability* of the doctrines of natural religion, he is making it clear to deists that many of the doctrines they may share with him are not known with certainty, and can only be held with a proper recognition that there is attendant mystery and counter-evidence. If he can establish this, he can undermine the contrast *they* wish to draw between the doctrines of natural religion and those of revelation, by showing that the objections they raised to the latter can be raised against the former also.

Such a tactic makes the ambiguities we find in his use of the notion of probability almost inevitable. For example, he will have strong motives, while talking of revealed doctrines, for assuming the doctrines of natural religion to be highly likely; for this, and only this, permits him to follow in Aquinas's footsteps and say that revelation supplements and completes them, and is rendered more rationally acceptable by the assumption of their truth. On the other hand, in persuading the deists that the doctrines of natural religion need to be augmented, he has to emphasise that there are features of them which the non-revealed evidence does not support unambiguously, but which are rendered more consonant with it if the claims of revelation are agreed to – for example, the doctrine that God rewards virtue and punishes vice, which is only partially supported by the evidence of this world, but is bolstered by the Christian proclamations about the hereafter. Arguments like this entail that the doctrines of natural religion, when *not* thus supplemented by revelation, are only moderately likely.

I do not suggest by this that the ambiguity we find in Butler is wholly excused, merely that it becomes more predictable. There is a secondary ambiguity that his anti-deistic strategy helps to account for, which I have also noted previously. This is his otherwise curious unwillingness to denounce the *a priori* arguments for natural religion which he so studiously avoids using himself. He does not seem willing to say that *all* the doctrines of natural religion are merely probable. His comments in the Introduction and elsewhere make it clear that he thinks it has been proved that there is 'an intelligent Author of Nature, and natural Governor of the world', both 'from this argument of analogy and final causes' and 'from abstract reasonings'. If we take the latter, as I have previously done, to refer to arguments like Samuel Clarke's version of the Cosmological Proof, we seem to have Butler telling us at the outset that the existence of an author and governor of nature is something he will assume to have been shown to be probable in the highest degree from the evidence, *and* proved *a priori* by metaphysical argument. No doubt he has every motive for beginning in some such way, since it would not suit his tactics at all to open a way for his deist readers to evade his case for revelation by retracting their own commitment to the existence of God, even if this had been a culturally open option when the *Analogy* was written! But it is a vulnerable starting-point in two obvious ways. First, if the analogical method only yields a moderate degree of probability when Butler uses it to show the moral character of God's governance, then it is likely that he has over-estimated the degree of likelihood with which this same method can establish the very existence of a God who governs us. This is what Hume showed us, *in extenso*, in the *Dialogues*. Second, if it is really true that *a priori* argument can establish the being of God, can it be so clear that it can do no more, and that only analogical argument can succeed thereafter?

So there is inevitably an arbitrariness in Butler's starting-point: in his assuming it to be established that there is a God who governs nature, but denying the possibility of anything more than a probable knowledge of his purposes. This is the starting-point that Hume nominally adopts in the *Dialogues*, but progressively destroys as he proceeds: that there can be no doubt of the being of God, but there can be dispute about his nature.[21] The explanation of it is historical and tactical; but there is no doubt that its arbitrariness gives plausibility to the judgment of Mossner and others that the *Analogy* is now obsolete. If it is not obsolete, this will be in spite of Butler's procedure here, not because of it.

When Butler passes from the doctrines of natural religion to those of revealed religion, he uses four main lines of argument to persuade his readers that the claims of revelation are credible. (1) Revelation includes within it the proclamation of doctrines that are already part of natural religion. If these doctrines are agreed to be probable, this lends credence to the proclamation of the additional doctrines revelation contains. (2) These additional doctrines are not at odds with those of natural religion, but supplement them in plausible ways. For example, the claim that Christ is our mediator supplements the doctrine of God's justice by showing that our fumbling attempts at virtue can be acceptable to him. (3) The claims of revelation are supported by special evidences, such as miracles, fulfilled prophecies, and spiritual testimonies. (4) Objections raised against the claims of revelation are readily comparable to objections that can be raised to the claims of natural religion, and even to some well-accepted claims of common sense and natural science. Parity of reasoning requires that if we accept these latter claims in the face of the objections to them, we should be willing to do the same for the claims of revelation.

Argument (1) is reasonable, but of limited value. If someone argues a complex position to me, and includes within it some propositions I already accept for independent reasons, I would probably be foolish to ignore him, but I might be justified in rejecting what he says if the propositions he adds are inconsistent with those I accept. Argument (2) addresses this, but does not help us if the new propositions have internal difficulties, or even absurdities, of their own. Only argument (3) is designed to give positive probability to the content of revelation, and it is an argument that has little relation to the analogical reasoning of Part I. Argument (4), which so much affects the structure of the *Analogy*, is wholly defensive, but extremely important. I shall return to it below.

All four arguments are set in a pragmatic context by Butler's discussion, in Chapter i of Part II, of the *importance* of Christianity. His purpose here is to stress the frivolity of not attending to a proclamation which, if true, is vital to one's life. We are reminded here once more of the practical nature of Butler's argument throughout:

> The conclusion of all this evidently is, that, Christianity being supposed either true or credible, it is unspeakable irreverence, and really the most presumptuous rashness, to treat it as a light matter. It can never justly be esteemed of little consequence, till it be positively supposed false. Nor do I know a higher and more important obligation which we are under, than that of examining most

seriously into the evidence of it, supposing its credibility; and of embracing it, upon supposition of its truth. (*An* II i, 19/25)

5

It is now possible to make some preliminary comments about the probable value of Butler's apologetic, in his own time and in ours. I begin with his case against the deists.

Whatever their differences, they rejected the claims for revelation made by the Christian Church, except where the doctrines included in it were mere duplicates of truths they thought we could learn independently and include within natural religion. This effectively ruled out the key Christian teachings about the person of Christ, the work of the Holy Spirit, and the requirements of prayer and worship. In addition, some of them would have been more parsimonious than Butler in listing those doctrines that could be included in natural religion. Butler makes his case, as we have seen, by assuming God's existence, and the presence of some teleological order in nature, and then arguing, from evidence, that God's governance is moral, and that this life is a period of probation in which we are tested for our fitness to enter another. His case is not built up by ignoring counter-evidence. On the contrary: he is far more anxious than the typical deist to stress that the facts are not wholly unambiguous[22] – that although we can discern the general truths about God's governance and our future judgment that he urges upon us, they are, for us, only probable truths, for our world contains evils and obscurities that we can neither account for in detail nor disregard. Our knowledge of God and his purposes is pragmatically adequate, but not totally illuminating: it is, as he puts it in Sermon xv, more like twilight than sunlight. An unwillingness to recognise the limits God has placed on our understanding is a major spiritual obstacle. It is a particular obstacle for the deists, who acknowledge the reality of God, but are unwilling to admit he might have purposes they cannot fathom, even though those purposes they can fathom can be fathomed only in part. If they can be brought to see this, they can be made receptive to the additional insights into God's providence that he has made available to us in revelation. For the difficulties they raise about these are less than they suppose, and are comparable to those they choose to disregard in the realm of natural religion.

I think Butler's case against the deists is a powerful one. At least, for reasons that will emerge later, I think he has a powerful case against those who, like Tindal, agreed with him that we can discern the morality of God's purpose and demands by reason. They did not have a conclusive case against the specific claims of the Christian revelation; indeed these claims do something to accommodate difficulties for which they have no answer without it. But this is in itself of merely historical interest, since the deism to which he is responding was only a transitional period in the history of thought.

With the hindsight that Hume and Kant make possible for us, a hindsight of which I shall make frequent use, we can now see two things. The first is that the very difficulties about which Butler is so open, and which he needs to emphasise against the deists, are difficulties which have a much *simpler* resolution than Butler's, even if the minimal deism with which he starts his argument is accepted. Even if we follow Butler and his contemporaries in judging it unthinkable that our world could exist without a designing intelligence, the investigation of the conditions under which its inhabitants have to live suggest that this intelligence is not a totally moral one, and may even be devoid of moral purposes altogether. Butler is right in arguing, against those deists who assumed that God was moral, that the world as we find it can only be the way it is if a deity like that has broader purposes for us which are fulfilled beyond it. But the same defects that force someone already committed to the morality of God to postulate a future life and add a doctrine of probation, can be handled far more simply by denying that God's purposes can be seen to be moral at all. The ostensible (if not the real) position of Philo at the close of Hume's *Dialogues* is that we cannot disbelieve in the existence of an intelligence that guides our world, but can learn nothing about the morality of this intelligence from scrutinising the world it has designed, and have to make our own moral judgments without reference to it.[23]

The second, and more radical, judgment that hindsight makes possible for us, is the one that many readers take to be Hume's real position at the close of the *Dialogues*: that the rigorous use of the analogical method that Butler recommends should lead us to the conclusion that the evidence does not favour the hypothesis of divine intelligence at all, but rather the very atheism which Butler and his contemporaries found unthinkable. I say that this judgment is now possible for us, not that it is correct: my point is that the present-day reader cannot approach the questions with which Butler deals, with the assumptions that he makes, and in particular cannot assume that one can take a minimal deism for granted and then see what the evidence suggests God's purposes are. If one is to make one's judgments about God and his possible purposes by examining evidence as Butler does, it is not intellectually possible to close off the most fundamental question of all, that of God's very existence.

It is clear that for us the value that Butler's work may have is not affected by the power his arguments had, or should have had, against the deists. In such circumstances, what can he still teach us?

To begin with, if one sees it as a basic task of philosophy of religion to understand the logical structure of religious belief, then Butler's analogical arguments can be a valuable source of insight into this. Two illustrations may serve. First, Butler begins his case for natural religion by arguing that the fact that we can learn from our pleasures and our pains shows that God uses them to teach us. Someone who is unsure whether there is a God at all will find little nourishment in this argument; it may also well be the case that someone who accepted that there is some kind of divine governance or other, but was unsure what sort, would be only mildly disposed to accept it. So such readers might well not move much, after reading it, towards Butler's conclusion that God is a righteous governor who wishes us to come to a proper relationship with him by responding to his revealed teachings. But in arguing as he does, Butler makes something else clear: that for anyone who *does* accept Christian revelation, it is inconsistent not to view the natural world and our life within it as a source of moral teaching. This is unaffected by the fact that it is the revelation that has to be the source of the pedagogical principles that nature can be seen to illustrate, rather than the other way round as Butler suggests. Second, to clarify this last point, Butler tries to establish by analogical argument that the travails and difficulties that even the virtuous face in this life are intended by God as probationary: that they are here to give us the opportunity to exercise moral virtue in a way that consolidates it in our characters and thereby fits us for the next life. Even if his arguments for this are not persuasive, and the evidence we have does not alone make it likely that the travails of this world are there for this purpose, in selecting this as the supposed truth about our world that can be established before the claims of revelation are considered, Butler shows us how this part of human experience has to be subsumed under the cosmic and moral scheme that the Christian revelation presents to us.

These unsurprising truths about the inner logic of the Christian scheme do not show at all that the Christian scheme is true, or likely, or even in all respects coherent. They merely show how those committed to the Christian revelation must approach their day-to-day experience with an eye to those phenomena which are potentially revelatory for them. They show what Christians must see their world *as*, in addition to seeing it as their unbelieving contemporaries see it – as the context for business, recreation, and exploitation. But we can get more from Butler's analogical arguments than this.

We can, in the first instance, derive many contributions to a purely defensive apologetic. This is easy to illustrate. I take again the case Butler makes in Part I of the *Analogy* for supposing that God's moral government ordains that the evils the virtuous suffer are probationary trials that fit them for a future existence. Let us agree that he fails to show that the evidence makes this likely. Hume's discussion of evil[24] is the classic statement of the difficulty that a case like Butler's faces. Hume points out that if we are seeking to discern the nature of the divine mind from its handiwork in nature, the evils we find there force us to say that God is not all-powerful and all-good. But he is clear that this tells against the theist only if the case for God's power and goodness rests upon the evidence. If it does not, and the theist believes in them for other reasons, it might still be possible to *reconcile* these evils with the omnipotence and goodness of God, by supposing that there are morally satisfactory reasons for them in the scheme of God's governance. Although Butler may fail when judged in the light of Hume's primary criticism, since he has indeed tried to make a scheme of probation seem likely through the investigation of nature, he may still have presented a hypothesis which can reconcile the Christian view of God with many of the evils of the world.

Examples are even easier to find among Butler's defences of revelation in Part II. These can often be evaluated quite independently of their anti-deist context. It is immaterial that it was deists who said, at that time, that revelation would have to be available to everyone, or available all at once, or available sooner, in order to be genuine; whatever value Butler's response to these criticisms has, it has irrespective of their authorship. But even where his arguments take the form they do because of the deistic origins of the attacks he is trying to answer, they can be transposed into another key. For one example, we can consider an argument he offers in defence of the doctrine of Christ's mediation. He points out that in nature and human life we often find one being's good being acquired at the cost of the loss of another's, and often find that people escape the due consequences of their own foolishness or vice. The argument is that the deist, who accepts such a world as one which God governs, should not reject the doctrine of Christ's mediation out of hand. The argument is very weak indeed to someone who does not accept the deist's premiss. But an apologist for revelation could use the same analogy differently. He could suggest that the revealed doctrine of the mediation of Christ offers a model of God's mercy which can sometimes be used to suggest an interpretation of the sufferings of the just or of the prosperity of the unjust.

I do not urge these apologetic arguments, but point out merely that they are easy to construct using materials which Butler makes available to us for his more restricted purposes. In general, I think it is fair to say that where Butler thinks he has shown a religious doctrine to be probable on the basis of evidence, his case depends crucially on the prior acceptance of deistic premises; and that even these may not always be enough.

But, at the same time, readers who do not share these premises can find in these same arguments the components of effective apologetic defences of the doctrine he commends to us. This is what we would naturally expect to happen, given the character of his minimal objective. For it is the task of the apologist to show, if he can, not only that Christian doctrines are internally coherent and are formally consistent with the evidence of experience, but also that if they *were* true, we should expect our world to be pretty much the sort of place that it is. This is, of course, far less than showing that Christian doctrines are indeed true, or even that they are more likely than their extant competitors to be true. But it might be enough, when combined with the pragmatic considerations Butler urges upon us, to make a case for the kind of practical inclination towards Christianity that he seeks to bring about.

In expounding him in what follows I shall try, therefore, to indicate the quality of his arguments, both as responses to the deists, and as examples of a wider sort of apologetic defence.

7

These considerations still do not do justice to Butler's stature as an apologist. Throughout the work there are three recurring themes which are of great importance in determining the detailed arguments he presents, and which raise the deepest questions in the epistemology of religion. In view of their importance, I shall attempt to give Butler's position on them separate and sustained treatment.

(i) The first theme has already concerned us, and it is one to which Butler returns most frequently and at length. It is the theme of the limitations on our knowledge of God. Many religious writers, from the greatest to the least, urge this upon us. Butler's use of it is complex and subtle, and carefully qualified. A person inquiring into the subject of religion, he says,

> should beforehand expect things mysterious, and such as he will not be able thoroughly to comprehend, or go to the bottom of. To expect a distinct comprehensive view of the whole subject, clear of difficulties and objections, is to forget our nature and condition; neither of which admit of such knowledge, with respect to any science whatever. And to enquire with this expectation, is not to enquire, as a man, but as one of another order of creatures. (S xv 13/10)

Butler's stance on this theme is not a mere profession of humility or a mere demand for it. Nor is it a fideistic leaning towards scepticism. On the contrary, he is most insistent that at the levels of common sense, science, and religion equally, probable knowledge can be had, and that it is our urgent obligation to acquire it where it is available. But he also insists that this knowledge is limited, by God's choice and by our faculties. This limitation extends to common sense and to science as well as to religion, but it is more to be expected in religion. His use of analogical argument throughout is based on the view that in all these spheres we have to rest content with a partial and probabilistic understanding of a system which is in itself wholly intelligible, and understood in its fullness by God himself. If we pursue the clear, though partial, knowledge of God's purposes and demands, that he has made available in nature and revelation, then the world in which we find ourselves will make more coherent sense to us than it can if we demand a more detailed understanding than we have the right to expect, or if we resort to scepticism and fideism and refuse to seek the understanding that is within our grasp.

(ii) The second theme is the converse of the first, and is implied throughout Butler's analogical reasonings. His most general statement of it is the following:

> Upon the whole then: the appearance of deficiencies and irregularities in Nature is owing to its being a scheme but in part made known, and of such a particular kind in other respects. Now we see no more reason why the frame of Nature should be such a scheme, than why Christianity should. And that the former is such a scheme, renders it credible, that the latter, upon supposition of its truth, may be so too. (*An* II 4, 5/6)

Usually Butler deploys this form of argument against the position of the deists, who were prepared to see divine governance in nature, yet found it impossible to admit the moral and revealed governance on which Christianity rests. To them he says that they are demanding more clarity and freedom from difficulty in religion than they demand in their deistic metaphysic. But he does not always use the argument in this restricted form. His position involves an analogy, not merely between the deist accepting God's natural governance and the Christian accepting revelation, but between the need we all have in daily life and science to be satisfied with probability and the need he alleges we have to accept revelation. Nature, as a system whose rules we can only partially discern, is a realm where we are prepared to make confident decisions on limited evidence. If we are unwilling to accept similarly limited evidence in religion, we are reasoning inconsistently. This is Butler's version of what I have elsewhere called the Parity Argument:[25] the claim that religious scepticism is the result of the application to the claims of religion of a degree of rigour that we do not demand elsewhere. It can, and has, taken the form of arguing that it is mistaken to expect any grounds for religious conviction at all, since the key commitments of common sense and science are themselves said to be groundless. This fideistic version of the

Parity Argument is not, of course, Butler's. What he says is that in common life, science, and the deists' forms of 'natural religion', we find examples of commitments which rest upon a degree of probability which is often not as high as we would like. As created beings of limited capacities, we should be less meticulous than some of us are when confronted with the claims of the Christian revelation, since they possess a degree of probability which, though perhaps not very high, is high enough to warrant our practical acceptance if we apply to them the standards which readily satisfy us in matters of far less importance.

(iii) Finally, Butler makes it clear from the outset of his work that he wants its arguments to be judged, not only piecemeal, but together:

> If the reader should meet here with anything which he had not before attended to, it will not be in the observations upon the constitution and course of Nature, these being all obvious; but in the application of them: in which, though there is nothing but what appears to me of some real weight, and therefore of great importance; yet he will observe several things, which will appear to him of very little, if we can think things to be of very little importance, which are of any weight at all, upon such a subject as religion. However, the proper force of the following treatise lies in the whole general analogy considered together. (*An*, Advertisement, 1)

We can infer from this opening comment that Butler considers his argument to be a *cumulative* one. It is doubtful whether he has a clear view of the import of this. If he thinks that he builds up a case for the probability of Christian claims one step at a time, making the whole increasingly likely by showing each successive part to have a high degree of probability (and it is reasonable enough to take him to think this in his more confident moments), then his case is open to strong objections, both from the elementary logic of probability and from the weakness of many of his constituent arguments. On the other hand, we can approach the work, as a whole, in a different manner, asking ourselves whether we can take the Christian cosmic scheme, as he interprets it, *in toto*, and compare it, as a whole, with the deistic schemes that he combated, and with wholly secular understandings of human life. Such holistic comparisons cannot be subsumed under any formal probability calculus; yet it seems clear that at the level of world-views and ideologies men and women make such comparative judgments and decisions at crucial points in their lives, and have no alternative but to do so. They compare world-views that are incompatible, and they do so in the absence of neutral positions from which safe comparisons can be made from a distance. It is a counsel of despair to pronounce such judgments irrational, yet all the reasons one can give for the choice one makes seem question-begging to those who choose differently. I think there is no doubt that, in the long haul, it is this sort of comparative judgment that Butler (again, like Pascal) presses upon his readers; as long as he can show them that each element in his scheme is not irrational, he relies on their holistic judgment that although many elements may have low probability, the scheme as a whole is rationally persuasive.

The philosophical assessment of this sort of appeal is very difficult, but inescapable. In the case of Butler, part of this assessment will have to be concerned with the evaluation of an aspect of his case with which this chapter began: its practicality. There is no doubt that Butler (once more, like Pascal) considers that the rational persuasiveness of the Christian case is due to the fact that the low theoretical likelihood of many elements within it is offset by the practical urgency of the claims that it makes: in elemental terms, that if it should turn out to be true, it is frivolous and foolhardy in the extreme not to pay careful heed to it. No doubt all ideological decisions are pragmatic in like ways; but in the Christian case the claim is made, truly or falsely, that one's individual destiny is affected fundamentally by the decision one takes when faced with it. No assessment of the rationality of his total case can be complete without an evaluation of its essentially prudential character. This in turn requires a hard look at what, in such circumstances, acceptance of the Christian case as he presents it comes to. Can one, for example, accept it in the recommended way while still considering the theoretical likelihood of many of its component parts to be low, or must such theoretical reservations melt away in the process of practical consent?

I have already indicated that in expounding Butler's argument I shall try to assess its parts in the light of his debate with the deists, and in the light of the demands of a defensive apologetic. To add on to this, at each stage, the impact of the three major themes I have now raised would be to produce an impossibly multi-layered treatment of a work which is in any case complex in its details. I shall therefore concentrate immediately on the first two considerations, and attempt to deal with these wider matters separately in the final chapter.

V

Identity and the Future Life

Even those few who admire the *Analogy* tend to have a low view of its first chapter. This is partly because they expect more from it than Butler explicitly promises, but also because he claims more than he has delivered. I shall argue that Butler's arguments are enough to establish the logical possibility of some form of life after death, but not to give it any degree of probability. He thinks that they give it a substantial degree of likelihood; whereas a careful scrutiny of them is enough to show that at best they provide answers to common attacks on the belief in survival.

I have already noted that none of the arguments he offers in favour of a future life depend on making deistic assumptions. The assumption of a future life is fundamental to most of Part I, where he repeatedly argues that certain discernible features of our present life have their purpose in the way they prepare us for the next; but he does not try to persuade his readers that there *is* a next life by maintaining that no purpose could be found in this life without it. He confines himself to pointing out regularities in this world which suggest the presence of natural laws that extend into the future, and to arguing that common reasons for rejecting a future life are due to mistaken inferences.

The absence of any appeal to deistic assumptions may have another source. Butler never suggests that the fact of an afterlife, of itself, does anything to help prove the existence of God.

> That we are to live hereafter, is just as reconcilable with the scheme of atheism, and as well to be accounted for by it, as that we are now alive is. (*An* I i 24/32)

He considers it obvious, however, that a presumption against a future life is a presumption against Christianity. I think he is correct in both these positions, though I shall not attempt to support either of them here.

In arguing that Butler helps us to see the logical possibility of a form

113

of life after death, I am indicating a value that his argument has for us, in the light of recent debates on this topic. I do not imply that, for Butler, there are any doubts to dispel about its logical possibility. The Dissertation 'Of Personal Identity', which appears as one of two appendices to the *Analogy*, begins in fact with a vigorous assertion to the contrary:

> Whether we are to live in a future state, as it is the most important question which can possibly be asked, so it is the most intelligible one which can be expressed in language. (Diss I 1/1)

While he is interested in the 'strange perplexities' that philosophers have raised about our identity through time, he makes a point of relegating them to this appendix, in order to show that they can do nothing to undermine the clarity of the question he is concerned with in Chapter i. I think that some of his least effective arguments depend on premises that he only supports in the Dissertation, and that he is wrong to insist that the question of a future life is one that philosophical analysis cannot clarify. But I shall follow him in treating his arguments for a future life as he presents them, and then considering his discussion of personal identity afterwards.

1

The most obvious common-sense argument against the possibility of a future life is that death brings an apparently final end to all manifestations of the powers and personality of the dead person. The most painful of all human adjustments is the one we have to make to the fact that our habitual expectations of that person's characteristic actions, gestures, and words are hereafter doomed to be disappointed. It is the thinking involved in this human adjustment that Butler considers. He contrasts it with another fundamental feature of our thought about our world and about one another: the fact that we take it for granted that things, plants, animals, and people preserve their identities (remain the same things, plants, animals, and people) throughout their physical lives, in spite of the fact that they undergo very radical changes in size, shape, or capacity. Given this pervasive feature of all our thinking, he says, we should be prepared to examine with more care than we normally do the effect that death may have, or indeed may not have, upon people.

This looks at first sight to be a very odd way to approach our question. It looks rather like saying that just as frequent deposits and withdrawals, and alternative credit and debit balances, are stages that one and the same bank account goes through, so we should reconsider the common-sense view that the account does not survive my going to the bank and closing it out. Butler is fully aware of the oddity of what he is suggesting; he knows quite well that all of us much of the time, and some of us all of the time, think of death as an event that ends, or destroys, us. But his contention is that this belief depends on an *inference*: an inference from the observed discontinuance of personal activities to the inferred cessation of the agent. He holds that this inference is not self-evidently sound, and that there are some grounds for supposing that we might continue after death, radically changed but not destroyed. Such a possibility would be analogous to known occasions when we survive radical transformations during this life.

It is, he says, 'a general law of nature in our own species' that we have vastly different kinds of power and activity at different periods of our life – between the womb and infancy, between childhood and mature years. In this respect our species resembles many others:

> The changes of worms into flies, and the vast enlargement of their locomotive powers by such change: and birds and insects bursting the shell their habitation, and by this means entering into a new world, furnished with new accommodations for them, and finding a new sphere of action assigned them; these are instances of this general law of nature. (*An* I i 2/2)

In addition to this law, there is another:

> There is in every case a probability, that all things will continue as we experience they are, in all respects, except those in which we have some reason to think they will be altered. (*An* I i 3/4)

If we combine these two considerations, we should suppose that death is merely one more radical change which does not destroy us, but may redirect our powers, and even enlarge them. Broad points out that the second principle only applies to some objects of our experience, not to all; we expect tables and chairs to continue as they are unless there is some reason to think they are being interfered with, but we have the reverse expectation about lights or noises.[1] It is only experience that teaches us whether or not to expect continuance, and in the present case the point at issue is the very question of what experience should teach us about what death does to our powers. Fortunately, Butler does not rest his case on this weak foundation, but undertakes to show that there is no basis for the inference that death destroys us, either from 'the reason of the thing' (*a priori*) or from 'the analogy of nature' (induction).

The *a priori* argument consists in the production of an important distinction, on which Butler's whole case rests. This is the distinction between the possession of a power and the possession of the means for its exercise. At this point in his argument Butler does not offer examples, but it rapidly becomes clear what he has in mind, and that it is controversial. I will supply an example of my own. Most normally-provided humans have the power of speech. Someone who has had his vocal chords damaged as a side-effect of throat surgery, has lost the means to exercise this power. Butler would insist, however, that he has not lost the power itself. For the moment, we can perhaps say that we see what distinction it is that he makes. His intent is to argue that death, while it takes away the means of exercising our powers that we have had in this life, is not shown by this to take away the powers themselves; so we may, for all we know to the contrary, retain them as we retain most of our powers when we are asleep or unconscious. He expresses the distinction by saying that when we say death destroys our living powers, our statement is ambiguous: it may mean that death destroys the living being himself, so that his powers cease altogether, or it may mean that death takes away 'those means and instruments by which it is capable of its present life'. He says that the latter is best expressed by saying death destroys our *present* powers. We know that death indeed takes away many of our present powers (though it turns out that he will not admit even this to be known of all of them), but he says we have no reason to think it can destroy living beings themselves.

The inductive, or supposedly inductive, argument rests on observing that throughout nature we find death removing the 'sensible proof' that animals have this or that living power, but never see death taking away creatures' powers themselves, rather than their means to use them. It is obvious that, given the distinction Butler has drawn, it would be logically impossible for this ever to be observed; but he seeks to bolster his argument by pointing out once more that we do very commonly observe that powers persist through changes of the most radical kind.

It is easy to feel at this point that Butler's case is so feeble as not to be worth pursuing. Granted the validity of some distinction between my possessing a power like speech, and my having the means to exercise it, surely this distinction can have no application after *death*? Surely, by taking away *all* the known means for the exercise of my powers, death takes away the powers themselves also? In daily life, if we encountered someone who had lost the use of his vocal chords, we might well say without reflection that he had lost his powers of speech. If we were to reconsider this and admit that he had retained them, this would be because we recognised the possibility that he might acquire the use of some technical device which substitutes for his vocal chords and allows him to produce sounds resembling those that normal speakers can produce. We can observe that technology now preserves powers that people used to lose. But when death removes *all* the natural and artificial means for the exercise of our powers, what ground can there be for supposing we retain them?

Butler is aware of this natural protest, and the rest of his chapter is an attempt to disarm it. His argument amounts to saying that our ability to recognise the continuance of personal powers through organic change requires that the distinction between having a power and having the means to use it be understood in a way which is at odds with the protest – that if common sense admits such continuance through life, but denies it can go on through death, common sense is at odds with itself. (I do not think that Butler himself believes that it *is* the common-sense view that death destroys us; but I shall return to this issue much later.)

I think the case Butler mounts has some substance; but in the course of his argument he indulges in some very bad metaphysics indeed. Some of the weakest arguments to be found in his writings appear in this strategically unfortunate place, right at the start of the *Analogy*.

The bad metaphysics is the result of the fact that, in common with many other defenders of immortality, Butler chooses to interpret this doctrine as one of disembodied spiritual survival; and of the further fact that he elects to interpret the distinction between having a power and having the means to exercise it in terms of the soul's being the owner of the person's powers, and the body being the assemblage of means and instruments that the soul uses to exercise them. This strategy is easy to discern and to understand, but has little else to be said for it. If Butler's general argument has any weight, it points, I shall suggest, to a quite different sort of survival from this – one which, historically speaking, is much more in accord with primitive Christian teachings than the belief in the immortality of the soul. I refer, of course, to the expectation of a resurrection.

It is interesting that Henry Hughes attacks Butler's arguments for immortality on the ground that they would confine us too much to a material environment. When Butler stresses how much we are bound to the recognition that our identity continues through material change, Hughes says that this argument points, at best, to a future life 'in the world of nature'. He continues:

> Apparently the most that Butler can be said to make out is a probability that we shall live in the future, as we have lived in the past, as disembodied spirits, within the confines of the knowable universe – in some such place, say, as the planet Mars; and he entirely omits to show that this is not more than counterbalanced by the opposite analogical probability, that human life is dependent for its existence upon a material frame.[2]

I do not speculate about how disembodied spirits might be said to inhabit Mars rather than Earth. The major thrust of Hughes's point is that if the common-sense objection mentioned earlier is to be overcome, this would leave us with the possibility of a future life subject to the material conditions we know now, or to somewhat similar ones. He is clearly suggesting that such an expectation is unorthodox – that an orthodox expectation would be one of a disembodied existence beyond the confines of the physical universe. I shall argue that Butler's argument uncovers a logically possible way of supposing an afterlife, and that this is an *embodied* afterlife; that it does not show this supposition to be a likely one; that Butler is right to think that those who seriously entertain this supposition are indeed continuing their common-sense habit of ascribing identity through change and distinguishing between having a power and exercising it, in spite of his detailed misunderstandings of this habit and this distinction; and that the logically possible supposition that his argument suggests is more nearly orthodox than the apparent commitments that he and Hughes share.

I return to the actual course of Butler's argument. His fundamental point, once more, is that on those many occasions in this life when we recognise that people preserve their identity through change, we make use of a distinction between the persons themselves, who possess certain powers, and the temporary manifestations of those powers that we encounter on this or that occasion. When our bodies die, he holds, it is true that the familiar means of manifesting human powers seem to cease; but we cannot infer from this that the individual who has expressed his or her powers using those means, must have come to an end also. To infer this, we have to reverse our habit of distinguishing between the individual and his or her performances. The real, though restricted, force of this argument is obscured, in his text, by unwarranted accretions.

He begins, without warning, to write of the indivisibility of *consciousness*. For death to destroy living beings, he tells us, they would have to be compounded of parts and therefore 'discerptible' (divisible). But 'since consciousness is a single and indivisible power, it should seem that the subject in which it resides must be so too' (*An* I i 8/10). We now see that Butler wishes us to interpret the distinction between a subject and the activities in which that subject's powers are manifested in such a way that the subject is equated with a simple, uncompounded, spiritual substance. To deal with all the implications of arguments of this form one needs to invoke the many critical considerations that Kant made available to us in the Paralogisms of the *Critique of Pure Reason*. To see where Butler combines his insight with confusion we do not need to range so widely.

Butler is right to pick out for special consideration the fact that what, above all else, makes us ascribe identity through time and change to *human* individuals is something that we should indeed refer to as the unity of consciousness. Where he, and many others, have gone wrong, is in inferring from this unity the simplicity and immateriality of the subject whose activities in time manifest it. Both the truth and the error in what he and they have claimed has been recognised and demonstrated by Kant. The truth is that human consciousness manifests a particular

118

sort of unity amidst complexity that Kant calls the transcendental unity of apperception. The most elementary acts of awareness require that the subject hold before himself a number of distinct items which usually have to be apprehended successively. If I understand what you say to me when you utter a sentence, this is because each successively heard word is apprehended, and linked with the others, by one and the same continuing subject. No such elementary understanding would arise if each successive part of your utterance were heard by a different person, who did not hear the earlier and later parts of it. If the sentence addressed to me was the nine-word sequence 'There is a large dog in the bean patch', I might be expected, at least if I were a dedicated gardener, to respond with swift action. But such action would only occur if I understood the sentence, and it would be a condition of that that the nine words were heard by one and the same listener. If one imagined an experiment in which nine different people were placed in nine separate sound-proof booths, and each successive word was relayed into one of the nine, no comparable response could reasonably be expected. Similarly, for what I had heard to have been *meant* by anyone, it must have been formulated by one continuing conscious subject, not nine subjects each randomly pronouncing one of the words. The act of understanding, and the corresponding act of intentional utterance, are each, in a way which is clear though not readily definable, indivisible acts, which means at least that they have each to be performed by one continuing conscious subject.

Conscious mental performances like these take quite short periods of time. Others take much longer periods, but are susceptible to a similar analysis. Random examples are remembering to buy the groceries my wife asked me to buy on the way home, carrying out the resolution I made on 1 January, or lamenting the passing of my fiftieth birthday. Each of these acts straddles a long time: not only in the sense that it may take a long time to *do* it, but in the sense that the person who does it must be one and the same conscious being that my wife made the request to as he left for work, who made the resolution on 1 January, or was born a little over fifty years ago. In these cases it is not necessary that the conscious being in question be continuously and incessantly aware of the undertaking to his wife, or the New Year resolution, or the passing of the fifty years, throughout the whole period of time involved; but it must in some sense retain, or remember, or have inner access, to them. If it is this fact that Butler refers to when he says that consciousness is a single and indivisible power, he is not only right to insist upon its reality, but also right to assume it is the most important form of unity we recognise when we ascribe identity to human beings through time. He is also correct when he says that we can distinguish between the possession of conscious human powers (those powers, that

119

is to say, which, when we exercise them, manifest this unity of consciousness) and the possession of this or that physical means of their exercise. If my New Year resolution was to visit my ailing aunt once a month throughout the year, then the conscious act of carrying out this resolution is something I can perform by travelling on the bus if my car breaks down, by travelling in a friend's car if I sprain my ankle and cannot walk, and so on. He is also right that I can retain my power to carry out such acts as walking, even if the normally necessary physical means are permanently removed; for some people manage to walk with artificial limbs.

Where Butler goes astray, as Kant shows in the Second Paralogism, is in supposing that the subject which *has* or *manifests* such unitary consciousness must be a simple, uncompounded, spiritual substance. For there is no clear reason why such unitary consciousness should exclude from the subject which possesses it other features of the greatest complexity or the grossest materiality – such as the ownership of a divisible human body, or even of a number of simultaneous or successive human bodies. For a crude and easy illustration, let us suppose that there were nine human organisms in nine separate sound-proof booths, and the successive words 'There', 'is', 'a', 'large', 'dog', 'in', 'the', 'bean', and 'patch' were relayed into the booths so that only one word could reach the ears of each occupant; but that, in spite of this, just when the ninth word had been relayed, all nine occupants rose hurriedly and ran towards the garden. Let us suppose further that their behaviour showed similar interrelatedness in a systematic way over a period of time: that they uttered sentences in sequence, one word each at a time, that they broke into laughter simultaneously, and the like. We might start to entertain the thought that there was one shared consciousness distributed among the nine organisms, or that one and the same subject 'had' nine human bodies at once.

We cannot, therefore, infer from the unity of the consciousness of a human subject to the simplicity of that subject – that 'since consciousness is a single and indivisible power, it should seem that the subject in which it resides must be so too'. Nor can we infer, as Butler does, that the subject possessing such consciousness must be intrinsically non-material. He seems to think that this follows not only from the alleged simplicity of the subject of consciousness, in contrast to the compositeness of matter, but also from the unity of consciousness itself, at least if we add some extra premiss. The extra premiss would be something like 'It is as easy to conceive that we exist out of bodies, as in them', or 'We might have animated bodies of any other organs and senses wholly different from those now given us.' He makes both these statements later in the same paragraph. Here again, Butler is arguing something false while perceiving something true.

The truth he perceives is that if we ascribe the performance of some complex act of consciousness to a subject, that subject must include all the elements of that act in its history. So if we were right to say that nine human organisms are each an indispensable part of the performance of one unitary act of consciousness like that of the understanding of a simple sentence, it would indeed follow that these nine organisms all belonged to the one subject that performed that single act of consciousness. Similarly, if we were right to say that some person now remembers doing some past action that was done forty years ago in a particular body (as Butler would put it, using the limbs and members which composed that body), then this person now remembering it did that action, and had that body, forty years ago, even if he does not have that body now. Butler is right to say that we can easily enough invent stories to fit such extravagant specifications.

But this truth does not require that the subject of consciousness be immaterial, any more than it requires that it be simple. It may well be true that material predicates cannot be applied to acts of consciousness themselves (that they do not have weight or fill space), but it does not follow from this that their subjects cannot have such predicates applied to them. The fact that my memories have no height or breadth does not show that I do not. It is a truism that a being possessed of consciousness is not merely a physical being, but it does not follow at all that a conscious being must be a non-physical being. The evidence is quite to the contrary. So Butler is not entitled to conclude that 'our organized bodies are no more ourselves or part of ourselves, than any other matter around us' (*An* I i 8/10). He proceeds to use this supposed result to argue that in conscious activities like perception or deliberate motion, we (that is, the supposedly immaterial selves with which he has identified us) merely *use* our limbs and organs, so should not be said to lose our powers of perception or locomotion merely because a calamity like death has deprived us of the physical means of exercising them. For the immaterial self may well continue, after death, with these powers intact, as my power of locomotion can be shown to have been retained after my leg amputation when I walk about on an artificial limb. Butler's resort to the doctrine of the simplicity of the soul, then, is his key subsidiary argument against the common-sense objection I imagined earlier to his claim that death need not destroy our powers. Kant has made it easy for us to see that the doctrine rests on an elementary *non sequitur*.

But we must not reject all Butler says because we reject the immaterialist metaphysics he uses to support it. I think Butler does have, concealed within these unattractive wrappings, an adequate argument to show that there is no logical absurdity in the supposition that a person may, in spite of death, retain powers hitherto exercised in the expired

121

body. I emphasise again that I shall not attempt to argue that Butler has, in this chapter, shown that this supposition is likely to be true, or is supported by evidence.

2

I have said that a key part of Butler's case for a future life is his claim that if we follow the common practice of believing that death destroys a person, as distinct from destroying the present means a person has for using his or her powers, we believe something at odds with our constant practice of recognising and ascribing identity through radical change. For that ascription requires us, he says, to distinguish between the conscious agent and the acts that manifest the agent's abilities. The sceptical retort is to say that this distinction is not one that allows us to persist in talking of an agent when *all*, rather than only *some*, of that agent's performances cease. Butler's appeal to a general principle that things should be considered to continue as before unless there is particular reason to suppose they do not, is far from decisive; it is, after all, open to the common-sense response 'If death does not stop things from continuing as before, whatever could?' Butler's response to this apparent stand-off has to be found in his unhappy arguments about the simplicity of the soul and the separateness of the person from the body. While these arguments tell us something important about the nature of the continuance of conscious beings through time, they do not show any reason for supposing that consciousness to persist when the body through which it is manifested is dissolved. This does not prove that human consciousness without a human body is not a *logical* possibility, though there are some well-known reasons for doubting this.[3] What it does show, however, is that Butler has done nothing to improve his case for the probability of survival by using these arguments, or to show that if we could extend our practice of ascribing identity even beyond death, we would be justified in supposing *disembodied* survival.

Butler's arguments for the independence of consciousness from the body are at odds with the analogies he draws between personal identity and the identity of insects and birds, and also with the natural import of the familiar facts he mentions about our organs and limbs being capable of replacement by artificial substitutes. Broad points out that the animal analogies suggest that if we survive at all, we do so in some kind of body, rather than without one;[4] and, though they do suggest that the body in which we survive may be very different from the one we have had hitherto, they do not fit at all well into the argument he tries to mount for the belief that our survival is immaterial. Now it has been maintained very vigorously in recent biblical scholarship that the primitive Christian expectation was of bodily resurrection, not of the immortality of the soul, which has a largely Platonic origin;[5] and if that is the correct reading of what St Paul proclaims in the fifteenth chapter of the First Epistle to the Corinthians, Broad is right to remind us that Butler's analogies of insects and birds are reminiscent of Paul's figure of a seed being buried and reborn as wheat. I wish in what follows to make some suggestions which, while they carry us a distance from Butler, utilise elements in his argument, and show how many of the things he says can still illuminate the status of the Christian expectation he is commending to us.

I return to a passage from which I quoted two clauses earlier:

> And it is as easy to conceive, how matter, which is no part of ourselves, may be appropriated to us in the manner in which our present bodies are; as how we can receive impressions from, and have power over any matter. It is as easy to conceive, that we may exist out of bodies, as in them; that we might have animated bodies of any other organs and senses wholly different from these now given us, and that we may hereafter animate these same or new bodies variously modified and organized; as to conceive how we can animate such bodies as our present. (*An* I i 10/11)

Most philosophers familiar with the ever-growing literature on 'puzzle-cases' that has attended recent work on self-identity would hesitate to be as open as Butler is here about the conceptual possibilities available to us.[6] I have, in particular, suggested we should reject the claim that it is easy to conceive how me might exist without bodies, and the claim that matter is no part of ourselves. But Butler has provided us, though for another purpose, with reasons for believing that some of the possibilities here are conceptually available. I shall select one such possibility, which will seem at first to be remote from Butler's concerns, but which I hope to show is not.

I select the supposition that a human subject might perform acts which show him to have had, in the past, a physical body other than the one he has now. The popular name for this supposition, at least in cases where it is also part of the story that the body the subject used to have has expired, is 'reincarnation'. Cases that allegedly support belief in reincarnation are easily enough found in the literature of psychical research.[7] Let us imagine someone named Smith who claims to remember doing actions and having experiences which were part of the known life of someone named Jones, who did these actions and had these experiences fifty years ago, and died forty years ago; Smith, let us say, is only twenty-five. Let us suppose, further, that Smith's apparent recollections are systematic and accurate, and that we have the strongest reasons for supposing that he cannot have had access to the independent information that establishes for us, that they *are* systematic and accurate. Let us

123

suppose that the actions are actions which Jones is not known to have regretted, but for which Smith professes deep contrition, a contrition which passes all the usual tests for sincerity, and for which he seeks to atone (perhaps by making major financial payments to the descendants of those whom Jones harmed by those actions).

If we were to encounter such a situation, it would be attractive to some, and, I submit, quite natural for everyone, to say that Smith and Jones are the same person, that Smith is Jones in another incarnation. Anyone who does say this will be doing something which Butler says it is natural for us to do, and inconsistent for us not to do, namely talking as though Jones continues to exist after his death, and to retain at least some of the powers and characteristics that he manifested in his now-expired body. On this view he will have retained them because he now manifests them again, in another body.

But however *natural* it might be for everyone to say this, only some would be inclined to do so. Others, perhaps a majority, would be most *dis*inclined to do so; and for powerful reasons. Let us bear in mind that our story makes no case for assuming that Jones is an immaterial substance that has 'left' the Jones-body and 'gone' to the Smith-body. Let us then note that we are only committed to saying that Smith is (the reincarnation of) Jones if we accept that Smith really does *remember* the actions of Jones, that he really is guilty of them, sorry for doing them, and the rest. It is then obvious what form the case against reincarnation must take, even assuming the reality of the phenomena we have imagined. It must take the form of insisting that the phenomena do not have to be described in the way in which Smith himself describes them. Instead, Smith must be said to have a paranormal power of knowing the past of another that is analogous to the manner in which each of us knows his or her own past in memory: except that it is not, of course, *memory*, since we only have memories of *our own* pasts. The phenomena, even if admitted, never have to be described in ways that entail the reality of reincarnation. The price for avoiding such unwanted description is accepting that there are some persons who have occult retrocognitive access to the lives of others. We can easily imagine that Smith himself is persuaded to accept this way of seeing the matter. He might then cease to feel guilty about the actions he thought he remembered, since we should not feel guilty about acts we merely *retrocognise* another person doing, in the way we feel guilty about acts we remember doing ourselves.

I do not wish to pursue the fancy further, but to make a double point: that it is natural to describe certain easily-imagined phenomena as cases of reincarnation, but that it is not necessary to do so. Each of the two alternative descriptions of such imagined phenomena would be reasonable, and would have advantages: one would enable those who are willing to enlarge the customary boundaries of individual life to subsume novel

124

events under familiar concepts, and the other would enable those who prefer the familiar boundaries to retain them at the cost of enlarging their inventory of human powers.

I think it is also true, though I shall not attempt to prove it here, that with sufficient patience and care, one could tell stories which would similarly enable us to speak of one human consciousness inhabiting a group of human bodies rather than one, or of two human subjects exchanging bodies. In each case, though I shall not argue this either, two provisos would have to be added: the first, that if one were to adopt these ways of describing the situations imagined in the stories, one would not thereby do anything to establish the thesis that a human subject is an immaterial spiritual substance that is only externally related to the material bodies it inhabits, or can go 'from' one 'into' another; the second, that the description the stories would legitimise would have the same optional character as the description of Smith as a reincarnation of Jones. For nothing in the stories would prevent anyone who wishes to retain the logical connection between one human consciousness and one human body from doing so by inventing the concept of a new human power rather than accepting a new relationship between individual persons and their bodies. (The new powers in this case might be some capacity of collective hypnotism, or some combination of amnesia and retrocognition.)

What does all this tell us, and how does it relate to Butler's very different argument for an afterlife? To answer this, let us return to the supposed case of reincarnation. Let us imagine that we found examples of apparent memories of earlier lives occurring with moderate frequency, and let us suppose that we decided to call them cases of real memory. This would entail that at least some of the people around us had had previous bodies. (It is not news that there are major cultures in which this is widely believed to be true.) The sorts of conscious acts which would lead us to ascribe one or more earlier incarnations to people we knew would be acts which straddled more than one life, on this account of the matter – acts in which the person in his or her later life atoned for deeds done in the earlier one, grew in character in consequence of experiences undergone in the prior existence, and so on. To ascribe such acts to someone is to imply that he or she has preserved certain characteristically human powers (those involved in moral development, learning, memory, and the like) from one life into another: has retained at least some such powers beyond physical death. (Again, it is not news that there are major cultures in which such things are believed to be true.) So we can at least say that one logically possible way of interpreting certain supposed actions and events would be to accept Butler's suggestion that death would not necessarily destroy our conscious powers, but would merely remove their present means of expression.

To be able to imagine events which would fit Butler's suggestion does not carry us far towards Butler's conclusions. It does not make it *likely* that such imagined events will come to pass. It certainly does not show that it is even logically possible for us to exercise our mental powers beyond death in an incorporeal state, since the scenarios we have imagined all involve embodied people like ourselves. And it is obvious also that Butler has no interest at all in establishing the likelihood of reincarnation, in spite of one friendly reference to Hindu teaching in a footnote. He wants to show we have good reasons to expect to go on from this life to another, but he would not welcome evidence that suggested this transition would repeat itself in the future, or that we have come into this present life from an earlier one. But in spite of this, I would claim to have helped Butler's case. For if we turn our attention to the traditional Christian teaching of bodily resurrection, we can see that its logical structure is closer than one might at first suppose to the belief in reincarnation. One can treat the prediction that we shall be resurrected as equivalent to the claim that we shall be reincarnate – with the restrictions that this has never happened to us before this life, that it will not be repeated since the next life will be endless, and that it lies only in the future, and has not happened to more than one or two special individuals so far. If reincarnation is a coherent supposition, so is resurrection. The considerations that make it intelligible to suppose that people may be reincarnated in the future make it intelligible to suppose they will be resurrected to another life.

But none of the alleged *evidence* that has been supposed to support the belief in reincarnation can be used to support the Christian belief in resurrection, since the latter excludes the belief in *previous* lives. So Butler can be granted that it is intelligible to suppose the dead will in future resume the exercise of powers they have manifested in this life, but he cannot be granted that we have evidence for it. But there is more to be said than this.

3

Christians have expected the resurrection of man to occur in the future. This expectation has been based on claims quite distinct from the arguments Butler presents in the first chapter of the *Analogy*, and he properly does not include them there. But as a Christian, he does have an eschatological dimension to his view of human nature. This is a dimension that unbelievers reject. So they will disagree, perhaps, about the range of powers and possibilities that human beings have, and will certainly disagree about the time-frame within which human beings can exercise the powers and possibilities they agree that they have. In this respect, as in many others, the world-view of the believer differs from that of the unbeliever by *addition*. Throughout his writings Butler is clear that the view of human nature he himself holds is not one which *contrasts* with that of enlightened and reasonable secular men of his own day, but is one which broadens and deepens it, and can therefore be presented as a plausible extension of it. It is quite natural, therefore, that he should say that the expectation of a future life is of a piece with our common practice of ascribing continuance through radical change. The immaterialist metaphysics in which he chooses to engage at this point in his argument conceals from him the fact that there is no direct evidence to support the claim that we should treat the death of the body as merely one more radical change in life. But this is also, perhaps, concealed from him by the fact that someone who holds an eschatological view of man is committed to Paul's seed-and-plant analogy through the very concept of human nature with which he thinks. In particular, one who has the eschatological view of human nature is committed to what has been called a 'one-gap-inclusive' view of man.[8] To believe in the resurrection is to believe that we are beings who will continue in the future after a gap of nothingness that death brings upon us – indeed to believe that this fundamental fact about us is one which is consistent with the observed features of our lives, yet is not rendered obvious by them, but is learned through a special historical revelation.

There are many conceptual difficulties about the idea that a human person is the kind of entity that has a gap in its being. I do not think that these difficulties are insuperable; that is, I do not think they show this concept of the human person to be absurd. But to grant this is not to show we *are* beings of this kind, only that we *could* be, in the minimal logical sense of 'could'. Anyone who thinks we *are* one-gap inclusive beings, of course, is also bound to think exactly what Butler urges upon us: that the gap that death introduces into human existence, the period during which there may be literally nothing of us going on, is still a period during which it will be true that we still exist, and have, but do not exercise, many of our powers, namely all those that we shall resume *after* the resurrection. For a being that has such a gap in its existence is not a being that ceases to exist during that gap and then starts to exist once more, but a being that exists during and through the gap: just as the television serial continues *its* sort of being throughout all those hours during the week between its instalments.

Of course, whether, during a particular week, the television serial is still in progress depends on whether there is or is not a later episode to come. And whether or not the dead still exist and have the powers they have stopped exercising will depend on whether or not the future contains their reappearance. Either their dead state now is one of cessation and non-being, or it is a gap. Only the future will tell. At this point, we can say which we please.

Where does this leave Butler's argument? It permits a form of development which is present throughout the rest of the *Analogy*, but is concealed. What Butler erroneously thinks he has done is to show that a future life is quite likely, and that those who recognise this should scrutinise our condition to see whether some familiar features of it are not best interpreted as signs of how we should live in the light of that likelihood. Such an argument is as weak as its premiss. But the same considerations can be viewed another way. For they will be considerations that will be consequences of adopting the gap-inclusive, resurrection-oriented understanding of our natures and of our world, and as they are built up they will grow into an edifice which displays the main features of a total world-view (that of Christianity) and shows how it can interpret the familiar facts of our condition – facts which admittedly can be interpreted, throughout, in a wholly secular fashion. It is possible that such a comprehensive view of ourselves and our world might seem to some to be, as a whole, more likely than the secular one, even though this or that part of it cannot be shown to be likely solely by attending to evidence culled from within the descriptions of our world that the two world-views share in common. Someone who made this judgment would in fact come to judge the eschatological view of man to be more likely to be true, because of the total effect of those interpretations and understandings of our common world that it made possible.

I have already indicated that this form of argument, and the implied prudential pressure to consider it attentively, is one part of Butler's fundamental strategy. It is concealed, even from Butler himself, by his tactical need to start from the nominal belief in God that his target-audience professed; but not only does it not depend on that nominal theism, it is clearer if it is presented without it. I have called it Butler's cumulative argument.[9] In relation to the matter of the future life, its application is this. We live, as Butler tells us, in a world in which we ascribe continued active existence to one another through very radical changes. Our human attachments make us want to continue this ascription in the face of death, when all signs of the continued possessions of human powers and faculties vanish. The tradition which teaches that we can still continue this ascription, does so because it proclaims that at a future time we shall manifest many of those powers again, so that we and they have only temporarily ceased. The world in which those who believe this proclamation live, and the world in which those who do not believe it live, is the same world – but viewed in two radically different ways. Each, however, can develop his own interpretation of this one world's events, choices, and calamities. The choice of which of these two views of humanity, and of the world it inhabits, is the true one has to be based on the rational agent's serious comparison of the total competing world-views, and their alternative interpretations of the details of this shared, ambiguous world. It is imprudent in the extreme, as Butler sees the matter, for anyone who is aware of the existence of the eschatological alternative to confine his attention to the secular interpretations alone. For, even though the evidence does not compel him to abandon it, the alternative just might be true, and the evidence does not (he contends) show that it is false.

We must agree that if Butler is trying to base a case for Christianity on a prior proof that immortality is likely, his argument is very weak indeed. We have seen how the requirements of his anti-deist polemic require him to proceed in this way. But I hope to have shown, also, how his comments on identity through change can provide elements of an argument of a different sort which it is not anachronistic to suggest is also at work when the *Analogy* is viewed in its totality.

4

While Butler's case for a future life has had a poor press, the Dissertation 'Of Personal Identity', which appears as one of two appendices to the *Analogy*, is generally celebrated and judged to be required reading for those interested in its theme. It has, accordingly, been discussed with almost no reference to the work to which it is attached.

Butler himself could not consistently have deplored this, since he separates its arguments off into an appendix explicitly for the reason that it has nothing to do with the main purposes of the work. But we should treat this with caution. The reason he has for thinking that a discussion of the nature of personal identity is irrelevant to his argument for a future life, is one which is highly controversial, and affects both discussions. He states it as follows:

> Whether we are to live in a future state, as it is the most important question which can possibly be asked, so it is the most intelligible one which can be expressed in language. Yet strange perplexities have been raised about the meaning of that identity or sameness of person, which is implied in our living now and hereafter, or in any two successive moments. And the solution of these difficulties hath been stranger than these difficulties themselves. For, personal identity has been explained so by some, as to render the inquiry concerning a future life of no consequence at all to us the persons who are making it. And though few men can be misled by such subtleties; yet it may be proper a little to consider them. (Diss I 1/1)

The perplexities of the philosophers about personal identity are irrelevant, in other words, for two reasons: they suggest what we know is false, that there is some doubt about the clarity of questions about a future life, and they generate analyses of personal identity which, if true, would show the question of a future life to be of no importance to us – which we also know to be false. Butler considers it to be a *reductio ad absurdum* of a theory of personal identity that it should imply either that we do not understand the problem of a future life or that the answer to it could turn out to be of no concern to us. This is a very sweeping assertion, for it amounts to a rejection, *a priori*, of the possibility that we can be concerned about the question of survival, even in part, because we are *confused* about the concepts we use in expressing it. While it is undoubtedly true that we can talk sense with concepts, very commonly, without being able to talk sense about them, or analyse them, this does not show that the idea of a widespread, even universal, confusion is absurd, though the burden of proof lies with those who claim to find one.

Butler goes further than this. He adds something that in no way follows from the above, but would serve also, if true, to demonstrate the irrelevance of philosophical analysis to the question of survival. He tells us that the idea of personal identity, though wholly clear and familiar, is indefinable. He does not have to say this, since an idea could be clear, and the questions it is used to formulate could be important, while it is susceptible of quite straightforward definition. Though Butler has already said that the idea of personal identity is one we can use clearly without having an account of it, he does not have to say that this is because no account of it can be given. But he does say this. He compares the idea of personal identity to those of 'similitude' and 'equality'. In each of these cases, 'all attempts to define would but perplex it'. This is a dark saying; for if 'perplex' here is supposed to mean 'confuse', then we have his own word for it that we can manage to use these ideas without confusion irrespective of the analytical efforts of philosophers. He has to mean that such attempts will always, for some reason, become involved in misleading confusions, and fail. He does not say why. Instead we get three illustrations of how we understand important ideas that in his view we cannot define; and then we get a famous argument to show how one attempt to define the idea of personal identity fails.

Butler illustrates his contention that an idea may be indefinable, yet clear and familiar, in a threefold way. When we compare two triangles 'there arises to the mind the idea of similitude'; when we compare twice two and four, we have the idea of equality; and, when 'upon comparing the consciousnesses of one's self, or one's own existence, in any two moments, there as immediately arises to the mind the idea of personal identity'. It is not as clear as it might be what Butler means here by saying that these ideas 'arise to the mind'. Probably he just means that when faced with these facts our intellect is stimulated to *make use of* these ideas. It is easier to understand him in the first two examples than in the third, but perhaps an example of the third might be my being reminded by my feelings of joy when I see my birthplace after a long absence, of the way I felt on the day I left it, and being stimulated by this recollection to make some such judgment as 'How I have changed since I was last here!' Butler goes on to say that these kinds of occasions do not merely 'give us' the ideas in question, but *show us* that two triangles are alike, or two sums equal, or that the two moments are separate moments in the life of the self-same person. So occasions like this are occasions when we not only use the ideas in question, but are specifically aware that they are occasions when the ideas have application.

From this point onward, Butler confines himself to the idea of personal identity; and he says that the understanding of it that his illustration gives us is one that shows it cannot be defined – or at least cannot be defined in one particular way. To assess his argument, we should look very carefully at what I feel is a very implausible claim embodied in his illustration. He says that in the case of identity the comparison of the two 'consciousnesses' shows us 'the identity of ourselves in those two moments'. The only way I can read this is that Butler is telling us that when I compare a present conscious state of mine with a previous one, I 'discern' that they are both states of one and the same person. This means that when I am conscious of, or remember, some past state of mine, part of what I remember is that it was I who had this state.

This is plainly false. It may well be that I could not recall some previous state of mine, and compare it with a present one, or with another, more recent, one, unless I knew that it was I who had it; but this is not at all the same as saying that when I make such a comparison part of what I am conscious of, or remember, is *that it was I who had it*. There are cases where this might be true. If I am thrilled by a performance of *Hamlet*, and am stimulated by this fact to recall previous performances of *Hamlet* that I attended, I might, in so doing, recall that it was I, rather than someone else present, who expressed a particular opinion about the lead actor's interpretation of the role. But in most cases, when I recall some part of my past, I will not remember, even though I might well have to know, that it was I, who am now recalling it, who had that experience at that past time. My own presence is not part of what I am remembering, as a rule, though it *can* be. Butler, however, seems to infer from the fact that I cannot recall an event in my past without knowing that it *is* part of my past, that when I recall it I must be *conscious* of the fact that it belongs to my past and not another's.

This becomes important immediately. For Butler goes on to say that this supposed fact proves that my consciousness of events in my past cannot be what *makes* them part of my past. And the reason he gives is not the one usually attributed to him. The one he gives is, simply, that I cannot be conscious of something that is not independently so; so my

131

being conscious that something is part of my past cannot be what makes it that. It is this that he has in mind when he says that personal identity cannot be constituted by consciousness, but that consciousness *presupposes* it.

This argument has been much discussed. There are those, such as Reid and Flew, who judge it to be a decisive refutation of the previous account of personal identity given by John Locke.[10] Others, such as Grice, Wiggins, and Perry, have attempted to defend analyses like that of Locke from what they take to be Butler's criticism.[11] Much of the importance that this criticism has acquired in the literature of personal identity may be due to crediting Butler with a better argument than the one he actually offers us. The common view is that Butler accuses Locke of circularity in attempting to define what the identity of a person consists of by using the notion of 'consciousness'. This term is a generic one covering both the sort of awareness a person has of his or her present mental states, and the sort of awareness a person can have now of mental states in his or her past; since the latter is the more critical in discussions of self-identity, Locke is usually taken to be trying to define this relationship in terms of *memory*. Butler is read as saying that any attempt to do this will involve us in circularity. Indeed he does believe this; but not in the manner commonly ascribed to him. When contemporary writers present the 'problem of circularity' in their own words, they tend to interpret it as a point about the concept of memory itself: for example, that when we analyse what it is to remember having a past experience, we find we have to include the identity of the remembered and the original subject as part of our analysis. This has led neo-Lockeans to see whether or not memory could be defined without this, or whether some analogous notion might be developed that differed from that of memory only in the absence of this apparent requirement.[12] (My own discussion of the idea of reincarnation in the earlier part of this chapter has connections with these discussions.[13]) But however fruitful this reading of Butler has been, it is a misreading of him. I quote the key paragraph (Diss I 3/3) in full:

> But though consciousness of what is past does thus ascertain our personal identity to ourselves, yet to say, that it makes personal identity, or is necessary to our being the same persons, is to say, that a person has not existed a single moment, nor done one action, but what he can remember; indeed none but what he reflects upon. And one should really think it self-evident, that consciousness of personal identity presupposes, and therefore cannot constitute, personal identity; any more than knowledge, *in any other case*, can constitute truth, which it presupposes. (Italics not in original.)

The circularity problem is stated in the last sentence, which I shall therefore discuss first. Butler is manifestly not making a point here about the concept of memory, or consciousness, as he is commonly thought to be, though certainly what he says *has to do* with memory. The 'And' with which the sentence begins indicates that the point made in this sentence is not the same as the one made in the preceding one. What, then, is it? I find no difficulty: Butler tells us that personal identity is presupposed *in the way that other forms of knowledge presuppose truth* – a way which would prevent our defining truth in terms of knowledge. What way is this? Again, there is no difficulty, in view this time of the clause that 'consciousness of personal identity presupposes, and therefore cannot constitute, personal identity'. Truth is presupposed by knowledge in the sense that truth is, necessarily, a feature of *what is known*. As the reference to 'consciousness of personal identity' makes clear, remembering here presupposes personal identity because personal identity is *part of what is remembered*. So when I remember doing something in the past, part of that experience is my remembering that I am the agent who did it. I have already argued that this claim is implausible, once we distinguish it from the (true) claim that I have to *know* I was the agent involved in order to remember doing the action. But it is clear from all Butler's (unambiguous) phrasing, that it is this implausible claim he is making, not the more plausible and interesting claim that we cannot define what it is to remember without including personal identity in the definition. I shall therefore not yield to the temptation to explore how far Locke's analysis of personal identity could be rescued from the 'circularity' problem as others have presented it, since this will take us too far from anything Butler says.

In the first sentence of the quoted paragraph Butler makes another, and justified criticism of Locke: that it is quite impossible to understand personal identity in terms of memories, if these are to be understood as *actual* memories. For this would imply that no one can have done anything that he does not remember doing, and would turn forgetting into self-destruction. The point is developed with rather heavy-handed force by Reid, and more subtly by Flew. But even my statement of Butler's point is slightly misleading. It suggests that Butler shows some cognisance of the fact that a Lockean could respond to the criticism by invoking possible, rather than actual, memories. But Butler's sentence suggests no such cognisance or interest.

Butler next says that Locke's 'wonderful mistake' is due perhaps to something Locke has perceived correctly: that 'to be endowed with consciousness is inseparable from the idea of a person'. While Butler agrees with Locke in this, he not only rejects Locke's attempt to define personal identity in terms of it, but rejects an important contribution that is allied with it. His unfortunate line of reasoning here is what leads him to adopt the position on the simplicity of the soul that mars his treatment of immortality in Chapter i.

Locke's analysis of personal identity, in Chapter XXVII of Book II of the *Essay concerning Human Understanding*, is a profound but confused one. In fastening on some of Locke's confusions, Butler manages to miss some of Locke's insights as well. One of these is the general insight that the concept of identity has to be joined to some substantive notion, like that of a tree or an animal or a person, to have a clear use. As David Wiggins has put it, 'if someone tells you that a= b, then you should always ask them "the same *what* as b?" '[14] From this Locke concludes that what 'comprehends' or 'determines' identity will vary from one sort of entity to another. He also concludes that in many cases unchangingness is not a necessary condition of identity through time. In particular, the radical change that takes place in the parts that compose organisms does not destroy their identity, because (as we might now express it) these changes are characteristic of entities of those sorts, and are allowed for in their concepts. For example:

> That being then one plant which has such an organization of parts
> in one coherent body, partaking of one common life, though that
> life be communicated to new particles of matter vitally united to the
> living plant, in a like continued organization conformable to that sort
> of plants.[15]

It is interesting that it is the same fact of organisms enduring radical change without loss of identity to which Butler draws our attention when arguing for a future life. Yet he takes strong exception to Locke's argument, saying it is irrelevant for understanding personal identity.

> The inquiry, what makes vegetables the same in the common
> acceptation of the word does not appear to have any relation to
> this of personal identity: because, the word *same*, when applied to
> them and to person, is not only applied to different subjects, but
> it is also used in different senses. (Diss I 5/4)

Butler claims, then, that the notion of identity has a different *sense* when applied to organisms and to persons. He goes on to say that the former are only identical in 'a loose and popular sense'. He contrasts this with 'the strict philosophical sense' of the word 'same'. He makes it very clear what this strict sense of sameness requires – that there can be no change in the parts of the entity to which it is applied. He then tells us, giving no reason, that 'sameness is used in this latter sense, when applied to persons'.

If Butler were right about this, it would follow that all his examples of organisms surviving radical change are cases of identity only in the loose and popular sense, not the strict sense. This would make them valueless (as in fact they are not) as analogies for a personal identity that might persist even through physical death. (It would also be less than a compliment to the perspicacity of St Paul.)

His unargued assertion that personal identity is strict identity (later to be rejected by Hume[16]) has had its defenders.[17] Taking it himself as obvious, Butler proceeds to dismiss as absurd a question Locke tried to answer, and answered insightfully. Locke's question was this. Since identity is determined differently for different entities, we find that the identity of a *man* and the identity of a *person* are determined differently. For men are biological organisms, and their identity is determined, like that of plants and animals, by the retention of a certain kind of biological organisation. Persons, however, are bearers of reflection and responsibility; hence, Locke says, *their* identity depends on *consciousness*: roughly, awareness and memory. This makes it possible that the spatial or temporal dimensions of a person should be wider or narrower than those of a man. There might be living human bodies that have lost personal identity. There might be persons whose identity persisted through two human histories: if I should remember Noah's Flood, I should have been there in an earlier organism. There might be persons who exchanged organisms with each other: a cobbler and a prince might switch bodies. Having made this point, Locke goes on to consider the relationship between the two expressions 'same person' and 'same *substance*'. Locke's understanding of the idea of substance is a well-known source of confusion in the *Essay*, but for present purposes it is enough to say that he thinks substances, material and spiritual, are the ultimate metaphysical components of things, and do not change through time.[18] A material being, then, that is now composed of different particles of matter from those which composed it earlier, cannot be, or contain, the same material substance, even if we correctly say it is the same tree or house. In the case of persons, Locke, having located the source of their identity in consciousness, decides that if there is spiritual substance deep down in us, it cannot be the bearer of personal identity. He recognises that this would seem puzzling to many of his readers, because they think that an act of consciousness is performed by a single thinking substance, and my present consciousness of my past actions obviously involves a numerically different act of consciousness from the one performed in each of those past actions; hence we seem to have the paradoxical result that what we usually think of as one biography is a sequence of distinct substances – perhaps not a unitary self at all. Locke replies, essentially, that spiritual substance, if a reality, is an unknown one, so we simply cannot tell whether there is one or whether there are many, in each biography; but whatever the answer is, it is irrelevant to the continuance of *personal* identity. That extends as far as consciousness reaches.

Locke's sharp distinction between the identity of men, persons, and spiritual substances, gives rise to many problems, and no doubt Butler is right to feel dissatisfied with it. But the critique he offers is unhelpful, even to himself. It is clear that the identity Locke thinks that substances have is what Butler calls strict identity, and is inconsistent with alteration in composition. (Butler says, in fact, that the bearer of consciousness, like consciousness itself, must be 'indiscerptible'.) He scores quickly by saying that if, as Locke says, a person is a rational being, and 'being' and 'substance' are synonymous, one cannot ask whether the identity of a person could persist without that of substance. Perhaps Locke would have felt wounded by this hit, but it is doubtful, since it involves insisting upon a use of the term 'substance' which Locke argues against elsewhere.[19] Butler proceeds to impugn the reality of Locke's problem by repeating his earlier argument that consciousness cannot constitute personal identity. It is strange, he says, that anyone should suppose our identity is called in question by the fact that our present consciousness of our past life is a distinct act from past consciousnesses: two perceptions of the same object are necessarily two, while it is one. Once again he clearly says that our identity in the two conscious states is part of the content of those states:

> And thus though the successive consciousnesses, which we have of our own existence, are not the same, yet are they consciousnesses of one and the same thing or object; of the same person, self, or living agent. The person, of whose existence the consciousness is felt now, and was felt an hour or a year ago, is discerned to be, not two persons, but one and the same person; and therefore is one and the same. (Diss I 6/5)

In spite of the potential ambiguity of the phrase 'consciousness of one and the same person', I do not think that a wider version of the circularity problem is even hinted at here. Butler is repeating his earlier contention that when we remember our pasts, our identity is part of what we remember, and in *that* sense a condition of our now remembering it. It is for this reason that we can dismiss as absurd any philosophical worry about our not now being identical with the past person whose acts or experiences we now recall.

Butler concludes with some arguments designed to show the absurdity of thinking that a person's life could be split into a series of discrete selves, each constituted by the bounds of a single conscious act. Such a view would imply that my present self could not be held responsible for the deeds of my past selves, or take interest in the prospects of future ones. He makes three objections. (1) No one 'in his wits' can alter his plans on the premiss that although he will live tomorrow, yet he might not be the same person he is today. Since this is manifestly absurd to contemplate with regard to our 'temporal concerns', it would be equally absurd to contemplate with regard to 'religion' for anyone not sunk in 'secret corruption of heart'. (2) Consciousness is a mental act, and it is not such an 'idea, or abstract notion, or quality' which is the subject of life and action, but the being that *has* or *does* it. Beings that have life and perform actions have an identity through time, and come to their actions already provided with pasts. These pasts are theirs, whether they remember them or not; but if they do, the past they remember is the *object* of their memory, and is not *made* theirs by the fact that they remember it. (3) Every person is as conscious of the fact that he did some past action that he remembers, as he is of the fact that the action was done: indeed, he is often only aware that it was done because he remembers that 'he himself did it'. If he, a person, is a substance, then this shows that he knows he is the same substance; if only the property of some substance, since a property cannot be transferred from one substance to another, he knows that the substance of which he is the property is the same. And anyone who wonders whether we could be deceived in supposing we existed as far back as our memories carry us must be reminded that in the end memory has to be its own justification.

These three arguments deserve brief comment, but no more. (1) It is easy, and perhaps fair, to convict many statements that express scepticism about personal identity, of manifest absurdity. But, while it is not to the point to explore this here, discontinuities between the inner lives of persons at different stages of what is commonly regarded as one life can generate perplexities that can be expressed without the glaring infelicities Butler exposes. (2) This passage (in Diss I 9/9) is probably the nearest Butler himself comes to a statement of a more general version of the circularity problem, but even here it is too cryptically expressed to be identified with certainty. He quickly reverts to his familiar contention that memory of a past presupposes that past as its object. (3) The third argument is fallacious. Even though it is true that the only reason I have for claiming that some action was done is that I remember doing it, and even though it is true that I cannot remember doing it and be ignorant of the fact that it was I who did it, it does not follow that in remembering it I remember that I, now remembering, am the person who then did it. And even if it *were* the case that I remember I was that person, and also the case that persons are substances, it would not follow that, in remembering all that, I am conscious I am the same substance as that substance. This would not follow any more than it would follow from the fact that the person who did it was the 389th to have been born in 1929, that I would be conscious of being, then or now, the 389th person to have been born in 1929.

To summarise, Butler's criticisms of Locke's analysis of personal identity are these. (1) He accepts that 'consciousness makes personality': that persons are essentially the subjects of awareness and memory. (2) He also accepts that personal identity goes 'as far back as our remembrance reaches'; that it is a sufficient condition of my being identical with a person who did some past action or had some past experience, that I should remember doing the action or having the experience. But he rejects Locke's attempt to show that consciousness determines personal identity. (3) Memory is a sufficient condition of personal identity only in the sense that when I remember a past action or experience, part of what I remember is that it was *my* past action or experience. Since identity is in this way a part of all my memories, these memories presuppose it and cannot constitute it, any more than they constitute the actions or experience themselves. I have argued that this thesis of Butler's is mistaken, even if Locke is guilty of circularity in some other way Butler has not identified. (4) Butler further rejects Locke's fundamental thesis that identity is determined differently for different sorts of entities. He claims that this is only true if the word 'same' is used in a loose and popular sense, not if it is used in the strict and philosophical sense. The strict and philosophical sense is one which excludes the possibility of change in the entity's composition. This thesis is stated without argument. (5) Personal identity, according to Butler, is identity in the strict sense. This also is unargued, aside from the argument based on the unity of consciousness found in the body of Chapter i, which I have criticised earlier. The combination of arguments (4) and (5) generates Butler's contention in Chapter i that the identity of persons is the identity of something which is unaltered by changes in the actions they do or the experiences they have, and in particular is unaltered even by the most radical changes in the bodies that persons have – death included. This argument is not only devoid of visible support, but is directly at odds with the analogies Butler draws between persons and those organisms that survive radical change, as these can only be examples of identity in the loose and popular sense. (6) Identity in the strict sense is identity of substance, so that Locke is mistaken in arguing that identity of substance is irrelevant to the identity of persons. While many of the puzzle-stories on which Locke relies to make his point may be open to a different interpretation from his, the organic examples which he and Butler both use for their different purposes are enough, in my view, to illustrate the correctness of Locke's opinion that even if there is substance, its identity is irrelevant to that of any of the entities with which it may be connected. (7) Finally, Butler maintains that the debates about personal identity are irrelevant to the case for a future life because personal identity is indefinable, though clearly understood by all of us. He relies here upon an intuitive appeal, and to alleged absurdities in scepticism about personal identity.

It is noticeable that Locke and Butler both seem to assume that if self-identity could be defined, it would have to be defined in terms of one necessary and sufficient condition, not more than one. It is now a truism of the literature of personal identity that we ascribe it on the basis of at least two such possible conditions (or more, depending on how these are understood). These are bodily continuity, and what Swinburne calls 'similarity of memory and character'.[20] Given that this is so, many of the puzzle-stories that have been invented have been told with the purpose of asking what we could say if they appeared to clash. Locke's theory would require us to say that only memory was definitive of the identity of persons, and bodily continuity is definitive of that of men, or of human organisms. If we do not make this sharp separation, we open up the possibility of apparent cases of deadlock, where there is no clear case for deciding which standard should take priority. If, for example, two men wake up one morning expressing astonishment at the faces they see in the mirror, and each having apparent memories that fit the past of the other's body and none that fit the bodies they have, we seem able to say that they have switched bodies (thus giving priority to the memory standard of identity), but also able to say that each has lost his own memories and acquired retrocognitive access to the past of the other (thus giving priority to bodily continuity). The fact that an impasse like this can easily be generated, plus the fact that Butler correctly points out that if memory alone constituted personal identity we should lose identity when we forgot segments of our pasts, has led some to defend Butler's claim that personal identity is indefinable, and that all such factors as memories and bodily features can do is give us evidence for it. A consequence of this view is that there will always be an answer to the question 'Is this the same person or not?' even though the answer will sometimes be impossible to get. Indeed, it is the fact that attempted definitions of personal identity might open up the possibility of there not being an answer in certain circumstances, or of such an answer being a matter not of discovery but of *decision*, that is thought to demonstrate such enterprises to be mistaken in principle. For sometimes widespread hopes and fears would be made incoherent, or shown to be mere matters of decision, if personal identity were constituted by those factors philosophers have selected in the definitions of it. Some of those hopes and fears involve hopes and fears of a future life. I shall return to these shortly, but when Butler dismisses arguments about self-identity as beside the point in his discussion of immortality, he does this on the ground that some of the theories these arguments produce would make our hopes and fears about a future life unclear ones, or make a future state of no concern to us when its nature is articulated. Now if a philosophical theory would have this consequence with respect to a very widespread human hope or fear, this would seem, on the surface, to be a reason to think it very important, and to examine it carefully, if only to refute it; not a reason to judge it irrelevant. It is only irrelevant if it is self-evident that the hope or fear it would put in question is clear and urgent. I must dissent from such an appeal. It seems to be based on the strange belief that a hope or fear could not be virtually universal but confused, and on that even stranger belief that a confused hope or fear is somehow not a *real* hope or fear. No doubt philosophers, especially those of an empiricist or analytical bent, are far too prone to deal with hopes or fears by suggesting they are incoherent when they are not. But it is just as dangerous to suppose that deep concerns cannot be based on confusions because all of us have them. One does not remove confusions, if they are really present, by banging the table.

I therefore reject Butler's stated reason for relegating discussion of personal identity to an appendix. It is just possible, however, that his insistence that the hope for a future life is 'the most intelligible one that can be expressed' in language masks a particular contribution to the debate about the nature and identity of persons, in spite of these difficulties. I turn to this possibility in conclusion.

5

In sections 2 and 3 of this chapter I attempted to construct a case for supposing that there could be an intelligible expectation of an afterlife that was closer in its character to the traditional Christian expectation that the incorporeal future life that Butler argues for. It is now clearer that this construction relies upon making use of the two theses that Butler accepts from Locke (that persons are beings endowed with awareness and memory, and that their identity reaches as far back as their memories), and utilising also those organic analogies that both thinkers appeal to, even though Butler nullifies their value by insisting that persons are incorporeal substances. The constructed expectation is that of a future resurrection. Since the kinds of events that would make us all want to talk in the language of this construction do not appear to have been taking place around us, I have not argued that the expectation is a likely one; the biological analogies that Butler uses are at best useful conceptual resources, and do not add to the probability of it in a non-negligible way. Of course, expectations that *are* likely ones can only get their likelihood from past and present events. If the expectation of resurrection is to gain any likelihood in this way, it has to be from the fact that it is the consequence of an overall world-view and estimate of human nature that provides a more plausible understanding of the past and present than its alternatives. Though I judge it to be one of Butler's purposes to give us such an overall interpretation in the *Analogy*, the argument in Chapter i is not of this nature, and cannot be judged to do more than make the logical possibilities clear to us.

The discussion of personal identity just ended, however, brings into sharp focus a problem which I have hitherto deferred, or not mentioned explicitly. The doctrine of resurrection is notoriously open to what I shall call the Replica Objection. It is an objection to which Butler's doctrine of incorporeal survival is not obviously open; it may perhaps have been designed to avoid it. His belief in the indefinability of personal identity is probably intended to circumvent it also. I begin by presenting the difficulty in the words of Richard Swinburne, who is a Christian philosopher who accepts what Butler says on this point. He rejects what he calls 'empiricist theories' of self-identity: theories which attempt to say what self-identity is in terms of the facts about memory and the body which, in his view, are merely the evidences for it.

> Consider, to begin with, the resurrection of the dead (whose dead bodies have decayed). Most people, I suggest, uninfluenced by philosophical theory, would allow this to be a logical possibility. The affirmation that there is life after death in another world or reincarnation on earth is widespread. Perhaps equally widespread is the denial that these things happen. Yet most who deny that these things happen seem to allow that it makes sense to suppose that they do happen, while denying that in fact they do. Now an empiricist theory which allows life after death must claim that in such a case personal identity is a matter of similarity of memory and character. A man survives death if and only if there exists after his death a man with similar memory and character to his (subject, possibly, to the proviso that there is no more than one such man). We saw earlier that there are difficulties in such theories. But here is a further one. If it is logically possible that I should survive my death, I have a coherent hope if I hope to do so. On an empiricist theory, for me to hope for my resurrection is for me to hope for the future existence of a man with my memories and character, that is a man who will be able to remember the things which happened to me and will react to circumstances somewhat as I do. But that is not at all what I hope for in hoping for my resurrection. I do not hope that *there be* a man of that kind – I want it to be me.[21]

Swinburne's point here is that unless personal identity is understood to be an ultimate fact distinct from the similarities that normally reveal it to us, we cannot describe the future state in any way that would ensure that its inhabitants are ourselves; they would only be replicas of ourselves, whose futures we could contemplate with quite detached interest. I have presented a similar thesis myself[22] as a problem in any doctrine of resurrection, and must return to it here as one who is unconvinced that it can be dealt with by the mere assertion that personal identity must be indefinable because the doctrine of resurrection is coherent. It is, I think, a genuine theoretical problem to determine whether any imaginary account of a future state can be produced that avoids the charge that it is merely a world inhabited by duplicates of ourselves rather than by us.

In approaching the idea of resurrection via that of reincarnation, I expressed the view that the sorts of events that would prompt us to speak of reincarnation would always be susceptible of another description. This would be a description that presupposed Locke and Butler to be right in thinking that self-identity reached back as far as memory, but insisted that however systematic and accurate the representation of past events a contemporary of ours might have, they could not be *memories* if the events and acts represented took place before the body this person has was born. They might be a form of occult knowledge of a personal past, but could not be the memories of a past belonging to the person now experiencing them. In a word, all such possible events are ambiguous: they *can* be called memories, thus demonstrating reincarnation, but they can also be called mere forms of retrocognition, thus retaining a world-view in which reincarnation does not occur. I would myself put the Replica Objection to resurrection in the same way. One could always insist upon describing the future events expected in terms which made them descriptions of a world containing replicas of ourselves rather than ourselves.

Such descriptions would be unlikely to be made by anyone experiencing such events – if only for the reason that they would, one supposes, not be detached about the pasts of the persons they claimed to be in the way in which we, looking forward, could, if we chose the replica description, elect to be detached about the futures of those we would decide we were *not* going to be. But the logical possibility remains. Does it have an answer? In what follows I shall suggest a possible response. I am unsure of its merits, but I think it has some, and that it is hinted at by Butler. I have been stimulated to recognise this by a fine essay of Robert Herbert's, in which the Replica Objection is examined with great elegance and humour.[23]

I begin by recalling how Butler starts his case for immortality. He does it by pointing out that we continue to ascribe identity, and the attendant retention of powers, through radical changes in organisms, and then suggests that, by analogy, we ought to be willing to consider that death does not destroy us, or our powers. He then offers arguments against the obvious retort that death is different. The case he offers leads him at once into the immaterialist metaphysics to which I have taken exception. As noted earlier, Butler's move at least recognises that there is a strangeness in the suggestion that death is in the end merely a radical change like many others; but to many readers of our own day, the very suggestion will seem patently absurd. To others, it will not seem so. The division will be largely, though not wholly, coincident with that between those who do not believe in a future life and those who do; I say it will not be wholly coincident with this latter division because some who deny a future life may think that the case against it is not one that makes it absurd, as distinct from just false, to think of death in this way. Although Butler argues that his suggestion is wholly in accord with our common conceptual practices, he does not seem to envisage the sort of dismissive response that a case like his would provoke now. This connects, I think, with the additional fact that more readers today would be unsympathetic to Butler's dogmatic insistence that the question of a future life is wholly clear, than would have been when the *Analogy* was written.

As a result of many cultural and philosophical developments that have accelerated since Butler's time (including the transition among religious sceptics from deism to atheism or agnosticism), the difference between those who have, and those who do not have, a Christian or near-Christian world-view has grown sharper, even though they share a common scientific understanding of the secular world for the most part. For the believer adds on many interpretations of our common world that the unbeliever no longer feels are warranted. One such addition, of course, is the expectation of a future life; though it is vital to remember that this is added on only as part of a whole world-view including claims about God and his intentions for his creatures, and is not a mere predictive hypothesis, as Butler feels obliged to represent it in Chapter i. In our day the sparer, secular understanding of our world is the commoner one.

The sharpness of the difference between the believer and the unbeliever is a fact I wish to express by saying that they now have clearly different *conceptions* of what a person is. They share many common understandings of what a person is, that they derive, equally, from biology, medicine, economics, and all the other human sciences, but in the believer's case these understandings are all subsumed under certain perceptions of a person's relation to God and of a person's future. This means that even when they agree – about some social or political issue, for example – they will be agreeing about what should be done by or to or for beings whose natures they envisage differently. 'Conception' is a vague notion, but 'concept' will not quite serve: for to suggest that the believer and the unbeliever differ in their *concept* of a person suggests that they may not disagree about what will happen, only about how to describe it; and of course they do disagree about what will happen, since one expects a future life and the other does not. On the other hand, their difference is not merely one about facts and expectations, for the differences they have in this realm imply, and are implied by, the difference there is between them about what sort of a being a person is.[24] I cannot dwell on the relation between conceptual and factual issues further, but I hope to have said enough to justify my suggestion that the division between believers and unbelievers is a complex mixture of the two.

I submit that Butler's calm in suggesting that death might turn out on examination to be merely one more radical change in the history of persons, comparable to that from chrysalis to butterfly or from seed to plant, is due to the fact that he normally thinks, and believes that his readers think, with the conception of persons that the Christian tradition embodies, so that his problem seems to him only one of persuading his readers that there is no reason to dismiss the possibility of events and changes that this conception of persons implies. He is sensitive to the fact that his readers are more inclined than earlier generations to dismiss doctrines that have no relation to evidence, and indeed he is more inclined that way himself than previous theologians. But he is not sensitive enough to the fact that this inclination will generate a new and more restrictive understanding of what persons are. This is also the reason, I submit, why he is so dogmatically dismissive of the relevance of those analyses of personal identity which could imply that a future life is irrelevant or inconceivable to us: that he has a conception of persons which is manifestly inconsistent with such theories, so that they could be disregarded as analyses of the idea of a person that he has.

The idea of a person that the believer has is, I have suggested, not of an incorporeal spiritual substance as he claims. It is of a corporeal, but one-gap-inclusive, being, that has two major stages: the first coming to a sharp end at death, and the second commencing at the Day of Resurrection and then continuing indefinitely. (Perhaps one should say that this conception is of persons as beings who go through three stages, not two. For during the intermediate stage there may be *nothing of the person* in the world, yet he or she will not have ceased to exist, since the final stage is still to come. The second stage would then be one of nothingness, but not of non-being.) The unbeliever's conception of a person is of a being whom death destroys for ever.

What has all this to do with the Replica Objection? I recall, first, what that objection is. It is to the effect that an imagined resurrection world is one which can be described as a world of replica persons as well as being described as a world in which we are resurrected. So there is no way of describing it that unambiguously satisfies the supposedly clear hope that *we* shall be resurrected. Let us recall Swinburne's unsatisfactory future world in which everyone seems to be a duplicate of a pre-mortem person, and ask, 'What has to be added to this to make it a world that contains us?'

Given the fact of death, no other detail can be added that would appear to guarantee this. For whatever detail one adds, the ambiguity infects it in turn. This seems to leave us in a position where we can easily enough describe a future world in a way that permits, but would never require, the language of resurrection. And how could the hope of resurrection ever be a real one, if no description could be given that unambiguously required it?

Let us approach this by imagining ourselves to be a select group that had lived up to, and through, the Day of Resurrection, and had not died before it. We encounter all these beings who say they recognise us, greet us, and go through all the behaviour of persons who have met each other again after a long separation; we find no one who does not identify himself or herself as a pre-mortem person and have the apparent memories and character of the person so identified. According to the Replica Objection, this is an ineluctably ambiguous situation, and the persons in it are not unambiguously our former acquaintances.

But perhaps this does not state our fancied situation fully or correctly. Perhaps the alleged ambiguity should be characterised further. For those of us living survivors who had the conception of a person as one-gap-inclusive, there would be no ambiguity at all. For speakers with that conception, nothing need be added to confirm that the Resurrection had arrived; all details requisite for this would have been supplied. On the other hand, for those who have the concept of a person as a being that is not one-gap-inclusive, but ends at death, there is no ambiguity either, it seems. For them, they have entered a world in which replicas of their former acquaintances fill the landscape. There would only be real ambiguity, in the sense of a potential for real indecision, for someone who was unsure which conception of persons is the right one.

But of course this is ridiculous. If we ever were to find ourselves in this situation, that is not how it would strike us at all. The reason why so many have adopted the naturalistic, no-gap conception of the person is that they see no reason at all to expect such fancied events to occur. If they *did* occur, while it would still be logically possible for one of us survivors to say 'These are all replicas, not our friends', such a response would be comparable to philosophical fantasies like solipsism or universal shamming. It would be wholly irrational, if such events took place, to retain the naturalistic conception of the person if one had had it previously, or to continue to hesitate about adopting the Christian conception of the person if one had been hesitating. The only reason why it is not irrational to do either of these things now is that these events have not happened, and are still in the future even on the Christian view.

The Replica Objection, then, is perhaps merely a philosophical worry in the vicious sense. Butler may be right about the matter after all, when he says that a doubt about whether the future life could be of real concern to us is 'owing to an inward unfairness, and secret corruption of heart'. While I am not free of qualms about this argument, I think at the time of writing that it provides a reason for thinking that the Replica Objection amounts in the end to no more than a negative dogmatism.

I cannot ascribe this line of thought, as I have formulated it, to Butler. But I think it can be constructed out of elements in his case, and makes his presentation of that case less objectionable in important respects. He assumes, first of all, that he and his readers share the Christian conception of what a person is, and that his problem is to convince his readers that the expectations dictated by that conception are not as severely threatened by lack of evidence as they thought. He is, however, conscious of the beginnings of speculation about self-identity that open up the possibility of this conception of personality being replaced by one that precludes a future life. His instinct is to dismiss such speculations as irrelevant to the concept we actually have, since the doubts he seeks to allay are not, of themselves, conceptual ones. He fails to produce any good evidence that it is likely the expectations dictated by the Christian conception of the person are true. But he does manage to produce some analogies that reinforce the fact that this conception of the person behaves like our conceptions of other sorts of living creatures. He fails to see the implications of these analogies, however, because he feels obliged to interpret the absence of visible human continuance as a sign that the expectation of our preservation through death is an expectation of an incorporeal future. In common with many others, he overlooks the gap-inclusive corporeality of the conception of the person with which he operates. Once we recover the realisation of this, we can see that the lack of such visible evidence does not refute the expectations associated with the Christian conception of man, though it clearly robs them of the sort of probability Butler thought he could show them to have. In such a situation, our world is ambiguous in the sense that both this conception of man and its naturalistic competitor can be used to interpret the evidence that we do have. If my argument above has weight, however, it is easy to imagine what would remove *this* ambiguity, and mistaken to think it would persist in the circumstances that Christians predict.

In conclusion, I would repeat the comment at the close of section 3. Although Butler does not show a future life to be likely in Chapter i, this would not preclude the cumulative case that he offers us in the *Analogy* as a whole being strong enough to make the Christian worldview, as (allegedly) revealed, more reasonable to adopt than its alternatives. Adopting it, of course, would entail adopting the conception of a person that is central to it.

VI

Divine Government and Human Probation

When we pass from Butler's arguments for a future life to the development of his case for natural religion, we find two important presuppositions constantly present. The first is that a future life is likely, so that the significance of our experience in this life must be judged in a wider context that includes it. The second is that nature does not merely have an intelligent author, but its author has made of it a teleological system: that we live in a world in which the regularities we find have been placed there for special purposes. Butler assumes that even if God does not interfere with the natural order he has established (and the possibility of miracle is not discussed until Part II of the *Analogy*), the results to which natural regularities lead are, in general, results to which God intends that they should lead. While we may not be able to discern all the purposes thus fulfilled, or understand those we can discern very fully, Butler thinks it follows from this that the investigation of nature is a necessary, if uncertain, way of finding out God's purposes.

In accordance with my previous analysis of Butler's apologetic method, I shall examine the main arguments of the remainder of Part I, with the dual objective of seeing how convincing they should have been to the deists, and of determining what value they have for those who cannot assume what he assumes.

1

Butler starts by saying that the reason the prospect of a future life is of interest to us, and deserves reflection, is that we may be able to affect the sort of life we shall have in it by the way we conduct ourselves now. If we find that there is reason to think that God plans the world as we find it in this life in a way that makes earlier choices determine the nature of later experiences, this will give us grounds for thinking that this same pattern may apply to the relation between life here, in its entirety, and

147

life hereafter. So he sets out to show that we live in a world God has so planned that, on the whole, good choices are rewarded and bad choices punished. He divides this into two stages: the attempted proof that in this life prudence is rewarded and imprudence punished, and the attempt to show that this pattern is also one in which *virtuous* acts are rewarded and *vicious* acts punished.

It is an obvious and pervasive fact of our life here that 'all which we enjoy, and a great part of what we suffer, *is put in our own power*' (*An* I ii 2/2). This does not mean that we can experience pleasure or pain by some direct act of will; but that we are able to learn what events produce the one or the other, and choose our actions in order to encourage the first and avoid the second. We are not able to make ourselves secure or happy without at least some attention and effort; and the very powers God has given us for this can be misused so that we make ourselves knowingly miserable. Why God has chosen to provide for us in this way, and has not so arranged things that we are happy without regard to our own actions, and have no power to make ourselves miserable, is a matter of speculation. Perhaps, says Butler, such a possibility is logically impossible, or would necessarily lead to less happiness than one in which our actions play the sort of part they do; or perhaps God values the rewarding of virtue more than the mere distribution of happiness; or perhaps God's purposes are quite beyond us. However these things are, 'it is a certain matter of universal experience, that the general method of Divine administration is, forewarning us, or giving us capacities to foresee, with more or less clearness, that if we act so and so, we shall have such enjoyments, and if so and so, such sufferings; and giving us those enjoyments, and making us feel those sufferings, in consequence of our actions' (*An* I ii 3/3). In one of his common-sense broadsides, Butler insists that anyone who agrees that God is the author of nature must also agree that such obvious features of the natural order as this one are present in it because God has put them in it. The fact that they are 'to be ascribed to the general course of nature', as indeed they are, does not show that they are not to be ascribed to the purposes of God, but, on the contrary, that they must be.

This does not mean that God intends us to choose every action that we find leads to pleasure, or avoid every action that we find leads to pain. We can see this when we reflect that we have obviously been given eyes to see with, but are not thereby being told to stare at everything we can turn them towards. What we should rather infer from the way we can learn from pleasure and pain, is that God governs our lives in the way in which 'civil magistrates' do: he teaches us through rewards and punishments. We can see, 'prior to the consideration of His moral attributes', that God is our 'master or governor'. Butler draws the following conclusion:

And thus the whole analogy of Nature, the whole present course of things, most fully shews, that there is nothing incredible in the general doctrine of religion, that God will reward and punish men for their actions hereafter: nothing incredible, I mean, arising out of the notion of rewarding and punishing. For the whole course of Nature is a present instance of His exercising that government over us, which implies in it rewarding and punishing. (*An* I ii 8/8)

How should we respond to this argument?

We must bear in mind that Butler has not yet said anything about the *morality* of God's governance; only that the divinely ordained system in which we find ourselves is one that encourages us to cultivate *prudence*.[1] There is an air of verbal necessity about saying that in this life prudence leads to happiness and imprudence leads to misery, since we would have to define prudence as a disposition to choose courses of action which lead to happiness, and imprudence as the lack of such a disposition. Butler is not trying to say something as vacuous as this, even though he does think that what he is saying is obvious. He is saying we live in a world where prudence is a disposition we can develop, because we find that our happiness and misery are substantially affected by the choices that we make, and can develop a capacity for good judgment if we choose. We develop it by noticing which experiences are pleasant or painful, and what actions lead to them. But he is not, of course, saying only that we live in a world where we can *learn* from our experience. He claims that we live in a world in which God *teaches* us; and that he does it by rewards and punishments, as a magistrate does. A magistrate inflicts experiences he knows are painful on offenders whom he hopes to deter from repeating their offences. The burnt child who fears the fire is, in relation to God, like the chastised child who has been slapped on the wrist by its parent for going too close to the oven. Offenders, and children, can of course choose not to heed their lesson, and can wantonly continue to do foolish things if they so choose. But in the end (this argument implies) the objective has been to *teach* them rather than to *get them to do* beneficial things.

For those of us today who have been influenced by Hume, there is a natural and immediate response to this argument: to say it involves Butler in generalising from a selected set of instances, and ignoring the special characteristics that make them what they are. We know that *magistrates* teach by rewards and punishments, because we know that the pleasures and pains that accused persons undergo in the legal system come about as a result of the orders that magistrates issue. We know *this* because we have observed magistrates issuing such orders. But this is a very small class of pleasures and pains. Observation suggests that *most* pleasures and pains are not *ordered* or *inflicted* by any discernible agent at all.

149

Observation does not teach us that God trains us by rewards and punishments; merely that we learn (or fail to learn) from pleasant and unpleasant
experiences that happen to us.

This response would be mistaken. Butler is not Cleanthes, and is not
trying to prove the existence of God. He is trying to persuade someone
who accepts the existence of God that nature is a system of rewards and
punishments, whose function is to encourage us, if we choose, to develop
good judgment. For this, he thinks it enough to point out that nature is
a realm where we find we have a significant degree of control over our
pleasures and pains, and where we find it conducive to a more pleasant
and less painful existence to exercise our wits and develop good judgment. Since nature is such a place, and can be assumed to have been
made so by God deliberately, we can properly say that God has arranged
nature in a manner that rewards and punishes us. The argument is not
from a supposed observation of natural rewards and punishments to a
divine magistrate, but from the existence of an intelligent governor of
nature to the conclusion that the pleasures and pains found within it
function as rewards and punishments for those creatures capable of
learning from them. To this argument the absence of observed agency is
no objection.

There are other objections, however. The first is that the argument
hardly establishes rewards and punishments in the primary senses of
those terms. Most would consider that the use of these terms, where
what is being taught is prudence and not morality, is a secondary use.
What Butler has in view is the expectation that God rewards and punishes
in the moral sense in the next life, i.e. as an overtly favourable or negative
moral response to our actions in this world. He is anxious to show that
the evidence points to God's being a 'righteous judge', rather than (for
example) an omnibenevolent being who spares us all suffering. The kind
of divine education that he speaks of in Chapter ii, however, is an
education in prudence – the sort of education that enables us to learn that
over-indulgence causes indigestion or ever-expenditure causes poverty.
While it is natural enough to say that such instruction is carried out
through reward and punishment, the elements of acknowledgment of
merit and infliction of retribution are absent. Butler needs to proceed as
he does, because he wants to persuade the deist that moral reward and
punishment, in which he does not yet believe, is of a piece with the sort
of reward and punishment that, on his principles, he should admit to be
part of the economy of the natural world. It is therefore important for
him to stress the similarities between the one and the other. But even if
there is no problem in urging the deist to discern prizes and sanctions
in nature, the analogy he tries to draw between these and moral rewards
and punishments is strained. (Butler does believe that prudence is a

virtue, and that conscience and self-love point the same way. But these, if truths, are not conceptual truths.)

A more serious objection could be based on some observations that Butler himself makes. He is quite clear that it is only a general truth, with many exceptions, that using one's best judgment leads to happiness, and ignoring it leads to misery. Indeed, so anxious is he to remove common deistic objections to eternal punishment that he is led to emphasise how hard the regime is in which God has placed us. He points out that in this world we find many who undergo long-term suffering for brief indiscretions; that the penalties of youthful mistakes are often deferred until the guilty person has turned into someone who would no longer do such things; and that some indulgences do not result in the penalties we think should follow them – in short, that the divine economy is one in which we can at most find a broad, but not a detailed apportionment of happiness to prudence. He holds, of course, that none of us is in a position to see all God's purposes in detail. But it is always possible for someone who accepts that the world contains some divine purposes, but who has no inhibitions in speculating what they might be, to use the hard cases Butler cites to argue that God amuses himself at our expense by so arranging nature that at least some of those who diet properly still become obese, or that some non-smokers still contract lung cancer. The plausibility of the prudential economy that Butler discerns is to be measured by one's judgment of how far our ability to understand the course of nature, and find what causes pleasure and pain in it, is conducive to our happiness when we follow this understanding.

Butler is not only concerned to establish that we live in this life under a system of rewards and punishments, but to argue that we should expect this system to extend into the next life. The argument is openly analogical: that because this is how we find the divine economy here, it is more likely than not that this is how it will be hereafter. This is one of the places where the text only delivers a defence, but Butler seems to think he has given grounds for more. Let us take him in his most careful vein, and interpret him as follows: that the distribution of rewards and punishments in this life is such that, assuming as we must that this life and the next are both under the governance of the same divine mind, we have no good reason to suppose the next life will not contain rewards and punishments also. What are we to make of this argument?

It is not clear, first, what its conclusion is. If the intent of Butler's reasoning is to persuade us that we can infer from the order of rewards and punishments that we find in this world, that God has a general policy of teaching rational creatures by reward and punishment, then this would suggest that we shall also find the next life to be one in which we can learn what is good or bad for us through pleasures and pains. The trouble with this conclusion is that it does not support Butler's belief that the decisions we make *here* will be rewarded or punished *there*, merely that decisions we will make *there* will be rewarded or punished *there*. To connect this-worldly acts with next-worldly rewards and punishments, he would have to show that there is a probable causal connection between the way our environment affects us here and the way it will affect us there, or between the way we develop our personalities and powers here and the way we enter the next life. There would have to be some reason to think, for example, that developing a resistance to sensual indulgence here would equip us for enjoyment of the opportunities for spiritual satisfaction there, or that a failure to cultivate higher pleasures here would lead to boredom or exclusion there. Butler attempts no such case; indeed, it would probably depend upon his drawing contrasts between this life and the next one, instead of emphasising likenesses. He later tries to show that this life is specially fitted for the consolidation of good moral *habits*; and this argument, to which I shall return, shows that he sometimes thinks of the next world as one in which there are continued challenges and difficulties, with which the right form of life here equips us to deal. But this is not the same as saying our experiences in the next world are rewards or punishments for our acts here, since it might merely amount to the view that our acts here, which have already been rewarded or punished here, can, in addition, habituate us to make the sorts of choices which will, in their turn, be rewarded or punished indigenously in the future.

There is no doubt that the most common Christian expectation has been of a future life which does not contain tests of its own, but rewards us or punishes us for passing or failing the tests we undergo here. Butler never directly disowns this expectation (and as an Anglican he cannot even qualify it by a doctrine of purgatory). This expectation contains an answer to those who point to those times in this life when prudence is not rewarded and profligacy prospers: the answer being that such inequities will be corrected hereafter. But this answer carries a price which Butler does not seem to be in a position to pay. If the next world differs from this one in not having tests and difficulties, and in correcting this world's inequities, what argument based upon the observed character of *this* world could give us reason to expect it? The character it has to have to serve such a purpose would prevent any predictions about it being based on analogies.

A second difficulty that besets Butler's analogy between this world and the next concerns the critical appeal that he makes to the supposed fact that both are under the same divine governance. It is easy to see that this appeal *is* critical. There would be no weight in an argument which said that because certain choices are good for us here, they will be good for us hereafter; this would be like arguing that because offering bribes to policemen is a good way to avoid a criminal record in one country, it will keep us out of trouble in another too. We need to be able to add that both places are under the same 'governance'. But this, too, is ambiguous. The fact that this life and the next have the same author, especially when his purposes are admittedly beyond us, does not give much assurance that he will govern us the same way in the next world as in this; or that, even if he does, it is because he has an overall plan that is beneficial to us. Why not assume, for example, that the author of nature, like other intelligent beings, enjoys relief and contrast, and designs a second life for us in order to have the diversion of observing the problems we have adjusting to an environment in which our previously acquired habits are valueless? There is no reason at all to suppose that the author of nature is like this. But if all that Butler is supposing is that there is an author of nature, who is intelligent and has purposes in what he has created, such a supposition is neither inconsistent nor absurd.

It does not help Butler's case here to notice that he goes on later to argue that God's governance is moral, so that the possibility that God is cruel or malevolent is to be ruled out subsequently. For the form Butler's later argument takes is one which assumes he has already shown that God teaches us by rewards and punishments, and in so doing equips us for the next life. All he adds to this is an argument that this divine plan has moral dimensions as well as prudential ones – that God equips us for the next life by making us potentially moral, as well as potentially prudent. For this argument to succeed, we must assume that *God's* actions, as distinct from ours, are already agreed to be moral and consistent.

The most we can concede is that if we assume an intelligent author of nature who has created a teleological system, and also assume the reality of a future life, it is not unreasonable to think that he teaches us to be prudent in this life by rewards and punishments, and in so doing helps us to prepare for the next – either because the next life will contain trials where our prudence will be needed, or because it will contain prizes for our earlier efforts; or, of course, both. This is not an unreasonable conclusion to draw, because it is not unreasonable to suppose that an intelligent author of a teleological system would have purposes which are consistent in the required ways. But although this is not unreasonable, Hume has taught us to see that equally reasonable, and less orthodox, speculations could fit the same observed facts of our world, even if God's intelligent governance is granted. We can agree, however, that Butler has succeeded so far in meeting his minimal objective of showing that someone who accepts deism and a future life is not irrational to expect that life to contain rewards and punishments which we can prepare for here. Since he is right to say that such a prospect is a vitally important one, he is right to insist that the very modest degree of likelihood we can accord to it is enough to show that the deists ought not to dismiss it. Tactically, since many deists assumed in practice that God's plans were consistent and benign, he should have seemed more persuasive than this to some of them.

What can we say about Butler's argument if we do not make the assumptions of his intended audience? Most fundamentally, we cannot say that the facts of life from which we know that we can learn are there *in order that* we should learn from them; for we cannot assume, and Butler has done nothing to show us, that there is any teleological ordering in nature at all. In our post-Darwinian age, it is intellectually adequate to recognise that our being here at all is a biological consequence of the fact that our remote ancestors found themselves able to learn from their environment and survived in it as a result. Human beings are in this world because they have learned; this does not show (even though it could be true) that they are here in part so *that they should* learn.

But this does not mean Butler has nothing to teach us if we see him as a source of purely defensive arguments whose purpose is to show that the Christian revelation is consistent with the facts of experience. To succeed in this, one has to show that if it were true that the Christian revelation indeed showed God's purposes to us, then we could expect the world to contain those phenomena we find around us, including those evils the Christian revelation emphasises. Part of the Christian proclamation is that our world is providentially governed, so that many aspects of it which are sheer given facts to the unbeliever, will properly represent intended opportunities in the light of Christian teaching. Since the Christian revelation does not represent God's purposes as being indiscriminately benevolent in the sense of sparing us suffering under every circumstance, but, on the contrary, as prizing states of mind and character which arise in response to suffering, we should expect to find our world containing unpleasant features that can provide a context in which such states of mind can be manifested, as well as pleasant features that can teach us other, easier things. It happens to be Butler's view that one of the states God wants us to cultivate is prudence, which Butler regards as a virtue. Not all Christians are as sure that prudence should be given this status. It is natural that Butler should select it as the first trait to consider, given the requirements of his anti-deistic argument. If these requirements are disregarded, we can still see, however, that what he says about it is otherwise a mere illustration of a particular form of apologetic that is influential today[2]: that our world is the way it is because God's central concern for us is that we should freely elect to become persons of a certain kind. If the emphasis is on our doing this (or failing to do it) *freely*, then it is not an argument against, but an argument for, this apologetic, that one can learn the wrong things, as well as the right ones, from the circumstances in which one finds oneself.

154

Someone who does not rate prudence highly can use the same apologetic, but maintain that prudence is one of the traits we should not cultivate; instead we should cultivate forbearance, meekness, and the willingness to go the second mile. Such an argument would have been hard for Butler to mount, since his deistic polemic required him to move from positions his non-Christian readers would accept to others that he had to assimilate to them. But a purely defensive apologist has no need to identify himself with secular morality – only to show that the values the Christian scheme espouses are, if ascribed to God, likely to lead to the sort of environment in which we find ourselves. (In fact, contemporary secular morality is, since the end of the nineteenth century, disinclined to admire prudence in any case.)

So I think we can say that Butler's argument in Chapter ii is one which, though claiming that certain observable features of our world make God's pedagogical governance likely, succeeds rather in illustrating a more successful apologetic procedure – the procedure of showing how the revelation he is defending can interpret salient aspects of human experience. He also teaches those who accept that revelation that they should be able to discern signs of the purposes they ascribe to God in the most unlikely places.

2

The next stage in Butler's argument, to which he devotes Chapter iii of Part I of the *Analogy*, is an attempt to show we have good reason to think that God's government is a moral one: that the system of rewards and punishments that connects this life with the next is one in which *virtue* is rewarded and *vice* punished, so that the cultivation of virtue in this life is the wisest preparation for the next. This stage is critical; but it is notable for an uneasy combination of two theses that are not wholly compatible with each other. The first, and more clear, thesis is that in this life God makes it plain that virtue has an inbuilt tendency to triumph over vice and adversity, and that we can infer, by analogy, that this tendency pervades both realms. This is very much like his contention in the moral Sermons that conscience and self-love point in the same direction. The second, and less clear, thesis is that God 'declares' in favour of virtue by building a bias towards it into our natures, so that we find it naturally unacceptable that it should *not* triumph over vice and adversity, even though it often seems not to do so. He connects these two theses by the claim that our natures make us uneasy in the presence of vice in ourselves and others, so that it is psychologically imprudent to be vicious. But there is bound to be tension between proclaiming that this life rewards virtue and punishes vice, and proclaiming that we are so constituted that we are unhappy when vice prospers: for the uneasiness that vice generates in us, even if it is a penalty attaching to vice, can only come about if vice has *not* been deterred.

Butler's case for the first thesis rests upon reminding us, first, that man is a part of the natural order, and then saying that man is more successful in this world if he lives in a virtuous society than if he does not. He points out that societies single out virtuous actions for rewards, and vicious actions for punishment, and in so doing show that they recognise the well-being of society to depend to a large degree upon the virtuous behaviour of its members. He emphasises that the rewards and punishments that society attaches to virtue and vice are themselves part of nature, since society is. He is very much aware that virtue does not always flourish, and that vice often seems to pay, for societies as well as for individuals, but he insists that there is an intrinsic strength attaching to virtue, both in individuals and in groups. To support this, he draws a comparison between virtue and reason. The fact that reason may lose a contest against brute force in some circumstances (where the contest is between a small number of rational agents on the one hand and a vast number of irrational creatures on the other) does not show that reason does not have an intrinsic superiority over force. Similarly, the fact that virtue often fails to prosper does not show that it is not intrinsically superior to vice. He supports this further by imagining a mythical kingdom that is perfectly virtuous; the reader is supposed to see that such a kingdom must come to rule the world.

I think these arguments are very weak. (1) It may be true that society singles out virtuous actions for reward, and vicious ones for punishment; but this does not show, to begin with, that society is thereby rewarding virtue *as such*, as Butler puts it, or is punishing vice *as such*, unless this is merely a way of saying that virtue has to be correctly identified and not confused with other states that simulate it. If a society wants to encourage virtue because of its beneficial effects, this is consistent with its also valuing virtue for itself; but it is equally consistent with its not caring about it one way or the other except as a means to the social benefits it brings. Honesty in business may be prized as leading to prosperity, without being valued for itself alone, as Plato saw. Butler is, of course, right in saying that a society that is anxious, for economic reasons, to encourage honesty in business, has to be able to recognise it and not confuse it with its mere appearance, but this does not mean that when it finds it and rewards it, it shows it values honesty *per se*. That would depend on whether or not it would continue to prize it if no connection between honesty and prosperity could be established. (2) It is notorious that a society with high internal standards of conduct may have very low external standards. These can be combined very readily by the use of some convenient public hypocrisy, which allows a country held together by honest dealings between its own citizens to gain pros-

156

perity by behaving agressively to other nations and plundering their
wealth. This is known as imperialism. The very success of virtue often
comes about through the imposition of severe limitations on the sphere
of its exercise. (3) As Hughes points out, within a society many of the
beneficiaries of virtue are themselves not examples of it, and many of
the exemplars of it may not be its beneficiaries. Robber-baron tycoons
may prosper because of an honesty in their underlings which they themselves do not practise.[3] (4) There is less substance than there appears to
be in the claim that virtue, or reason for that matter, has an intrinsic
tendency to prevail over the forces which sometimes defeat it. If this
means merely that virtue, and reason, are useful weapons in the battle
for survival and prosperity, then the case for this is strong – although
the case for reason looks considerably stronger than the case for virtue.
But the wording suggests it means more than this. The example of a
small number of rational agents falling to a horde of irrational brutes
shows that reason is only overcome when faced with an *immoderate*, or
exceptionally large, amount of force, and this amounts to little more
than the question-begging statement that reason will only lose out when
the powers that happen to defeat it are present in greater degree than
they have any right to be! (5) The myth of the virtuous kingdom (I iii
21/29) is quite ineffective if we read it as the kind of appeal Butler says
it is. Such a kingdom, he tells us, 'would plainly be superior to all others,
and the world must gradually come under its empire'. There are few
obvious inductive grounds for such a judgment, if we treat it as an
assertion about how the world has been seen to progress in history. It
is hard to suppose that this myth is not a thinly disguised introduction
of the idea of the Kingdom of God. But the proclamation of the Kingdom
of God was, and is, a proclamation that the defeats righteousness suffers
will be overcome in some imminent future domain. This proclamation
explicitly appeals to the morality of God's government in a way that
Butler, who is still supposed to be offering us an independent case for
believing in it, cannot imitate.

So Butler makes a poor case for holding that the present life rewards
virtue and punishes vice, even though there is no reason to doubt him
when he tells us that virtue often strengthens individuals and societies,
and vice often weakens them. I turn now to his second thesis, that our
natures have an inbuilt bias towards virtue and away from vice, and that
this shows that God 'declares' for virtue and against vice. In part this is
a reassertion of what he tells us in the moral Sermons about the authority
of conscience. But the import of his making this assertion again here is
not clear.

To some extent it appears to be intended to supply supplementary
evidence for the first thesis. In so far as this is so, Butler's argument is
not hard to follow, or to evaluate. He tells us that acting virtuously

generates a special kind of satisfaction that is distinct from the satisfaction of those wants which the virtuous action is initially intended to fulfil. He expresses this, once again, by saying that we value virtue and deplore vice, as such. If we combine what he says here with the Dissertation on Virtue, we can say that his position is this. For the most part, each and every action that I perform is the outcome of some inclination, or 'affection'. To say of any such action that it is a virtuous one is not ever to deny this prior fact about it, but to say also that it is an action that is enjoined, or at the very least allowed, by conscience. This view implies that sometimes the judgment of conscience will be enough of itself to prompt me to do what it judges to be right, even though it will not be necessary to resort to this purely moral motive in the case of most virtuous actions. Most morally good actions are actions to which we have an inclination irrespective of their morally good character. This analysis makes it likely that the performance of a virtuous action will please us in two distinct ways. It will satisfy the inclination that initially gave rise to it, and it will also give us the satisfaction of having done what we see to be right. The situation with vicious actions is only partly analogous. They too are generated by inclinations, and will satisfy those inclinations and so give us pleasure. But this pleasure is likely to be offset by our recognition that we have done something which our consciences forbid. Butler speculates briefly on the possibility of there being a pleasure in having acted viciously to correspond to the pleasure at having acted virtuously, and says merely that if there is such a pleasure, it is clearly 'monstrous'. If the moral character of a vicious action produces any hedonic tone at all, therefore, it is likely to be negative, and to spoil the pleasure of satisfied inclination by mixing it with 'uneasiness'.

So Butler wishes to use the existence of moral satisfaction and remorse as additional evidence that virtue is rewarded and vice punished, since these inner results often follow from them. As evidence for this conclusion, these facts are of only modest value, because they are offset by two other facts. One is that heeding our consciences causes us not to satisfy inclinations that run counter to them, and this generates its own irritation and resentment in less-than-perfect souls. Another is the fact, which Butler admits himself, that the degree to which we feel remorse at vicious actions does not correlate well with our need for reform: the person who feels most remorse at vicious acts he has performed is not the person who is hardened in his vice, but one who has at least begun to shed it – one, that is, whose conscience is beginning to win him over. So remorse is as much a consequence of virtue as it is of vice. Although Butler admits this, he does not seem to think it matters very much; but if his argument is, as it seems to be, an attempt to connect virtue with satisfaction and vice with unease in the way we connect exercise with health and drinking with headaches, then it affects its success considerably.

I do not think, however, that in this part of Chapter iii (paragraphs 10–16/13–21) this is all that Butler is up to. In particular, let us consider the following vital passage:

> It is not pretended but that in the natural course of things, happiness and misery appear to be distributed by other rules, than only the personal merit and demerit of characters. They may sometimes be distributed by way of mere discipline. There may be the wisest and best reasons, why the world should be governed by general laws, from whence such promiscuous distribution perhaps must follow; and also why our happiness and misery should be put in each other's power, in the degree which they are. And these things, as in general they contribute to the rewarding virtue and punishing vice, as such: so they often contribute also, not to the inversion of this, which is impossible; but to the rendering persons prosperous, though wicked; afflicted, though righteous; and, which is worse, to the *rewarding some actions*, though vicious, and *punishing other actions*, though virtuous. But all this cannot drown out the voice of Nature in the conduct of Providence, plainly declaring itself for virtue, by way of distinction from vice, and preference to it. For our being so constituted as that virtue and vice are thus naturally favoured and discountenanced, rewarded and punished respectively as such, is an intuitive proof of the intent of Nature, that it should be so: otherwise the constitution of our minds, from which it thus immediately and directly proceeds, would be absurd. But it cannot be said, because virtuous actions are sometimes punished, and vicious actions rewarded, that Nature intended it. For, though this great disorder is brought about, as all actions are done, by means of some natural passion; yet *this may be*, as it undoubtedly is, brought about by the perversion of such passion, implanted in us for other, and those very good purposes. And indeed these and other good purposes, even of every passion, may be clearly seen. (*An* I iii 15/20)

This passage makes it clear that we do less than justice to Butler's case in Chapter iii if we only consider his attempts to show that the personal and social consequences of virtue are mainly good in this life. There is another appeal in this paragraph also, and it is one that is present thoughout his treatment of this theme. The problem is to identify it accurately. To do this we must first note, once again, two features of Butler's position.

First, his apologetic strategy towards the deists requires him to make a case for God's moral government of the world, but also to make it clear (and not merely *concede*) that the reality of his moral government is frequently concealed by events like the sufferings of the virtuous. Only such a stance can make use of analogous ambiguities in God's natural government (such as the waste of animal lives), and only such a stance can provide a basis for looking to the next life to remove the moral ambiguities of this one. For such a stance to be plausible, however, we have to be persuaded that the negative facts we encounter can be identified as 'perversion' of the right and proper natural order – as *unnatural* phenomena. The difficulty is not so great if God's moral goodness is taken as given. But here it is not. So Butler has to look elsewhere for the basis of the judgment that the morally negative features of our world are perversions of divine teleology.

Second, we must be quite clear what is meant when Butler speaks of God's moral government. It includes two distinguishable elements. The first of these is the doctrine that human beings are so constituted by God that they are taught what virtue requires and have the freedom and power to follow this instruction in practice. This is Butler's familiar doctrine of conscience and its place in human nature, viewed as an instance of God's teleological government. This is reiterated, rather than re-argued, in this part of the *Analogy*. The second element is the doctrine that God apportions happiness to virtue (and misery to vice). It is the second element that is problematic at this stage of Butler's argument, rather than the first. The fact that we reward virtue, and punish vice, is not, as we have seen, a sure sign of the truth of Butler's teaching about the moral constitution of human nature, but it is still a plausible inference from it. It is not so clearly plausible, however, to say that the same fact shows that *God* apportions happiness to virtue; for although Butler is quite right to insist that we are part of nature, the extent to which virtue prospers depends on much more than the presence of conscience in us. It also depends on the extent to which we choose to follow it in our dealings with the virtuous, and it depends on many circumstances beyond our control, such as physical health, natural forces, and the limits of our knowledge.

In the passage quoted, Butler tells us that the moral constitution of human nature is itself a clear sign that God apportions happiness to virtue. Here he does not seem to mean that we feel better when we follow our consciences, and worse when we violate them. We have already commented on that argument. Here he says that if God did not apportion happiness to virtue, the moral constitution of human nature would be 'absurd'. How are we to interpret this? I suggest there are two possible readings.

The first reading is that God could have no purpose in creating human beings with natures that are morally constituted as ours are, if he did not also intend to apportion happiness to virtue. This argument cannot stand examination. Let us assume that a God who constitutes our nature morally and also apportions happiness to virtue, is one who conforms to the Christian view of what God is. Let us also assume that a world in which we are constituted morally, but where happiness is not regularly apportioned to virtue, is an *unfair* world. What Butler has to show us is that we have good enough reason to think the world is not unfair in this way. But there is every reason to suppose that it is. We must remember that Butler's view of conscience would require us to say that we should follow it, that is, be virtuous, even if the world *is* unfair. He has done nothing to show that we do not live in a world ordered by a God who values virtue in us, and therefore encourages us to practise it by giving us consciences, but feels no obligation to see that every time we do practise it, we prosper. Fostering virtue may only be one of his purposes, and it may be one that he feels is adequately fulfilled if there are some virtuous creatures in the world, whether they prosper through their virtue or not. In the language of Butler's moral philosophy, while self-love may only gain expression if we are taught what is good for us by rewards and punishments, the fact that conscience can tell us what is right or wrong without scrutiny of consequences may indicate that God wishes us to follow it, but takes no care to reward us if we do. It is even possible to speculate that God's purposes are still less fair than this: that he sometimes finds the travails of virtue amusing. To say that such theoretical possibilities are impossible is to *assume* that God's government is moral in the Christian manner, and it is this very thing for which Butler is seeking evidence.

A second, less likely, reading is that the moral constitution of our natures in some way includes an intuitive recognition that happiness and virtue are ultimately apportioned (not merely that it would be unfair if they were not). On this view our natures enable us to perceive the 'necessary tendency' for virtue to succeed and vice fail, and to recognise occasions when they do not as natural, not merely moral, anomalies. If this is what Butler means, it must, in its turn, be divided into two possible doctrines. It might be a claim that God would not permit us to intuit the ultimate fairness of the world unless the world were a fair one. But this would be, once more, an appeal to the morality of God's government rather than an argument for it. For a God who wanted us to be virtuous, but did not see fit to make this world a fair place, might well so constitute us that we were enabled to act virtuously more frequently than we might otherwise be, by being gifted with a natural (though false) conviction that virtue prospers. There are many signs in Butler's system that he thinks we need such reassurance, and that his claim that conscience and self-love coincide is his attempt to support it; but as far as the present argument goes, it might well be that we were naturally endowed with the conviction of the world's fairness, for purposes which did not include its reality. I think it is more likely, however, that Butler is appealing directly *to* this intuition, rather than arguing from the supposed fact of it. This would put him in good company: one is reminded of Socrates' conviction that a good man cannot be harmed. If that is what he is about, he is departing from his announced procedure of appealing to evidence, since the evidence is clear and strong that sometimes good men (such as Socrates himself) are harmed, and harmed exceedingly. A principle that helps to reassure us in the presence of unpleasant facts cannot be inferred from the facts alone, but has to be known independently. Another reason for supposing that Butler might be appealing to this common intuition is the weight he places upon the allegedly obvious triumph of a wholly virtuous kingdom (*An* I iii 21/29–30). We are supposed to need no argument to see that such a society would come to reign supreme in the world. In fact, any conviction that this would be so would not only lack support from secular history; it would depend upon a prior acceptance of the New Testament proclamations, or of a claim like that of Socrates.

I would argue further that the demands of his anti-deistic apologetic have led Butler into misunderstanding the real function of an appeal to the conviction that virtue will win out in the end – if, indeed, he is making that appeal here. We do not need to believe in the ultimate triumph of virtue in order to see that the claims of virtue apply to us. Here the deontologists like Prichard have always been right, and for all his talk of the coincidence of conscience and self-love, Butler is at one with them. Nor is the belief that virtue will triumph one which it is necessary to have in order to *be* virtuous, for there have been many who have held on to the demands of morality in the face of ill-fortune; though in trying to persuade the more unspiritual of his contemporaries to take morality and religion seriously, Butler sometimes talks as though this is so. The belief that virtue must win out has a more fundamental function, that is certainly central to the proclamation of the Kingdom of God. This is the function of reassuring the hard-pressed moral agent that what he does will not go for nothing, that his achievements will not be lost in spite of contrary appearances. It is an antidote to despair about the satisfaction of moral objectives, not to frustrated prudence.

On its own terms, the argument of Chapter iii is largely a failure. Even assuming a divine intelligence and a future life, Butler has not succeeded in making an observational case for believing that the cultivation of virtue has the key importance as preparation for the next world that he says it has. In trying to make amends for the evidential weakness of his case, Butler has indirectly made clear the moral core of the Christian eschatology towards which his argument is intended to carry us: the claim that our moral struggles here are not hopeless, since the failures and obstacles we encounter are not permanent parts of God's order, but features of the present life which will be corrected in the later scheme of things and subsumed within the understanding of that order which we may ultimately expect. This claim, by its very content, makes appeal to wider considerations than Butler can properly introduce within the confines of his anti-deist polemic, or indeed of any form of 'natural religion'. Having introduced it, however, he is able to appeal to the pedagogical comparisons he has used before to show how this vision of human life provides us with a more specific way of approaching those obstacles and trials which we find in this life. He is able to introduce the apologetically fruitful concept of probation.

3

In Chapters iv and v of Part I of the *Analogy*, Butler produces a set of arguments designed to persuade the deist that the next life is not merely one in which God rewards and punishes us for our conduct in this one, but is also one for which we need opportunities to prepare ourselves here by developing dispositions which the next life will require of us. In spite of his aversion to merely speculative theology, he makes an important suggestion about why a creator whose government is moral places us in situations where virtue has such a difficult time of it. The suggestion is that the difficulties virtue encounters are necessary for its real possession: that to fit ourselves for the next world, we have to confirm our possession of virtue by *exercising* it. Hence this life is a period of probation, or testing. Those who pass the tests it imposes are fit for the next life, and those who do not, are not. His position incorporates at least the outline of a theodicy. I shall first sketch his argument in these two chapters, and then comment on its strengths and weaknesses.

He returns, first, to the fact that God has placed us in a world where our well-being is partly in our own hands. This means that we are able to make ourselves happy or miserable by our own choices. If we confine ourselves in the first place to purely prudential considerations, we find that we have a nature which embodies inclinations and aversions which, though not of themselves harmful, need to be under the control of prudence, or self-love. There is, for example, nothing intrinsically harmful about a natural desire for food, or possessions, or sex, or a natural aversion to pain or injury; but for our actions to lead to our welfare, we have to ensure that we follow these desires or aversions only when doing so is to our benefit. Inevitably there will be times when the desires or aversions will arise inopportunely: these will be times when circumstances present us with objects we naturally find attractive, or prospects we naturally dislike, and our desires or aversions are aroused accordingly, but should not be indulged. There are both internal and external sources of 'trial' or temptation. We need to make our choices in such ways that inopportune inclinations do not get the better of us over time because we have not built up a resistance to them when we could. We need to develop the right dispositions in order to prosper. What is true of our prudential development is equally true of our moral development. If we are prepared to agree that God has made us so that we need to develop a prudent character to prosper, we have no reason to reject the religious claim that he subjects us to moral temptations so that we can develop good moral character also.

But the religious claim that Butler is pressing is that God wishes us to develop good moral character 'as the requisite qualification for a future state of security and happiness' (*An* I v 1/2). So he draws an analogy between the way in which our early years can equip us to deal with the demands of adult life, and the way in which, according to religion, our life here can equip us to enter the life to come. All species of which we have knowledge, he says, are endowed with the capacity to develop abilities which are necessary for their mature ways of life; these latter abilities do not attend them at once, but have to be built up. An essential part of this development in our own case is the formation of *habits*. These may be passive (as in habits of perception such as the nearly unconscious ways in which we come to respond to sensory cues in distance perception) or active, when we respond to the demands of our environment by habitual outward behaviour. This behaviour will consist of *actions*, but actions which we have become accustomed to perform. As we grow accustomed to performing them, we will be less and less involved in lively reflection, or in emotional responses to the situations that require them; but this will serve to reinforce, not weaken, our capacity to act effectively. For example, the recognition of danger will generate fear, and this in turn will make us careful to respond wisely to the danger; but when such response becomes habitual, this lessens the fear. Similarly, perceiving distress in others generates pity and leads to charitable actions; when these become habitual, the practical response to the distress of others is reinforced, but the inner suffering associated with pity lessens. We acquire a facility in action, while losing the need for lengthy reflection, great effort, or emotional attachment.

The early years of life are the years in which those habits we need in order to meet the challenges of the adult world can be built up, by a combination of training from others and effort from ourselves. Similarly, we have reason to suppose that our present life taken as a whole is suited to be a period of preparation and discipline to fit us for the next, since this life is one in which we can develop good moral habits and consolidate them in the face of temptations and difficulties. Butler is careful not to speculate about the nature of the next world, but he emphasises that if we expect it to be a 'happy community', it may still be a realm where we will need the virtues that the trials of this life can consolidate.

He makes clear how this could be so. Our nature makes us chronically liable to temptation, so that a habit of virtuous decision-making is always necessary; he even says that 'it is scarce possible to avoid supposing' that these features will always be present, even in the next life. Temptation is an inevitable consequence of the fact that we are so constituted that we 'have in our inward frame various affections towards particular external objects'. These desires and aversions are amenable to the direction of reason (that is, to self-love and conscience), but their amenability consists in the fact that self-love and conscience can permit or forbid their gratification. They do not permit or forbid their *occurrence*, since this is a function of the presence of the external objects to which they are naturally directed. So when these objects present themselves, even though they 'cannot be obtained innocently', we are still liable to find ourselves *wanting* them. So even the most controlled person is liable to be tried by temptations:

> And when the objects of any affection whatever cannot be obtained without unlawful means; but may be obtained by them: such affection, though its being excited, and its continuing some time in the mind, be as innocent as it is natural and necessary; yet cannot but be conceived to have a tendency to incline persons to venture upon such unlawful means: and therefore must be conceived as putting them in some danger of it. Now what is the security against this danger, against their actually deviating from right? As the danger is, so also must the security be, from within: from the practical principle of virtue. (*An* I v 13/23–4)

The very structure of our natures, then, leads even the best of us to the disturbances of temptation. From his previous remarks about the way in which the formation of habits lessens the turmoil associated with the proper response to trials, we can see that Butler does not wish to deny that virtue lessens inner stress; indeed, its very essence is to make the right choices easier. But it is also clear that even when thinking about the next life, he supposes that there will always be some inner disturbance potentially attendant upon right choices. It is just that the more nearly perfect an agent is, the less this disturbance is liable to interfere with his choices. He argues at some length that 'creatures without blemish, as they came out of the hands of God', can easily be understood to be tempted into wrongdoing, and to need the fortification of moral virtue. So creatures like ourselves, whose characters have all been harmed by some degree of wrongdoing, need this discipline even more. He commits himself, then, to the view that the disturbances of temptation, as distinct from the sin of yielding to it, are inevitable features of human nature, not merely likely ones.

So the essence of probation is protracted resistance to temptation, born of a clear awareness of the danger of yielding. Butler says that virtue does not always require self-denial, since what virtue teaches us to do may sometimes be attractive to us in itself; but self-denial is necessary for 'discipline and improvement'. So the consolidation of virtue requires the exercise of good dispositions over a period of time.

Butler's position on the place of probation in the building of character suggests one possible resolution of an ambiguity I have noted in his theological scheme. This is the ambiguity concerning the relationship between this life and the next. At times his argument suggests that the future life will be one in which we are free of the sufferings and setbacks that we endure in this life. At other times it suggests that the future life will have trials and difficulties of its own to match those we encounter here. On the surface, the former sort of future life would need strong moral character less than the latter sort; but the latter sort would embody fewer rewards than the former. This might be resolved by utilising Butler's view that a being with desires or aversions can always experience temptation. For such a being, temptation can arise easily in a world without pain or disease or danger: it would be temptation to such things as covetousness, discontent, or nostalgia for vicious excesses. A world without suffering or struggle could then generate what Hick has called 'the problem of heavenly boredom'.[4] However trouble-free the next life is, persons without characters that enabled them to enjoy its goods would suffer mental torment and disorientation. Hence a perfect future life would require the right sort of pre-built character for its proper enjoyment, not merely as a ticket of entry. It could, equally, be a place of punishment for the wrongly-disposed.

Butler considers two objections to his doctrine of probation. The first is that although some people respond to temptation by improving in virtue, others respond in the opposite way, and make their present state 'a discipline of vice'. Butler emphasises that he has not sought to explain all the evils in the world, but merely tried to show that many of them provide an opportunity for moral development if we will avail ourselves of it:

> That which appears amidst the general corruption is, that there are
> some persons, who, having within them the principle of amendment
> and recovery, attend to and follow the notices of virtue and religion,
> be they more clear or more obscure, which are afforded them; and
> that the present world is, not only an exercise of virtue in these
> persons, but an exercise of it in ways and degrees, peculiarly apt
> to improve it: apt to improve it, in some respects, even beyond what
> would be, by the exercise of it required in a perfectly virtuous
> society, or in a society of equally imperfect virtue with themselves.
> But that the present world does not actually become a state of moral
> discipline to many, even to the generality, i.e. that they do not

improve or grow better in it, cannot be urged as a proof, that it was not intended for moral discipline, by any who at all observe the analogy of Nature. (*An* I v 18/34)

He says that the high mortality among the young of plants and animals does not prove that seeds and infants were not intended to develop into healthy adult plants and beasts – even though we may be puzzled at the fact that so many of them fail to develop at all.

The second objection he considers is that the scheme he discerns in our present world is in fact one that would only generate ostensibly virtuous behaviour, caused by hope and fear, rather than genuine virtue. His answer appears to be that habitual performance of actions that virtue requires begets the genuine article itself, and that the habitual doing of the will of God, and refusal to act resentfully in the face of misfortunes, begets an inner attitude of submission to God – even though, in both cases, the original motives behind the right behaviour may be self-regarding. These are both, to say the least, questionable assertions. The general issue of how far prudential considerations can lead anyone into a true form of religious life is difficult and important; but Butler need not tangle with it here. For his argument has merely been that we can discern this life to be a place where we can acquire the habit of following the dictates of virtue, and that this will serve to prepare us for the next life. This argument does not depend upon assuming that the motive for following the dictates of virtue is self-interest. To assume this would be to suppose that because (as Butler thinks) self-love and conscience point in the same way, the man who follows conscience must also be motivated by self-love. Butler's case for the value of habituation would hold just as well if the reasons for choosing right actions were conscientious ones as if they were selfish ones: in both cases people are tempted by contrary desires to do otherwise, and refusing to yield once makes it easier to act well the next time.

Butler's discussion of probation is one of the most carefully presented and extensive parts of his religious apologetic. If we consider it as an argument directed to a deist who admits a future life, I think we must admit that it has some force. It amounts to saying that if such a thinker holds that our moral intuitions are given, or at least sanctioned, by God, he is better able to make sense of the fact that we do not always appear to prosper by following them if he defers the expectation of prosperity or reward to the next life, and sees the adversities of this life as a training-ground for those willing to respond to them appropriately. Morality and self-interest look much more likely to be coincident if the next world is included in one's calculations, than if it is not. A similar message can be expressed another way: just as the apparent wastage of nature is baffling for anyone who discerns the workings of divine intelligence in the natural order, so the apparent failure of morality to pay off is a problem for those who see God's plan as a moral one. But if the notion of probation is introduced, the divine plan as a whole looks more obviously moral; and the apparent moral wastage in human life becomes more readily intelligible than the natural wastage of the vegetable and animal kingdom is for someone who sees the perpetuation of species as a sign of God's intelligence at work in nature. Since the most reticent deist seemed to concede the latter, the Christian scheme of things should have been easier for him to consider.

Good or bad, however, this argument is of little value to those post-Humean readers who are unsure of that which the deist would have accepted. But it is clear that for such readers the probationary view of our state is one which can still have considerable apologetic usefulness, if it is offered purely defensively. Let us assume, with Butler, that the Christian proclamation is of a God who wants us to practise 'virtue'. Whatever this notion includes, it certainly must embrace the consistent (rather than the merely occasional) performance of morally obligatory actions. For someone who is told this, the fact that those who most exemplify virtue are not the ones who prosper most, is a theological problem. Part of the answer to the problem is that God will value the exercise, and not merely the nominal possession, of virtue – so that there have to be occasions which require fortitude and resignation and forgiveness and courage and integrity. These will, necessarily, be occasions where there are actual evils to which the virtuous person is responding. So some evils will have to exist in order that the states which God is said to value and enjoin can be exercised. In the face of those occasions, easy success is not enough, since the exercise of real courage is (again, necessarily) exercise of unflinching behaviour in the face of significant danger and stress. So virtue is not merely consolidated by being practised in the face of ongoing adversities, but to some degree logically requires them.

A second part of the answer is that virtue is a disposition to act in certain ways, and if that is so, it is always possible for the agent who acts in those ways to choose to act in other ways. So it is logically impossible for God to have created an order in which we have opportunities to exercise the virtues without also having created an order in which we have opportunities to exercise the vices.

A third part of the answer is that when the two features of our world just outlined combine to produce anomalies which are inconsistent with the justice the Christian ascribes to God, it is necessary for him to invoke the further Christian claim that such injustices, though their origin is intelligible, need to be corrected. For this a further realm, either of reward and punishment, or of continued moral progression, has to be expected as a consequence of the allegedly just nature of God. For example, the fact that some people choose to act viciously rather than virtuously in the face of their temptations and opportunities may create a situation in which others are confronted with adversities which are overwhelming and not merely probationary. For them, forced to live out the evil consequences of the freedom of others, a future state of regeneration and opportunity might be required. Such speculations are of course no more than possibilities. What is not speculative is that certain understandings of what God's general purposes might include, would render intelligible some of the evils which human beings have to undergo; but that they could not do so without its being held that God's providence extends into another life. To say this is not to say that such a cosmic scheme is true; only that, if it is true, the world would be, in these respects, about the sort of place that it is. To argue this is to present the sort of cosmic scheme that Butler outlines for us, but to present it as a defence of Christian theism to a sceptical audience; not as a probable hypothesis about the observed order to a deist.

VII

Revelation and Miracle

When Butler moves on, in Part II of the *Analogy*, to make his case for revealed religion, we might expect him to concentrate on the special evidences in history and Scripture that have been the standard bases of argument for Christian apologists both before and since. Had he done this, Part II would have suffered gravely from the fact that it pre-dates the whole of modern critical biblical scholarship. In keeping with his modest defensive stance, he does not do this. Only Chapter vii of Part II is addressed directly to these evidences, and even there the treatment is one that involves him in general considerations that we would class as philosophical ones. Most of Part II is designed to answer popular attacks on the credibility of Christian revelation, and most of these are arguments which would cause their hearers to disregard the evidences rather than scrutinise them carefully. In Butler's language, they are arguments that state 'presumptions' against the reality of any revelation, and arguments that point to alleged failings in the 'scheme' or content of the Christian revelation in particular. Butler uses all the dialectical powers at his command to change the attitude of his opponents. He considers this attitude to be frivolous, since if there is any chance at all that the Christian revelation is true, nothing could be more important than attending to it. He also considers it to be presumptuous, in that they are prepared to lay down *a priori* standards that revelation has to meet, without regard to the inevitable mysteriousness of divine things and the manifest limits of human understanding. He therefore emphasises the pragmatic importance of Christian claims, and tries to show that if the mysteriousness of God and the limits of the human mind are taken into account, the supposed defects in the Christian revelation are to be expected, and are not the barriers they are said to be. His procedure parallels that of Pascal, whose eloquent accounts of human weakness and of the limits of the human intellect are designed to get his reader to 'listen to God' and not be deterred by the obscurities which this weakness and those limits help make intelligible.[1]

The criticisms that Butler seeks to answer are typified by the following passage from Tindal:

> As far as divine wisdom exceeds human, so far the divine laws must excel human laws in clearness and perspicuity; as well as other perfections. Whatever is confused and perplexed, can never come from the clear fountain of all knowledge; nor that which is obscure from the father of inexhaustible light; and as far as you suppose God's laws are not plain to any part of mankind, so far you derogate from the perfection of those laws, and the wisdom and the goodness of the divine legislator.[2]

Both the tone and the content of this pronouncement exemplify Butler's target. The tone is the dismissive over-confidence expressed in the 'must' and 'can never'; the content is the dogmatic imposition of criteria which alleged revelations have to satisfy. They cannot be obscure. They cannot be less than plain to everyone. And, as this passage goes on to tell us, they cannot present us with moral difficulties. Butler directs his skills at the following criticisms in particular: that Christian revelation depends on miracles, and that miracles are incredible; that it lays great stress on the fulfilment of prophecies, and these are dubious and obscure; that it contains morally objectionable elements, such as the story of Abraham's being commanded to sacrifice Isaac, or of the Israelites being commanded to slaughter the Canaanites; that the key interpretative concept of Christ's mediation is obscure and morally questionable; and, most fundamental of all, that the Christian revelation is not clear and decisive and available to everyone, but has been made available only to some, and to them in differing degrees. I shall not attempt to trace all Butler's detailed defences. It is clearly the defence against the last criticism that concerns him the most, and engages his finest reflections. I shall defer what he says about it (which involves large tracts of Part I as well as of Part II) until the next chapter, where I shall deal with his position on human ignorance, and his version of what I have called the Parity Argument. In this chapter, I shall deal with his defences against some of the other, more specific difficulties. I confine myself to the defences of miracle, prophecy, and the doctrine of Christ's mediation. The space I accord to them will be due to their relative prominence in later philosophical discussion (which naturally prompts most attention to miracles), and to their relative accessibility to philosophical, as opposed to theological, comment (which permits less attention to the concept of mediation and atonement than these demand for Butler himself).

A final procedural remark. The criticisms Butler answers were mostly made by deists like Tindal. Here, as in Part I, Butler always has them in mind, and frequently reminds them that he has already shown that the beliefs about God's purposes which he shares with them require the recognition of obscurities in our understanding of the way God governs nature; he never tires of saying that these obscurities are often no less than these very deists object to in revelation. This argument, fair enough as applied to them, is irrelevant, most of the time, to the modern reader. In my judgment, however, the deistic presuppositions affect the value of the argument of Part II less often than that of Part I. This is because most of the criticisms are easily recast into a form that does not presuppose the truth of those propositions to which the deists were committed. One example will suffice: Tindal claims to know that God is the fount of all wisdom and desires human happiness for our sake, seeking nothing for himself. From all this he infers that if there were revelation, it could not be like the Christian one, because it would be universally available and free from obscurity. Someone who does not believe that God exists, or, therefore, that he is the fount of all wisdom and the rest, can still criticise Christian claims by saying that if there were the wholly good and loving God proclaimed within the Christian revelation, he would not have allowed such knowledge of himself to be as partial and obscure as it is. Butler's responses to this recast argument would undoubtedly have been much the same as they are when addressed in the form of a *tu quoque* argument to critics like Tindal. Their force, then, does not pass away with the doctrines held by the deists, but is still considerable. Indeed, arguments like Butler's are still common among apologists.

1

Of all the topics in philosophy of religion, that of miracles is the hardest to discuss without constant reference to Hume, whose treatment is generally taken to have defined the problems that belief in miracles has to face. There is no doubt that one of Hume's unstated objectives is to answer Butler. There is also no doubt that it is anachronistic to read Butler as though he is trying to answer Hume! I shall not attempt to avoid the questions that Hume raises, though I shall not expound or criticise him directly.

Butler discusses miracles in three places in Part II of the *Analogy*. The first is in Chapter ii, which has the title 'Of the supposed Presumption against a Revelation, considered as miraculous'. The second, very brief, discussion is in paragraph 4/4 of Chapter iv, where Butler makes the suggestion that although miracles are contrary to natural law, they might still be instances of supernatural law. The fullest discussion occurs in Chapter vii, where Butler deals at length with the historical evidences for the miracle-stories of Christianity. Hume's section 'Of Miracles'[3] is divided into two parts, of which the first addresses the general issues raised by Butler in the first two passages I have referred to, and the second examines the quality of the testimony to the miraculous that is actually available to us.

As we all know, Hume's conclusion is 'that no human testimony can have such force as to prove a miracle, and make it a just foundation for any . . . system of religion'. While he defines what a miracle is partly in terms of the agency of God, he is at pains to evaluate the likelihood of miracles without assuming that there is a God to perform them, and insists that it has to be judged solely in terms of the possibility of events that are contrary to natural law, and of the quality of the testimony to their occurrence. The testimony is to be judged 'not as the word or testimony of God himself, but as the production of a mere human writer and historian'. Hume assumes that the 'system of religion' with which the miracles are connected will be established *from* the miracles, not vice versa. What he says undoubtedly undermines the force of many of Butler's detailed remarks, but Hume himself is quite aware that Butler's arguments are made in a quite different context; and when we judge them we should be also.

Butler assumes that he and his readers agree that God exists; and, by this point in the book, he also thinks he has shown that there is a good case for believing that God's government is moral and will include a future life. Now most modern readers would assume that anyone who believed all this would have good reason to think the likelihood of miracles to be much greater than it could be if one did not believe any of it. If God exists, it might well be that he has special purposes that lead him to intervene in nature occasionally. Hume goes to some trouble to make it clear that he is not discussing the credibility of miracles in this way. Butler's purpose is very different. He was writing for an audience that claimed to believe in God, but to think that a rational belief in God *undermined* the credibility of miracles -- because, for example, they thought God would have created a world in which he did not need to intervene, or because they thought that there is no lesson a miracle can teach us that we cannot be taught better without miracles. Butler is trying to show readers who believed in God but rejected miracles that they had no good reason to do so. In arguing against them, he says many things about testimony and evidence that are open to Hume's criticisms. But he is not trying to do what Hume said cannot be done, namely to prove miracles and make them a foundation for a system of religion. He is trying to show that those who already accept part of the Christian system of religion on philosophical grounds, have no good reason to deny that the miracle-stories of Christianity support the remainder of that system.

But this leads us to an important likeness between Butler and Hume: both take it for granted that the credibility of the Christian miracle-

173

stories is important, because *if* the miracles were genuine they *would* 'prove' Christian doctrines. Since Hume is consciously proceeding on the assumption that there is none of the independent reason for expecting miracles that Butler believes there is, he naturally has a more stringent view of what would be needed to establish one; but both take it for granted that if miracles *have* taken place, they prove at least some of the doctrines of Christianity to be true. Neither imagines, it seems, that the miracle-stories could be true but Christianity false. (In Hume's case this comes out in his famous argument that the miracle-stories of the different religions cancel each other out, since if the stories of one religion are true, the other religions are thereby disproved, and their stories cannot then be true also.)

Neither Butler nor Hume says much that is helpful about *how* the occurrence of a miracle would serve to prove a religious doctrine, although Butler, as we might expect, says more than Hume does. Butler tells us that miracles *attest* Christianity (*An* II vii 4/3); he also says:

the fact itself is allowed, that Christianity obtained, i.e. was professed to be received in the world, upon the belief of miracles, immediately in the age in which it is said those miracles were wrought: or that this is what its first converts would have alleged, as the reason for their embracing it. (*An* II vii 10/8)

While Butler certainly thinks there are miracles other than those covered by these observations, we can assume that the miracles ascribed in the New Testament to Jesus and the Apostles are paradigms. He says that the early Christians were willing to face death for their beliefs, and must therefore have been totally convinced of the reality of the miracles attributed to them. Whatever value this argument has in persuading later readers that the miracles really took place, it has an important assumption built into it: that someone convinced of the reality of these miracles (whether through witnessing them, or through hearing reports of them) is not in a position rationally to reject the teachings of those who performed them. There is every reason to suppose that Hume agreed with this assumption. We can say, then, that for Butler, and probably for Hume also, a miracle, if it ever happens, is an event with a rationally overwhelming pedagogical force.

We can go further in unpacking the notion of 'attestation'. I think it implies that the miraculous event must itself be an illustration of the doctrines it supposedly supports, in the way, for example, that the healing miracles are illustrations of the love or mercy of God; and that a miracle would, therefore, be an event that somehow involved the resolution of some major human problem or concern, so that merely spectacular or intriguing events would not count as miracles. (If my shoelaces tied themselves up tomorrow morning merely on my command, this would be magic and not miracle, because it would be a *pointless* occurrence.) The notion of attestation implies another necessary condition of a miracle: it seems evident that for an event to instruct and illustrate, it has to be manifest and available to an audience, however small. The healing of a sick animal in an age when no human beings could be aware of it, for example, though an *instance* of divine compassion, would not *illustrate* it, because it could teach no one[4].

But the feature of miracles that has engaged philosophers' attention is none of these. It is that miracle-stories are accounts of events contrary to natural law. The word 'miracle' is sometimes used without this implication, so that it is intelligible in some contexts to say that certain biblical miracles were real historical events but have natural explanations. But it is clear that both Butler and Hume follow a stricter usage, and are not out of keeping with common practice in doing so. It is the violation of natural law that identifies miracles, and distinguishes them from other events of religious significance. Today this point might be put by saying that it is the fact that they violate natural law that distinguishes miracles (if there are any) from other revelatory occurrences (if there are any). Butler does not express himself in this way, and says that revelation is itself miraculous. It would take us too far afield to explore reasons for preferring more permissive uses of the words 'miracle' and 'revelation' than the ones Butler and Hume follow; it is enough to say here that anyone who accepts the possibility of there being miracles or revelatory events that are not contrary to natural law, incurs the obligation of telling us what it is about such events that identifies them as miraculous or revelatory, in this wider sense. For Butler and for Hume, it is a necessary condition of an event's being miraculous that it is contrary to a law of nature, and it is the fact of 'attestation' by such events that identifies a revelation.

Butler's statement of this feature of miracles is not as clear as Hume's, but is just clear enough:

> For a miracle, in its very notion, is relative to a course of nature; and implies somewhat different from it, considered as being so. (*An* II ii 6/7)[5]

I take this statement to imply not only that a miracle is contrary to some natural law, but that a person who does not know the law in question cannot recognise it to be a miracle. Since miracles are not commonly supposed to be performed for experts, but for the general public, this further implies that the laws miracles violate are laws of which most normally-informed persons are aware, even if they cannot state them accurately. We would not need a Newton to tell us that a case of levitation would violate the laws of gravitation. (On the other hand, a

Newton, or indeed a lesser expert, could make it clear to us that phenomena commonly thought to be miraculous are not.)

Given the above, I have to qualify my earlier comment that Butler and Hume use the word 'miracle' in such a way that miracles have to be available to an audience. This is true in most contexts: all those that concern Hume, and most of those that concern Butler. But Butler, in common with other Christians, wants to say that there are miracles, such as the Incarnation of Christ, which are 'invisible', and also to be able to state that the revelation that a miracle attests is a miracle itself. He does this by saying that the secret miracles, and revelation, are proved by the 'visible' miracles. Both visible and invisible miracles are acts of God contrary to natural law, but the proof or attestation of the invisible miracles is always due to the occurrence of visible ones.

I turn now to the details of Butler's arguments. These vary greatly in quality, from the perceptive to the sophistical. The most obviously sophistical come first, in Chapter ii. This chapter, and the brief discussion of miracles in Chapter iv, are intended to provide a general preparation for the treatment of the testimony to the Christian miracle-stories in Chapter vii. The preparation consists in attempts to remove the 'supposed presumption' against the miraculous, which would, in Butler's opinion, cause us to approach those stories with more scepticism than is appropriate. The first part of Hume's section is, of course, designed to reinforce this presumption and make the grounds for it clear.

Butler begins with the question, archaic to us, of the possibility of a primitive revelation at the beginning of the world. He thinks we need to postulate such a revelation to account for the existence of religious belief in prehistoric times, for 'there does not appear the least intimation in history or tradition, that religion was first reasoned out' (*An* II ii 10/10). The origins of religion may still be a matter of speculation, but Butler's assumption that they have to lie in revelation because they could not lie in philosophical reasoning is manifestly dated. Hume helped to date it in his *Natural History of Religion*, one of the first attempts to uncover the natural causes of religious belief and practice. To the modern believer, the problem is one of deciding how far such prehistoric practices, or their contemporary 'primitive' counterparts, could be judged revelatory – but such a question involves the assumption that revelation can take place through natural, rather than miraculous, processes. Viewing the prehistoric revelation as he does, however, Butler's concern is to argue that there is no presumption against it on the ground that it would have been miraculous. His answers are of less interest than his question, and can be dismissed very briefly. They are variations on the theme that at the time of man's creation there could not clearly be said yet to be a 'course of nature' to which the primitive revelation could be an exception; so that even if such a primeval event were outside natural

law as we have come to know it, this could not create a presumption
against its having taken place.

These are followed by an argument which is equally sophistical, but
of more interest, if only because it has been used quite commonly since
Butler invented it:

> There is a very strong presumption against common speculative
> truths, and against the most ordinary facts, before the proof of
> them; which is yet overcome by almost any proof. There is a
> presumption of millions to one, against the story of Caesar, or of
> any other man. . . . And from hence it appears, that the question of
> importance, as to the matter before us, is, concerning the degree
> of the peculiar presumption supposed against miracles; not whether
> there be any peculiar presumption at all against them. For, if there
> be the presumption of millions to one, against the most common
> facts; what can a small presumption, additional to this, amount to,
> though it be peculiar? It cannot be estimated, and is as nothing. (*An*
> II ii 12/11)

This defence has occasioned a good deal of comment. John Stuart Mill
says that Butler has confused improbability before the fact and improbability after the fact. ('The improbability, then, or the unusualness, of
any fact, is no reason for disbelieving it, if the nature of the case renders
it certain, that either that or something equally improbable, that is,
equally unusual, did happen.'[6]) Henry Hughes says Butler confuses
probabilities arising from ignorance and probabilities arising from knowledge[7]. These are apt comments; but here, surely, Hume has anticipated
everyone. Whatever the limitations of the first half of his section on
miracles, he is surely right in saying that if we are estimating the likelihood of an event that is contrary to the laws of nature, as distinct from
one that conforms to them but happens rarely, we cannot assign it any
positive degree of probability whatever; so Butler is grossly mistaken in
treating the 'peculiar' element of presumption against the miraculous as
all of a piece with the kind of presumption that arises from statistical
considerations. He has failed to see the implication of his own remark
that 'miracle, in its very notion, is relative to a course of Nature'.

In spite of this failure of insight, however, Butler follows with another
argument that contains within it the germ of a possible answer to what
Hume says. It is that if we take into account 'Religion, or the moral
system of the world', we see 'particular reasons for miracles: to afford
mankind instruction additional to that of Nature, and to attest the truth
of it' (*An* II ii 12/14). In other words, the special point that a miracle
might have offers us a reason for expecting one on occasion, or at least
considering that the report of one might not be false. This hint is spelled
out further in Chapter iv, where the argument is wrapped up in analogical

form. Butler states there that we commonly class strange events as accidental, even though 'all reasonable men know certainly, that there cannot, in reality, be any such things as chance; and conclude that the things which have this appearance are the result of general laws, and may be reduced into them' (*An* II iv 4/4). It may, he suggests, be a proper exercise of religious analogy to infer that 'God's miraculous interpositions may have been all along, in like manner, by *general* laws of wisdom'.

This suggestion is not much developed, but it is Butler's most perceptive contribution to the whole discussion. As a piece of analogical reasoning, it is highly controversial, as all religious analogy is. For a sceptic could easily say that what the comparison with strange natural events shows us is that apparent instances of miracles are merely contrary to the current *description* of natural law, and require us to revise it; once it is revised, these events will once again be seen to conform to natural law when the law is properly understood. This response involves an emendation of Hume. It is often said that Hume is too restrictive when he tells us that since a natural law is a universal regularity, the fact that a supposed event would be contrary to it amounts to a proof that it cannot have occurred. This conclusion would prevent scientific progress by forcing us to reject evidence for anomalous events, however often this evidence was repeated. A Humean can say, instead, that on those occasions when testimony to anomalous events wins out, as it sometimes must, the immediate consequence is that the events now agreed to have happened cannot be contrary to natural law after all: that we have hitherto misunderstood what the relevant natural law is, and must revise our account of it to accommodate events of the kind we now recognise. While this opens us to new evidence in a way that scientific progress demands, the openness does not extend to miracles, since no events admitted to occur are allowed to have that title. The sceptic can, therefore, say to Butler that our conviction that all natural events fall within a system of laws is one that closes us to miracles altogether.

In spite of this, Butler's suggestion is important. What we need is to detach it from its analogical wrappings. In the first place, he is really assuming that there are some events which, if they were to take place, would clearly be violations of natural law, and could not be accommodated to a revised science in the way a Humean sceptic might suggest. I submit that he is right about this. We all know perfectly well that if Jesus did walk on the water, or if Jesus did raise Lazarus from the dead, natural law was in each case violated. The sceptic has no rational option but to reject testimony to such events and deny they occurred. Butler tries to offer a rational alternative to the sceptic's position that permits the believer to take proper cognisance of the status of natural law, while saying that miracles do happen now and then. He says that the Christian view of God's dealings with mankind is one that at least allows us, and probably encourages us, to think of these dealings as following 'general laws of wisdom'. This notion is vague; it suggests that the laws of wisdom are what we would now call descriptive laws covering supernatural sequences in the way that statements of natural law are descriptions of natural sequence. This, not surprisingly, is left undeveloped. But the core of this suggestion is that God deals with men according to rational *principles*, and that these principles, unlike those that men espouse, are principles that God follows consistently, just as the natural world proceeds consistently according to natural laws. He is suggesting, then, that if we knew something of God's dealings and the principles he follows in them, we could see that these principles might lead him to intervene occasionally in the natural order. Such intervention would have to be rare, because its special sort of rarity would be a condition of its having the pedagogical function that God's purposes required. It would also be beyond the wit of men to predict, since God's purposes are not known to them in more than the dimmest way, and their awareness of natural law would always lead them, properly, *not* to expect such interventions.[8] But, when they happen, they can sometimes be seen to have had a special *point* that can be discerned to be congruent with God's purposes by those who are willing to be taught by them.

This argument is one Butler could reasonably suppose to have weighed against a deist, at least one who had come to agree that God's government is a moral one. If we approach it without deistic presuppositions, the argument retains most of its force as a defence of the rationality of believing that testimony could on occasion establish miracles. Such a belief is rational for anyone admitting that God has the sort of attitudes towards us that Christianity ascribes to him, since in a world where human freedom exists, occasions may well arise where men bring themselves into situations where divine intervention is necessary; for example, they may have reached such a point of corruption that their world is beyond their capacity to restore and their guilt beyond their capacity to expiate, and a deity who is compassionate as well as just would have to intervene in somewhat the way the New Testament says God did intervene. Such intervention would among other things provide signs of God's having that combination of attitudes, so that the intervention could be seen, even though only after the fact, as fulfilling general 'laws of wisdom' that God follows, though these are only understood dimly. So the miracles attendant on such intervention, though not predictable beforehand, make the kind of sense afterwards that enables us to see that past history was leading towards them, unknown to most of its participants. The belief that the world is in the hands of a God like this is, therefore, one which does not enable those who hold it to predict a particular miracle in advance, but permits them to have a rational presumption that miracles, though rare, are likely to occur occasionally. For them, this presumption can properly balance the general presumption against miracles that comes from the fact that it necessarily contravenes natural law.

Hume, of course, assumes that his readers do not have grounds for such a presumption when they approach testimony to miracles. For someone who does not believe that we live in a world governed by a God like the Christian one, the fact that a reported event is contrary to a law of nature is an overwhelming reason for rejecting even the strongest testimony to it. If the testimony cannot, in one's judgment, be gainsaid, or if, worse still, one witnesses the event oneself, then the only thing to say on atheist or agnostic principles is that we must have a mistaken understanding of what the natural laws in this area of experience really are, and need to revise our statement of them to show that this event conforms to them in spite of appearances. This last move is obviously unavailable for the raising of Lazarus or Jesus' walking on the water, and the sceptic, once more, *must* reject all testimony to them, and must reject the evidence of his own eyes if he ever thinks he sees events himself.

Something follows from this that is important. Believers and unbelievers share the same scientifically ordered world; in this respect they are even closer together in their daily expectations than in Butler's time. Hence, if one has a rational presumption in favour of the occasional miracle, and the other does not, this entails that they have different conceptions of what a natural law is.[9] I think this indeed is the case. Those who believe in miracles do not believe that admitting them *undermines* the formulation of natural law; someone who believes the story of Lazarus, or, more importantly, that of the Resurrection of Christ, does not suppose that the natural laws relating to decomposition are thereby under threat; someone who believes that Jesus walked on the water does not believe that the laws of gravitation do not hold after all. They think of miracles as special, necessarily rare, visitations from God into a world which is otherwise ruled by the law that these special visitations set aside. This is why miracles, if there are any, do not have to be unique, only rare. There are a small number of resurrection-stories in the New Testament, and a larger number of healing-miracle stories, but even the latter are rare in the context of human history as a whole.

The believer's conception of natural law allows for exceptions, but only at God's behest. The unbeliever's conception allows for none. It is as rational for the one to accept the possibility of adequate testimony to miracles as it is for the other to insist, with Hume, that such testimony must always fail. Who is right has to be judged as part of a judgment of their total competing world-views. But their two conceptions of natural law can co-exist quite peacefully on all other occasions, since both, equally, imply that the secular world that we share is a law-abiding world in which we can make our predictions, and give our explanations, with a confidence that is equal on both sides.

I do not claim that all of this can be found in Butler. But his suggestion that miracles can follow general laws of wisdom seems to me to be a suggestion that can quite naturally be developed in this way. Since, in making this suggestion, Butler is setting the stage for his detailed comments on the historical evidences for Christianity, our discussion can assist us in estimating the value of those comments. It does not follow from what I have said above that a believer must be inclined, on pain of irrationality, to look with favour upon *all* testimony to miracles, only that the unbeliever must be inclined, on pain of irrationality, to reject it.

When he turns to the particular evidences for Christianity Butler argues that the quality of testimony to the Christian miracle-stories is high. In conjunction with his earlier arguments, he considers that this gives the doctrines which these miracle-stories attest a substantial degree of probability, since there is no significant presumption against them *as* miracle-stories, and there is some modest general presumption *for* the occurrence of miracles, on the argument just discussed. Given our judgments, he is right to claim that the deists were in no position to reject miracle testimony out of hand; but he cannot persuade anyone who does not hold a world-view that includes benevolent divine purposes to entertain even the best testimony, save in the interests of reconsidering what the laws of nature are. Hume, who has taught us this, claims also that the actual testimony available to us is of low quality, even though it would not help if it were better. The truth lies somewhere between them.

Briefly, Butler says that the miracle-stories of the Old and New Testaments are not introduced as embellishments, but as sober parts of historical narratives. The New Testament testimony includes the claims made by Paul to have witnessed and performed miracles himself, in addition to knowing those present at the miracles of Jesus. The miracles were, he maintains, the grounds of the beliefs of the early Christians; their numbers, and the intensity of their conviction in the face of great danger, and their recognition of the fundamental importance of being in the right about the truths Christianity claimed to reveal to them, outweigh the fact that men can be moved to credulity and self-deceit by 'enthusiasm'. What Butler says is still a good counterbalance to Hume's patronising portrayal of the early Christian witnesses as ignorant purveyors of exciting tales. But of course it is no match for his fundamental argument that when a story is a *miracle*-story, it is never irrational to reject the supposition that a witness to it must be mistaken, if this argument is amended in the light of our previous discussion.

Hume's veto on miracle-stories does not apply to someone with the prior conviction of the existence of a God with the sort of attitudes the miracle-stories would attest. Given, however, that such a prior conviction does not enable one to predict that a miracle would be forthcoming on any given occasion, the testimony to such an event has to be of the highest quality, and deep reservations are always in order when approaching it, even for those suitably predisposed to consider it. Present-day Christians have many explanations of alleged biblical miracles open to them, beside those available to Butler, for all his candour and realism. His arguments do not establish, for example, that there is a strong reason for Christians to believe that all Jesus' healings took place as reported, or that those which did occur were all miraculous. Many seem clearly to have been cases where what is reported as the miraculous power of God combating demonic possession was probably the effect of an uniquely strong and compassionate personality alleviating the sufferings consequent upon hysteria, schizophrenia, or epilepsy. Christians will always differ on which miracle-stories in the Bible are doctrinally essential. The most Butler's arguments show is that testimony to those that are so judged must not be disregarded.

I conclude by considering an important objection to my argument. It would be as follows. 'You are perhaps right that Butler's case against the deists is persuasive, since anyone who already believes that the world is created by God, and that God is moral, is ill-placed to insist that he could have no cause to suspend natural law on any occasion. Perhaps you are also right that someone who believes God has the character Christianity proclaims should be open to continuing testimony to miracles in the way the Catholic Church claims to be with regard to stories of cures at Lourdes, for example.[10] But this is of no relevance to the uncommitted twentieth-century inquirer who approaches the *biblical* documents, which were, after all, Butler's primary concern. For such an inquirer cannot, on your account, be rationally open to the miracle-stories in the documents, since he lacks the antecedent commitments that make such openness rational. Yet it is these very documents, and the tradition founded on them, that in the absence of a viable natural theology have to be the source of theistic belief. The result of this is that Butler's defences are of no value to such a person, and are therefore as dated as his critics say they are.'

This objection is, I think, entirely well founded, but requires only that I return to a general position I have maintained throughout. The position is that if the deistic presuppositions that Butler makes are abandoned, he has to be judged as a defensive apologist who does not make Christian claims likely, but shows how they can accommodate the agreed realities that obtain in our world. For a contemporary reader, who is not poised in deism's half-way house, the fact that the Bible contains miracle-stories, and that some of them at least (such as the Resurrection) seem indispensable, is an *obstacle* to acceptance of Christian claims. For such a person, the sort of openness that Butler argues for, and that I have suggested is rational, cannot *precede* an acceptance of the claims the biblical documents make, but can only follow upon a positive response to them. Butler is indeed irrelevant, then, if we think he can only teach us how to think of miracles in advance of such positive response. But he is not irrelevant if we view him as showing how to accommodate the otherwise difficult fact of the miracle-stories (biblical and other) for someone who has responded positively. This value is indeed purely defensive. The positive response is something that has to be made (or not made) in reaction to the accumulated case for the Christian world-view that the contemporary inquirer considers to have been made. I shall argue in the next chapter that Butler's contribution to that case is not a negligible one.

2

One of the many signs that Hume is trying to answer Butler even when he does not mention him by name, is the fact that he says at the conclusion of his section on miracles that 'What we have said of miracles may be applied, without any variation, to prophecies.' This comment, though cryptic, is true, and helps us to estimate an ingenious argument that Butler makes about the biblical prophecies as evidences of the truth of the Christian revelation.[11]

The main defence Butler offers here is in response to the 'common objection' that 'considering each of them distinctly by itself, it does not at all appear, that they were intended of those particular events, to which they are applied by Christians'. For example, Christians have held that the mission of Jesus was the fulfilment of the famous Suffering Servant passages in Second Isaiah. Scholars have often maintained that these passages refer in fact to the nation of Israel, or to some individual contemporary with Isaiah himself. A sceptical critic would infer from this that it is erroneous to read them as prophecies of Jesus, even if they 'fit' his mission, or Christian understandings of it. Butler's own example is a prophecy contained in Chapter 7 verse 7 of the Book of Daniel, which was applied to later events by Christian readers, but itself refers to the age of Antiochus Epiphanes.

Butler's defence is that 'the meaning of a book is nothing but the meaning of the author'. To assume that if the human writer did not intend to speak of certain later events, these events are not referred to by the book, is to assume that the human writer is the author. But those who think the book is inspired by God suppose that the human writer has a merely subsidiary role in its composition, like that of the compiler of the memoirs of someone greater in knowledge and importance than himself. Such a writer cannot fully understand what he writes, and the meaning of it is not confined to that part which he *does* understand. To reject alleged prophecies that fit later events in telling ways, merely because the human writers of those passages did not themselves intend to refer to those later events, is to prejudge the question of prophecy against them.

This argument is a clever defence of traditional readings of the Scriptures, and has some weight against the deists in suggesting to them that if they ascribe benevolent intentions to God they might expect him to reveal his purposes in history through the sort of inspiration which can be recognised after the occurrence of later events. It has no value as part of a case for Christianity that proceeds *from* the fulfilment of prophecies identified without any such expectation, *to* the acceptance of the Christian view of history. For such a case requires that the alleged prophecies be treated, at least methodologically, solely as human writings, and to recognise them as prophecies on that assumption requires them to contain clear references to the future events they are alleged to foretell. The situation here is parallel to that of miracle-stories.

Butler is not trying to make this latter argument, so he can hardly be faulted for not showing that he recognises the limitations it would have. He is trying to urge on deists that *they* should be more open to the possibility of inspiration and prophecy, that for *them* the fact that an Old Testament passage fits later New Testament narratives is a good enough reason to think the one may have been intended by God as a prophecy of the other.

For twentieth-century readers, Butler's argument, like his defence of miracles, shows that someone already predisposed to expect that God might intimate his purposes in one era in the statements and hopes of an earlier one, can reasonably conclude in some cases that he has done so – namely in those cases where later events given special religious illumination when so interpreted. Someone not so predisposed will, properly, be untouched by this argument, though he may be able to see from it that the believer's reading is not an irrational one. The transition from the sceptic's stance to the believer's, however, is one that is made in response to the *whole* proclaimed tradition of which the biblical stories are a part; so the judgment that prophecies have been made and fulfilled will be a consequence of that response, not a cause of it.

3

Since the belief in Christ's mediation has been at the centre of the Christian proclamation since the earliest times in the Church's history, and since the claims of the institutional churches have centred on their making the benefits of this mediation available to their worshippers, it is not surprising that this belief was one of the deists' main targets, and that Butler devotes a chapter to defending it. What he says can be judged in a parallel manner to what he says about miracles and prophecies.[12]

Butler's defence of the doctrine of Christ's mediation leans heavily on religious analogy, and upon his having supposedly satisfied his readers that we live in a world that is governed by God morally. He suggests that religious analogy renders it likely that there is a supernatural law of which Christ's mediation is the result. His reasoning is as follows. The moral government of God should lead us to expect that each of us will be rewarded or punished according to his or her deserts, in the next life. The Christian revelation teaches us that this scheme is mitigated by a special act of God's compassion, in response to the unmerited sufferings of Christ. This act of compassion enables us to escape the ordained penalties of our misdeeds through repentance; since repentance does not remove the misdeeds we regret, it would not otherwise prevent the punishment that would await us. This revealed truth is analogous to certain features of God's known governance of this world. (1) There is, first, the fact that God never deals with us in nature wholly separately, but makes us dependent on one another; this is analogous to the revealed truth that our personal destinies are critically affected by the actions of another person. (2) Since in nature the punishments of imprudence and vice often come about through the operation of natural laws (so that someone 'trifling upon a precipice' will fall naturally to his destruction, or someone guilty of overindulgence in youth will endure a sickly old age), it may well be that the penalties of sinfulness follow in the next life in an equally lawlike manner. (3) In nature the normal bad consequences do not always follow when we behave foolishly; so we have intimations in our life here that God's rule is compassionate as well as just. (4) Societies do not remit misdeeds solely for repentance and reformation, but exact penalties; the widespread practice of propitiatory sacrifice among the heathen suggests that mankind has a deep recognition that somehow God's justice also requires punishment – a punishment that is borne, according to the Christian revelation, by Christ's unmerited suffering.

What the Christian revelation shows us, then, is that Christ's death makes it possible for us to attain salvation through repentance. It does not tell us the metaphysical details of *how* it makes this possible, apart from the intimation that his sufferings are acceptable in place of ours. Butler even adds that it does not tell us that God's compassion is only available to those who know of Christ's sufferings and accept him. We have no right to pronounce on questions like these. But we can see that there is nothing incredible about the claim that such mediated salvation is available to us. We can even infer some degree of likelihood for it by analogy with the tokens of divine compassion nature provides when imprudence and vice occasionally pass unpunished.

The analogy on which Butler relies can only begin, however, if we take it as given that he has already shown that God's scheme is one that rewards and punishes us hereafter for good and evil done here. If that is given, then one can mount some sort of argument that just as penalties for folly may come by natural law here, so they may do hereafter; and that just as the penalties for folly here are sometimes remitted, so they may be hereafter. Even if this argument is accepted, it would carry the old ambiguity that afflicts all Butler's inferences from this life to the next: that perhaps the outcome is not that we can expect punishment in the next life for ills done in this, save for future remission, but that we can expect punishment in the next life for ills done *in the next life*, save for remission. But this ambiguity is the least worry. The very remissions that Butler points to are arguments against holding that God does have a general plan of punishing evil and rewarding good hereafter, since it looks as though he only sometimes does it now. An argument that professes to begin from observation of nature, and to establish that God is impartially just on the basis of such observation, and then suggests that the counter-evidence to universal justice is the evidence for a secondary dispensation remitting penalties for those who repent, and says this last in spite of the fact that repentance does not usually produce remission in this world, is being described charitably when it is called circular. As Hume might have said, evidence of natural rewards, punishments, and remissions (or, more accurately, good and bad consequences) cannot be used to form the basis of a system of religion teaching supernatural punishments and mediation.

So although the argument might have some worth as a case against a deist who had accepted Butler's earlier case for divine justice, it has none whatever for anyone who recognises the weakness of that case, and the sources of it. I would suggest, however, that even here something can be salvaged from what Butler tells us. Someone who judges, as Christians do, that the view of our world and our natures found in the Gospels is the true one, and is convinced by them that the redemption and promise of a new community that are taught there are realities, can then rationally approach the inequities of this world and interpret them accordingly. This would permit, though it would not require, that certain cases of unpunished folly and wickedness could be judged as examples of the sort of forgiveness that is taught in the Christian tradition, while still making it possible to insist that no kind of suffering, however obviously unmerited and unrelated to moral development, is outside the divine justice or compassion. But it is beyond the scope of this work, and quite out of keeping with the mood of Butler's, to pursue a speculative theodicy any further.

VIII

The Ignorance of Man

In the two preceding chapters I have tried to assess the most important of the detailed arguments of Butler's apologetic in the *Analogy*. While the assessments have inevitably varied, I think they can fairly be summarised as follows. In the first place, the various uses of religious analogy by which Butler seeks to persuade us that there is probably a future life, that we are probably rewarded or punished in it for our actions here, and that the Christian revelation is shown by miracles and prophecies to hold the key to our future salvation, are quite unsuccessful. They are unsuccessful even if one approaches them with the minimal deistic assumptions that the world is created by a divine intelligence, and is some sort of teleological system. Hume has made it abundantly clear that if one approaches them without such assumptions, the natural phenomena on which Butler bases his arguments do not suggest the Christian world-view at all. On the other hand, it has to be conceded that a reader who approached Butler's case presupposing not only that our world is created by a divine intelligence, but also that that intelligence is a moral and just one, would find good reason to treat Butler's doctrine of probation with seriousness, and little reason to resist his claim that the Christian revelation is a possible source of light regarding God's purposes, and is supported by testimony that merits consideration. The most important judgment to make, however, in the context of our own world, is whether a reader making no presuppositions about God can properly be persuaded by what Butler says.

For such a reader, two judgments have to be made. The first is a judgment on Butler's success in removing those intellectual obstacles to the reception of Christianity that cannot be dealt with by arguments that only apply to the deists. I have suggested that we can often allow him to have been successful in this. For example, we can see that a combination of his doctrines of a future life and probation is a viable response to some of the age-old difficulties about evil; and we can see that his defence of miracles is one that shows an openness to the occasional possibility of divine intervention to be a rational stance for someone who thinks our world is governed by a God who is just and loving. The second judgment that has to be made is whether or not Butler has anything within him of positive value, in addition to offering defences against objections. This is a difficult judgment to make, given that Butler himself places so much positive weight in his own mind on the religious analogy that we must reject.

To deal with this second question, I shall consider the three recurring themes which dominate both Butler's positive arguments and his defensive ones. He claims repeatedly that the major obstacles to the proper consideration and reception of Christianity are its critics' unwillingness to recognise the implications of our intellectual limits, their consequent insistence on applying to Christian teachings standards that are more rigorous than any we apply in secular matters, and their refusal to take with sufficient seriousness the essentially *practical* demand that the Christian proclamation, seen as a whole, makes upon them. These three themes are intimately connected, but I will try as far as possible to examine what he says about them in sequence.

1

The dangers that follow upon the neglect of human intellectual limitations form the major theme of no less than four of the fifteen chapters of the *Analogy*.[1] Butler's main contentions are all present earlier, in one of his finest sermons, 'Upon the Ignorance of Man' (*S* xv). It is convenient to expound them as they appear there.

Although it is certain that God made the world, our knowledge of the world he has made is fragmentary and incomplete. We know no more of the scheme of God's providential government than is necessary for practice, and we are quite unable to understand the full significance even of the small part of creation that we do know. Not only are we ignorant of God's ways through sheer lack of capacity to fathom them; there may well be aspects of his purposes that we are capable of understanding, but which he has deliberately chosen to keep hidden from us. He might do this to impose an intellectual form of probation, or trial, on some persons, in the way he imposes a moral probation on others through temptation.

In the light of this, we should approach our reflections on religion appropriately. We ought, first, to expect to find that there are many mysterious things in it, not insist that we have an unclouded view of the whole. In spite of this, we should not anticipate total darkness, but 'take up and rest satisfied with any evidence whatever, which is real'. Secondly, we should recognise that many popular objections to religion, especially those that centre upon the evils and trials of this world, are adequately answered by reference to our ignorance: we should recognise that we know too little ever to be sure that such objections are decisive. Thirdly, we should recognise that our primary purpose has to be a practical, not a theoretical, one: to discover and to discharge those duties that God requires of us.

As always, Butler's case is presented analogically; and, as always, this aspect of its presentation is the least valuable now. Butler maintains that our ignorance of God's purposes is paralleled in our understanding of the material world. His reason for saying this is briefly expressed in such comments as this:

> What are the laws by which matter acts upon matter, but certain effects; which some, having observed to be frequently repeated, have reduced to general rules? The real nature and essence of beings likewise is what we are altogether ignorant of. All these things are so entirely out of our reach, that we have not the least glimpse of them. (S xv 3/5)

The world around us, then, is a world containing objects whose inner essences are unknowable, but whose effects alone are available to us. This roughly Lockean view, from which Hume was to carry us so far forward in the quite near future, is part of the basis for Butler's insistence that our ignorance of the intention behind those events in which God reveals himself to us parallels a similar ignorance in our dealings with nature; and that neither form of ignorance need prevent us from acquiring, at the level of visible effects, a body of knowledge which is enough to base our actions upon.

When this argument reappears in the *Analogy* (especially in I vii), Butler expresses it in terms of a somewhat different comparison, between what we can discern of God's natural government, and what we can discern of his moral government. The assumption is made there that our world is a teleological system, and that the limitations of our natural knowledge are limitations on our understanding of how far phenomena in nature fulfil the purposes that God has laid down for them. An obvious example of such a natural mystery is the fact that God permits such apparent waste of seeds and animal bodies in the propagation of species. (See *An* II v 18/35.) This is compared to the limits on our understanding of how far the evils and trials of life may have a purpose within God's moral government. If we can accept the one with equanimity, we should accept the other.

Both versions of this argument date badly. While the vast increase in scientific knowledge since Butler has not removed all mysteries, it is not possible to describe it now in terms of an inescapably unknown realm of hidden essences. And the assumption that natural phenomena are part of a divinely governed teleological system is part of the deistic framework which has also passed from the scene. It is especially important to see what the deistic assumption provides for Butler's argument, and what it does not provide. Even on the most clearly minimal interpretation of it, it provides a recognition of creation and natural government; on this basis Butler is able to say that all natural phenomena have divinely given purposes, and that we can reasonably expect to discern some of them with a good degree of probability, by observing natural sequences. Purposes we cannot discern we already know to be there, since we already know God has placed us in a purposive universe. This is the ground both for his insistence that we have to recognise limits to natural knowledge, and for his insistence that we are able to learn sufficient of God's purposes for practical decision. It opens the way for him to argue that there is no reason to insist that the world is not governed morally, merely because some features of it do not yet make moral sense to us; and it adds plausibility to his doctrine of probation. It does not provide the clear insight into God's intentions that Butler took the deists to be demanding; on the contrary, it makes us cease to expect it, and to rest content with less. The fundamental reassurance that is provided, however, is reassurance that the most mysterious phenomena can be supposed, to an adequate understanding, to *have a point*. There is no doubt where Butler supposes this reassurance to come from: it comes from the fact that God's non-existence is unthinkable.

It is unthinkable no longer; many now assert it. The key issue is how far this fact undermines Butler's apologetic argument. It fairly obviously does not prevent us from taking seriously, as defences of Christianity, the claim that if God does exist, we might expect our world to be full of events that he could teach us how to respond to without always knowing why he allows them to happen, or the claim that if God wishes us to acquire Christian characters, this necessitates moral, and even perhaps intellectual, probation. These are important defences, and Butler expresses them with as much clarity and caution as anyone. But we have to recognise that the honest inquirer, conscientious in attending to his own limitations in precisely the way that Butler says he should be, is in a profoundly different situation if God's non-existence is an intellectual possibility for him than the one he is in if it is not. For if it is not an intellectual possibility, he knows that every fact, however mysterious, has a point; all that he has to concern himself with is whether the point it has could be one that is compatible with the Christian teachings about God and man, or whether it could not. But if it is possible for him to consider that there is no God at all, it is possible for him to be conscientiously unsure whether any natural phenomena, even the ones that Christians see as clear expressions of the love of God, have any point whatever. For he is no longer prevented by the premisses from which he begins from thinking that the world he lives in is not a teleological system of any kind, Christian or non-Christian. He has to judge the likelihood of Christian claims against that possibility, as well as against other teleological ones. Once again, this is the position from which the bulk of contemporary inquirers approach the claims that Christianity makes upon them. It is in the light of this that we must consider the apologetic case Butler builds around the fact of our ignorance, and in particular his important suggestion that it may furnish a form of probation for us.

'For, after all, that which is true, must be admitted, though it should show us the shortness of our faculties; and that we are in no wise judges of many things, of which we are apt to think ourselves very competent ones' (*An* II iii 2/5). Yes, indeed. But we must also remember that evidence of the shortness of our faculties has always been the weapon of the sceptic. The wise sceptic, such as Hume, has always avoided the deists' error of pronouncing confidently about what cannot be so, or about what God would not do. For he does not even begin with the confidence that Butler and the deists both had, that God exists. The question at issue is whether a proper sense of our intellectual limitations should make us more or less impressed by the counter-evidences to Christian claims, such as the evils of the world, or the obscurities of revelation, when we cannot claim to know that some purpose must be present in them.

If there is to be any presumption, or even inclination, in favour of the Christian revelation, it would have to come from the recognition of the moral depth of the diagnosis of human ills associated with it, of the personal impact of the historical personality of its founder, and of the potential for personal transformation that is seen to lie within its prescriptions. It is these and other features of the Christian world-view as a whole that have to be weighed by the inquirer against the evils that disfigure what is said to be God's creation. It seems to be a necessary condition of any such presumption or inclination, and of the plausibility of an appeal to ignorance based upon it, that the Christian world-view is not manifestly inconsistent with the fact of these evils, that they do not amount to what Butler would call a disproof of it. If they do not, such a presumption or inclination would at least be a rational option, though it would certainly not be the only rational option.

In order to show that the evils we encounter do not disprove Christian claims, it is enough to demonstrate that there is a logically possible explanation of these evils which is consistent with the Christian claims about God and man. Butler's doctrine of probation is a suggestion of this sort. He thinks that his analogical argument in Part I shows it to be a likely hypothesis; we are in no position to accept his grounds for this. But all that is requisite apologetically is the mere possibility that it may be true, and that it may fend off the sceptical argument from evil.

191

Butler's doctrine of moral probation, like the 'soul-making' theodicy of John Hick in our own time that so much resembles it in spirit, is a variant on the 'free-will defence' against the problem of evil. That defence amounts to saying, in general, that there are some good states and acts that cannot, in logic, obtain without the prior existence of certain evils; and others which cannot in logic, obtain without the open *possibility* of certain evils. Forgiveness cannot take place without actual previous injury. And forgiveness cannot take place without the open option of vengefulness instead, for forgiveness is a free act. The Christian God is a deity who is represented as wishing us to respond to him, and to each other, freely; so such a deity cannot, in logic, enable us to do this without also enabling us to choose to respond badly also. Butler's doctrine of probation tells us that many of the evils, such as temptation and failure, with which virtuous persons have to contend, are logically necessary conditions of the possession and exercise of those virtuous states on which Christianity sets such store. As an apologetic argument, its power comes from the fact that the values it ascribes to God are the ones ascribed to him in the Christian proclamations, and the policies it suggests God may follow are policies which would both express those values on God's side and offer a general explanation of the evils we have to contend with on ours.

I cannot discuss the problem of evil in depth here. I must content myself with saying that this sort of defence against it remains, in my judgment, the most obviously viable one in contemporary discussion, and that the main outlines of this discussion are all present in Butler. Let us suppose that our rational inquirer accepts that it offers an adequate defence. He could then reasonably agree further that some evils whose purpose remained obscure to him, might be accounted for within this general scheme, though no one's knowledge is adequate to subsume them under it so far. If he was deeply impressed with the Christian proclamations, he might then feel there was no barrier to presuming in their favour in his subsequent reflections.

But this would clearly not be the only course open to him. The most perceptive and morally impressive world-view can still be false; and the fact that it can provide a plausible framework for dealing with counter-evidence still does not show that it is true. At best, the intellectual situation is an ambiguous one: one in which it is not irrational to presume that the Christian revelation may be genuine, but also not irrational to suppose that the world is a mixture of good and evil because it is not the creation of a divine being at all, and that the reason we cannot discern God's purposes in nature is that there is no God to have them. If this is the situation of the honest and serious inquirer (as indeed I believe it to be), a question arises for the believer. The question is this: granted that the Christian understanding of our world and our lives is a rationally open option, why is it not the only rationally open option? If Christianity is true, why is it not more *obviously* true? This is, in essence, the sort of question the deists were asking, and I hope to have shown, here and elsewhere[2], that it remains. It is this, very hard, question, that Butler tries to address in his doctrine of *intellectual probation*.

2

There are important parallels to Butler's hypothesis. The most famous is Pascal's doctrine of the *Dieu caché*:

> It is true then that everything teaches man his condition, but there must be no misunderstanding, for it is not true that everything reveals God, and it is not true that everything conceals God. But it is true at once that he hides from those who tempt him and that he reveals himself to those who seek him, because men are at once unworthy and capable of God: unworthy through their corruption, capable through their original nature.[3]

It is God's hiddenness, Pascal tells us, that accounts at once for the uselessness of the intellectual proofs of God and the faith of those whose hearts are open to him; God speaks to those who listen, and hides from those who wish him not to be there, and wilfully distract themselves with social and philosophical frivolities. A contemporary version of the same view is to be found in John Hick's doctrine of 'cognitive freedom'.[4] The Christian tradition teaches, Hick tells us, that God does not compel us to respond to him, that faith is a voluntary state. This means that the evidences for God cannot be such as to compel us to acknowledge him, but must make it possible for us to refrain from doing so if we are so minded. This means that the 'proofs' of God will always fail, when judged as purportedly compelling arguments. Our world is not merely ambiguous (open, that is, to both a theistic and an atheistic interpretation); it is a world whose ambiguity is to be expected if God values the freedom of his creatures.

Butler presents his version of this view most clearly in responding to the deists' complaint that revelation is obscure and not universal. It is important to be accurate about the exact position he takes. He claims, first, that the difficulties that lie in the way of accepting the Christian religion are difficulties that permit us to be discouraged, to be frivolous, and to be distracted by our earthly preoccupations. These are all pitfalls in the way of inquiry in the same way that temptations and failures are pitfalls in the exercise of our moral duties; and both sorts of pitfalls are signs of our state of probation.

Thus, that religion is not intuitively true, but a matter of deduction and inference; that a conviction of its truth is not forced upon every one, but left to be, by some, collected with heedful attention to premises; this as much constitutes religious probation, as much affords sphere, scope, opportunity, for right and wrong behaviour, as anything whatever does. And their manner of treating this subject, when laid before them, shows what is in their heart, and is an exertion of it. (*An* II vi 8/11)

He develops this by pointing out that some people are placed in life in situations where the moral temptations that beset others are less of an obstacle to them. Where, then, is their probationary trial to come from? 'Now when these latter persons have a distinct full conviction of the truth of religion, without any possible doubts or difficulties, the practice of it is to them unavoidable, unless they will do a constant violence to their own minds; and religion is scarce any more a discipline to them, than it is to creatures in a state of perfection' (*An* II 13/18). For such persons, it may be (Butler is, as ever, resolute in making clear that he is only showing us what God *might* do) that 'the probation, in all senses, . . . may be the difficulties in which the evidence of religion is involved'. They will prove themselves, or fail to prove themselves, in the way they contend with these difficulties. The same difficulties provide the opportunity for more frivolous characters to refuse to consider the warnings that religion gives them, so that they take refuge in the objections that more serious persons have thought up. What Butler says about this is critical for understanding his argument and its limitations:

Common men, were they as much in earnest about religion, as about their temporal affairs, are capable of being convinced upon real evidence, that there is a God Who governs the world: and they feel themselves to be of a moral nature, and accountable creatures. And as Christianity entirely falls in with this their natural sense of things, so they are capable, not only of being persuaded, but of being made to see, that there is evidence of miracles wrought in attestation of it, and many appearing completions of prophecy. But though this proof is real and conclusive, yet it is liable to objections, and may be run up into difficulties. . . . Now if persons who have picked up these objections from others, and take for granted they are of weight . . . will not prepare themselves for such an examination . . . or will not give that time and attention to the subject, which, from the nature of it, is necessary for attaining such information: in this case, they must remain in doubtfulness, ignorance, or error. (*An* II vi 16/20)

Butler finishes his case by imagining an objector saying that a prince who sent directions to a servant would always make it plain where the directions came from, and not leave occasion for doubt. The answer, says Butler, is that such a prince would be concerned solely with making sure that his servant did what he wanted to have done, and would not be concerned with the motives of the servant when he did them. God, on the other hand, is concerned with the inner nature of our responses to him; and this concern might well cause him to reveal his wishes to us in a way that permitted questioning and hesitation.

I think we can agree that it is not unreasonable for Butler to extend his doctrine of probation to include intellectual difficulties. There no doubt are persons, perhaps those of philosophical aptitude and inclination, for whom the intellectual conundrums of scepticism are real trials of faith, and will serve as tests of their seriousness and of their devotion to God. We can also agree that there are many persons who do not believe because they frivolously avoid paying serious attention to the evidences in favour of the Christian proclamations. The maddening heedlessness of the public is a common refrain of the prophets, and is a real fact of life.[5] Both of these things indicate that we do have cognitive freedom: that is, that we do have voluntary control, in some manner,[6] over the state of our beliefs, that this brings us face to face with trials and that we frequently misuse the freedom we have. So the concept of intellectual probation is not an absurd one. (As philosophers might express it, we do have doxastic responsibilities.) But the very truth of this suggests that there is no clear need for the evidences of Christianity to be obscure, or for our situation in the world to be religiously ambiguous. For if we do have the freedom to respond or not to respond to the signs of God, this freedom exists if the signs are clear, as well as if they are not. It is very well known (and Butler, who says such wise things about self-deceit, certainly knows it) that people can ignore obvious facts, can fail to attend to what stares them in the face, and can invent, or eagerly grasp on to, difficulties that would not impress them at all if they were not biased against learning unwelcome truths. The very facts about us that make intellectual probation a real possibility show that it could exist quite well, in all the forms Butler suggests for it, if the signs of God's presence were clear. Admittedly, in such a world, heedlessness and scepticism would be irrational; but if they were not irrational, that would cast doubt on their being misuses of freedom. For if they were not irrational, it would be entirely possible for someone who studied the evidences with seriousness and conscientiousness to decide that they were inconclusive, and suspend judgment on their meaning.

It is not quite clear whether or not Butler recognises this possibility. He often writes as though all that he can demand of his reader is that he or she consider the natural and revealed evidences seriously; and this seems to allow for the possibility that serious consideration might still end up in suspense or rejection. If this is what he thinks, then it would follow from his statement that

> All shadow of injustice, and indeed all harsh appearances, in this various economy of Providence, would be lost; if we would keep in mind, that every merciful allowance shall be made, and no more be required of any one, than what might equitably have been expected of him, from the circumstances in which he was placed (*An* II vi 5/7)

that an honest doubt that survived scrupulous reflection would not be a barrier to redemption. This passage, however, is fairly clearly designed to exculpate only those who have not heard the Christian revelation, and concludes with an admonition that those who are in darkness should try to get out of it. The ambiguity remains if we compare two places in which he comments on the psychology of religious doubt. One reads as follows:

> But as I have hitherto gone upon supposition, that men's dissatisfaction with the evidence of religion is not owing to their neglects or prejudices; it must be added, on the other hand, in all common reason, and as what the truth of the case plainly requires should be added, that such dissatisfaction possibly may be owing to those, possibly may be men's own fault. (*An* II vi 14/19)

This should be compared with the extract from *An* II vi 16/20 above, in which far less hesitancy is expressed about the motivations of scepticism.

This ambiguity is not surprising. For what is it that is meant by the suggestion that intellectual obstacles to belief might be a form of probation? Presumably that they present us with a choice whether or not to exercise our freedom (in this case our cognitive freedom) in both good and bad ways; the bad ways being frivolous inattention, easy rejection, and heedless negativity, and the good ways being serious scrutiny, lengthy reflection, and wrestling with unwanted doubts. The obstacles to belief parallel temptations in the moral sphere. In the moral sphere we show we have virtue by persevering in the face of temptations, and not yielding. But it is hard to suppose that this analogy does not imply that a struggle which concludes with ostensibly conscientious agnosticism would be the equivalent of yielding to temptation rather than overcoming it. This is only plausible, however, if one says that such a negative outcome is due to frivolity and corruption in every case, so that conscientious rejection is impossible. This is something that Butler, a very charitable and gentle thinker, is clearly reluctant to suggest. But his doctrine of intellectual probation really requires it.

How can such a suggestion be made plausible? On one condition only: that for those with the right doxastic attitudes the evidences are not ambiguous at all. This is why, in introducing the theory of intellectual probation to us, Butler falls into saying that the available proof of Christianity is 'real and *conclusive*'. It follows from this that anyone who does not find it so is less in earnest about religion than about his temporal affairs.

Butler's instinct is, in a sense, right here. For this is the only way of holding that unbelief is due to a person's failing a probationary test, viz. that if he had passed the test and attended to the evidence in the right spirit, he would believe. But that can only be true if the evidence is such as to remove all reasonable doubt. The trouble is that such a thesis is exactly the opposite of what we need to make sense of the fact with which we began, and which Butler seems anxious to keep repeating elsewhere, that the evidence is unclear and full of difficulty, yielding at the most some degree of probability.

The problem is certainly reduced if one makes deistic assumptions. If God's existence and natural government is given, then a better case can certainly be made for the view that someone who recognises it will only refuse to ponder the Christian revelation if his motives are questionable. While I have no reason to suppose that *all* deists lacked conscientiousness, it is clear from my modest reading of them that many of them were complacent and obtuse. But this is irrelevant in an era where the deistic assumptions are at least as problematic as the revelation the deists rejected.

So while Butler is commendably sensitive to the ambiguities and difficulties of religious evidence, and makes many plausible and wise suggestions about the hindrances to accepting them, he seems to me to fail in answering the question that the deists posed: if Christianity is true, why is it not more obviously true? And the defects in his answer seem to me to be present in similar answers that are offered today.

I cannot argue this last point fully here. I will merely say two things. First, we must be careful to distinguish between some fact that places the truth of Christianity beyond reasonable doubt, and one which compels our submission by frightening us, or otherwise overwhelming us. There might be clear reasons why a God who wished faith to be a free response would eschew the use of the latter; but philosophical proofs, or even some miraculous healings, need not be in this overwhelming category at all. Second, it is quite mistaken to suppose that there are no moral tests involved in acknowledging a fact which we know for certain, as opposed to one which we judge to be merely probable. If the acknowledgment is a painful one, showing our failures and defects to the world, there are no limits to the ingenuity with which we will persuade ourselves that we do not know it after all, or will distract ourselves from paying attention to it.

I turn now to two other aspects of Butler's apologetic which I have singled out for special mention: his reliance throughout on a form of what I have called the Parity Argument, and his stress upon the reader's taking the case for Christianity together as an accumulated whole.

When Butler tells us at the onset that probability is the guide of life, part of his purpose is to reconcile us to the fact that he can deliver no more than probabilities in his detailed arguments. We should not despise the products of religious analogy, because all we can get in secular affairs are the probable judgments delivered by natural analogy. Hume has made it clear to us that any strength that religious analogy may have depends upon the assumption that our world is a teleological system, and that this assumption is not required by natural analogy. Does this mean that the Parity Argument, as Butler uses it, is relevant only to his own opponents and not to us?

I think that it still retains a limited defensive force. To see what this is, we must first be clear how far the argument that we find in Butler differs from the more common versions of the Parity Argument. These commonly appeal to sceptical considerations that Butler never entertains. They attempt to show, for example, that we should not be anxious about the rationality of religious beliefs merely because we cannot provide philosophical grounds for them through proving the existence of God; for a comparable situation obtains in our secular inquiries. We are unable to justify our fundamental beliefs in such things as the systematic regularity of nature. But just as we can, and should, go forward in practice without the unobtainable guarantees that rationalists seek in our secular life, it is equally reasonable to proceed without philosophical guarantees in the religious sphere. If one procedure is rational, so is the other.[7]

Butler does not argue like this, since he thinks we have rational guarantees of God's existence, and that we know that the natural world has systematic regularities, even though they may be unknown to us in detail. But there is a core feature of the above fideist argument which *is* present in Butler's. It is the insistence that it is arbitrary, and a probable sign of mere prejudice, to dismiss the claims of religion on grounds that we are not willing to apply at the secular level. The onus of proof lies with those who demand greater assurances of truth in religion than they would demand in the realm of secular knowledge.

Although Butler is manifestly right, the onus is one that religious sceptics will often accept. They are likely to say that we should adjust our intellectual demands to the magnitude of the epistemic claims made upon us, and to the importance of the supposed truths we are invited to believe. Since the subject-matter of religious claims is vast in extent and of the greatest human importance, we should demand much more rigorous proofs of them than we would require even in major secular matters.

Butler does have an answer to this. His answer is that the importance of the claims of Christianity is a fact that should make us *less*, rather than *more*, meticulous when we examine the grounds for them. I shall deal with this thesis below, when I discuss the pragmatic aspects of Butler's apologetic.

For the moment, we must return to the fact that Butler's non-sceptical form of the appeal to parity involves the claim that we can assign probabilities to religious doctrine that are comparable to those we find satisfactory for purposes of action at the secular level. Once again we are confronted with the fact that the religious analogies on which he depends when he tries to show this require us to take God's existence and natural government as already proven; without this assumption, religious analogy fails. And there is little use in appealing to parity if there is none.

Here I think we must recognise that the probable case Butler seeks to build cannot be properly represented if we see it solely as a series of distinct arguments, each of which has divine government as a concealed premiss. For Butler also says that the case for religion must be viewed as a whole. To judge his claim that Christianity can be shown to have a degree of probability sufficient for our practical assent, we have to see what he has in mind when he says this. This will perhaps enable us to see whether some holistic judgment of probability can be made that includes in its scope even those elements in the Christian religion that Butler takes as given before he starts.

4

Butler says at intervals that his argument is a cumulative one, which should be taken as a whole rather than piecemeal. For example:

> Thus the evidence of Christianity will be a long series of things . . . making up, all of them together, one argument: the conviction arising from which kind of proof may be compared to what they call *the effect* in architecture or other works of art; a result from a great number of things so and so disposed, and taken into one view. (*An* II vii 2/2)

This passage precedes his consideration of the biblical and historical evidences for Christian revelation. Whatever one thinks of them, it seems right for Butler to say that if there are a number of these (for example, a number of well-attested miracles) and they are independent of one another, their accumulation adds to the probability of the scheme of revelation that they are thought to attest individually. On the other hand,

Butler seems not to be aware of the fact that the accumulation of some of his other arguments has the reverse effect. Henry Hughes points out[8] that in Part I of the *Analogy*, where Butler argues, in sequence, (i) that it is probable that there is a future life, (ii) that it is probable that prudence here will be rewarded there and imprudence here punished there, (iii) that it is probable that virtue here will be rewarded there and vice here punished there, and (iv) that it is probable that probation here is intended to consolidate the virtue that we acquire here to ensure reward there: the probability of the propositions discussed progressively decreases, since each depends on the preceding one. So if the probability of a future life is 0.7, and that of a future reward for prudence (given a future life) is 0.6, and the likelihood of a future reward for virtue (given a future reward for prudence) is 0.5, and the likelihood of probation here (given a reward for virtue there) is 0.8, the ultimate probability of the doctrine of moral probation is a mere 0.168 (my figures). Yet there is no sense, in Butler's prose, of a progressive decrease in probability as the argument progresses. This fact, together with the inevitable shakiness of religious analogy, shows that we cannot grant Butler much success in building up a cumulative argument, if this has to be thought of as the result of a series of individually probable steps.

He undoubtedly has another sort of judgment in mind, however. It is what I have earlier referred to as a holistic judgment, pitting the Christian scheme as a whole against alternatives to it, among these now being not only the world-views of other religions but the various forms of deism that concerned Butler himself, and various atheistic world-views familiar in our own day. The detailed development of Butler's argument, shorn of its obsolete analogical form, has the effect of showing how Christianity subsumes under it those phenomena, like those of pain and evil, which seem on the surface to be counter-evidences to it, how its doctrine of mediation softens the harshness of its teachings on probation and judgment in ways consistent with the moral precepts it enjoins, and how the explanations it gives of our world and man's place in it do not remove the mysteriousness that must be at the heart of any doctrine of God, and which many intuit to be a constant feature of human life. With these accumulated clarifications of the Christian revelation, one is then as well placed as one can be to decide whether it is or is not more likely to be true than each of its competitors. It is very clear that this decision is one that cannot be based upon any standard of probability that is used to determine relative likelihoods in the secular sciences. But it is equally clear that this holistic comparison is one that people do make at critical points in their lives, and may make in different ways at different times also.

Butler's own interest is in showing that the Christian revelation as a whole is more likely than any of its deistic alternatives. In spite of the defects in many of his argumentative steps, I think it is clear that he is successful in this – at least for any form of deism which ascribes morality to God. It is interesting that Pascal comments with hostility that deism is as far from Christianity as atheism is.[9] The reason is that deism, which lacks the revealed doctrines of alienation and redemption, has to underplay the gravity of the evils of the world, since they suggest God is finite in power or benevolence. Christianity, on the other hand, while not eliminating the mystery of evil, and adding other mysteries of its own, is able, through these doctrines, both to make evil partially intelligible and to emphasise its full gravity. Hume shows us the same thing when he makes Cleanthes deny the seriousness of evil in order to preserve his version of the Design Argument.[10] Christianity is a more *resourceful* position than deism is.

But if we compare Christianity instead with atheism or agnosticism, its resourcefulness has to be matched against the greater economy of these positions. The honest inquirer now has to match simplicity against depth, the risk of credulity against the risk of blindness, the hazards of sensitivity against the hazards of sustained scientific detachment. Each side has resources adequate to account for the apparent foolishness of the other, and each side has ways of responding to the criticisms the other makes of it. Each can give reasons for its stance; but the reasons will seem question-begging to the other. This deadlock is a familiar one, and is not resolved for us by the historical fact of Butler's victory over the deists. So the appeal to a holistic judgment of probability is more indecisive for us than for him.

We cannot credit Butler with seeing the way in which religious scepticism would develop after him. But the very circumspection with which he has constructed his case against the deists provides us with an argument that has direct bearing on the deadlock to which we seem to be reduced. It is, I think, his ultimate appeal in the *Analogy* to the reader who is unconvinced by his attempts to establish theoretical probabilities. It is the appeal to prudence.

5

Let us recall Butler's initial statement of intent:

> Thus much, at least, will be here found, not taken for granted, but proved, that any reasonable man, who will thoroughly consider the matter, may be as much assured, as he is of his own being, that it is not, however, so clear a case, that there is nothing in it. There is, I think, strong evidence of its truth; but it is certain no one can, upon principles of reason, be satisfied of the contrary. And the practical

consequence to be drawn from this is not attended to by everyone who is concerned in it. *(An, Advertisement)*

The ultimate appeal of the work is not to the great theoretical likelihood of Christianity's being true, though Butler is convinced of that, but to the practical consequence of admitting much less than this: that it is not clear that there is nothing in it; that, on the contrary, it has sufficient probability for us to act on its being true, even though we are not persuaded that it is more probably true than its competitors. Provided we can see that 'principles of reason' do not refute it (by showing it to be incoherent or at odds with historical evidence), and provided it has sufficient explanatory powers to teach us some truths about our world that would not be possible without it, we have a sufficient pragmatic case for assenting to it.

The reason why this is so is a reason that I earlier suggested might well be offered by the sceptic as a reason for declining to assent, namely the magnitude and importance of the claims Christianity makes. Butler utilises this consideration, much as Pascal had done before him, as a decisive factor in *favour* of assent:

> Nor should I dissuade any one from setting down, what he thought made for the contrary side. But then it is to be remembered, not in order to influence his judgment, but his practice, that a mistake on one side, may be, in its consequences, much more dangerous, than a mistake on the other . . . in deliberations concerning conduct, there is nothing which reason more requires to be taken into the account, than the importance of it. *(An* II vii 43/61)

It is not easy to be sure of Butler's exact position here, and it is important not to rush too readily into equating it with that of Pascal in the 'Wager' argument.[11] There are two areas of unclarity. The first is an unclarity over what evidential situation Butler thinks is enough to require a positive response on prudential grounds. Is it enough that there be no clear disproof of Christianity, so that mere compatibility with known evidence is sufficient, or is some positive probability required? If so, how much? The other area of unclarity concerns the response that prudence indicates. Is it only careful attention, as opposed to frivolous negation? Or does prudence require some degree of positive inclination to believe? Pascal is clear enough in the 'Wager' fragment: if the sceptic concedes that there is no more reason to declare that God does not exist than to declare that he does, that is enough for him to be *'embarqué'*, whether he sees it or not; and in such a situation, prudence requires him to acquire *belief*, by whatever means are necessary. These means include participation in religious practice and worship, said by Pascal to be a proven means of inducing the belief that it expresses for others.

But Butler is not as unequivocal. There is no doubt that he sees the importance of Christianity to be something that follows from what it tells us about man's need for salvation and the way it is to be attained, just as Pascal does. In the face of this, inattention is patently irrational, since it would bring down ultimate punishment if Christianity is true. (See *An* II i, *passim*.) But there are places where he contents himself with saying such things as

Christianity being supposed either true or credible, it is unspeakable irreverence, and really the most presumptuous rashness, to treat it as a light matter. (*An* II i 19/25)

But treating it seriously is a long way from assenting to it. I think the bridge between them, for Butler, is to be found in a passage like this, taken from his Charge to the Clergy of Durham, of 1751:

Were the evidence of religion no more than doubtful, then it ought not to be concluded false any more than true, nor denied any more than affirmed; for suspense would be the reasonable state of mind with regard to it. And then it ought in all reason, considering its infinite importance, to have nearly the same influence upon practice, as if it were thoroughly believed. For would it not be madness for a man to forsake a safe road, and prefer it to one in which he acknowledges there is an even chance he should lose his life, though there were an even chance likewise of his getting safe through it? (Charge at Durham, 4/6)

Here Butler says, differently from Pascal, that if we are at a point where theoretical suspense is the only reasonable outcome, we ought still to *act* as though Christianity is true. This passage has to be put beside his comments about probability in the Introduction to the *Analogy* (especially 4/6) where he stresses, as we have seen, how life may force us to act on an assumption which we see to be less probable than its competitors, because of the risks we run if we ignore it.

Without denying the untidiness of the texts on this important question, I think it is fair to summarise Butler's position as follows. The importance of the claims of Christianity is so great that it is prudentially foolish to ignore them unless they are disproved. If they are not disproved, and a serious examination of them shows them to have even a low degree of probability, this is prudentially sufficient to prove that we should act upon them. This demands an element of positive probability that Pascal seems not to require; but, on the other hand, it allows Butler's prudential case to proceed even where the probability of an incompatible theory, such as atheism, is thought to be greater. (Pascal's argument would not proceed at this point.)

But what is involved in *acting on* the claims of Christianity? Does this include trying, somehow, to *believe* them, when the evidence is so far from conclusive? Butler never says anything like this. What he does say, over and over, is that religion is a *practical* matter, not a theoretical one. 'Religion consists in submission and resignation to the divine will' (*S* xv 9/8). Religion is something we *practise*. On the surface, this suggests that Butler is telling us that the importance of the claims of Christianity is such that we should *do* what Christianity tells us to do, even though it only has minimal probability to us theoretically. And this seems to entail practical conformity without belief.

Here again, Butler is less than clear, even to himself. But it is easy to see that his views imply something more than mere conformity. I shall try to construct a position that seems to me to be close to his real intent, and conclude with a response to it.

Beginning on the practical side, it is important to remember that, for Butler, the special practical demands of religion consist merely in an expansion of those included in secular virtue. It is *virtue* that is demanded by the moral deity whose government he tries to establish by argument in Part I of the *Analogy*. Virtue is a state of habitual and regular performance of those actions which conscience tells us are right. Conscience is a natural endowment which identifies for us what God wants us to do. The special (or 'positive') duties of revealed religion, such as those of worship, fall into two categories: those which our unaided conscience would show us to be obligatory as soon as we had independently concluded that God had done those things for us which the Christian revelation tells us about, and those which are to be done merely because God commands them. In the former class come the obligations to give thanks and ask forgiveness; in the latter class come sacramental practices. But even the latter are binding upon us because of our manifest moral duty to obey a God who has saved us in the way Christianity proclaims.[12] We do not need revelation to show us our normal moral duties; nor do we need it to show us any more than the facts from which our conscience can infer our special religious duties. But just as we may need to see that self-love points the same way as conscience to help us to follow conscience when it is not enough to move us alone, so prudence can help us see that we are wisest to perform the religious duties Christianity identifies, even if we are not as sure as we would like to be that Christianity is true.

As a man of his time, Butler is much more concerned with the moral aspects of religion than with its doctrinal features, or with private forms of spirituality. So we can expect him to be less sensitive than he might be about the gap that exists between doing those deeds that religion requires and having the faith. But a problem can be raised in his own terms, in the language of the inner and outer obligations of religion. If religion consists in submission and resignation to the divine will, this must be more than doing what the divine will commands through our conscience. For, given Butler's views about the autonomy of conscience, that is something we can do without thinking of God at all. But to be *resigned* to God's will, to *submit* to God's will, is more than doing it, even from a sense of duty. It is doing God's will *as* God's will: recognising that the commands one follows, however mediated through conscience, come ultimately from God. It therefore entails having those very beliefs about God and his dealings with oneself that have to be true if the commands of conscience can really be the commands of God. So his view of what it is to act on the claims of Christianity requires, in the end, that one believes those claims.

But one would not have to *start off* by believing them, only by acknowledging they have some chance of being true – as long as one hoped or intended that performing the duties commanded might, as it became habitual, positively affect the degree of one's belief. It naturally helps if the parallel scrutiny of the historical evidence turns up more and better grounds for assent; but that cannot be guaranteed. Butler's position does, in the end, point the same way that Pascal's does – to a path of conformity that is intended to issue in faith.

When discussing moral probation in Part I, Chapter v, Butler considers an imaginary objection to his hypothesis that we live under divine moral discipline. The objection is that attention to rewards and punishments cannot produce *virtue*, only 'materially virtuous' behaviour, motivated by self-love. His response is interesting for our present purpose.[13] He says, in effect, that regular materially virtuous conduct, however begun, produces real virtues. He also deprecates 'this great nicety' of deploring hope and fear as religious motives. The best way to make these responses compatible is to say that we should not be too fussy about hope and fear as motives for bringing about religious conduct, because a regular practice of such conduct will generate the genuine virtues religion requires. Applied to our present question, it does not seem to me fanciful to suppose that Butler would say the same thing about the practice of special religious duties: that, begun out of proper prudence, they may well lead to a greater degree of belief in the doctrines that justify them.

If this is a correct understanding of where Butler's practical apologetic leads, an adequate assessment of it requires examination of the nature of belief and the ethics of it. Such an examination is out of the question here. I would offer the following comments in its absence. There seems to be a tension between Butler's obvious integrity as a thinker who wishes to make proper allowance for every aspect of a complex problem, and his anxiety as a religious spokesman to commend a course that will orient his readers towards salvation. The question is how far what he recommends to them involves him in direct conflict with his intellectual integrity. There are three possible situations in which an inquirer might find himself that could generate Butler's recommendations. I suggest that only in one of them would this inconsistency actually result.

There is, first, the situation in which the inquirer considers that the objections to Christianity have adequate answers, but thinks that there is no more reason to think it true than to think it false, and none of its competitors seems to him to more likely to be true than it does. The theoretical situation is one in which, as Pascal put it, reason can decide nothing. In such a case, theoretical considerations can, with integrity, be put aside in favour of practical and prudential ones, since, *ex hypothesi*, these latter have the field to themselves. There is no inconsistency here.

There is, secondly, the situation in which the inquirer, while conceding that the objections to Christianity have answers, still feels that one or more of the alternatives to it have a significant degree of probability, though in every case this is less than the probability he ascribes to Christianity. Such an inquirer could follow Butler's practical recommendation without loss of integrity, for he already has stronger positive reasons to accept Christianity than not, and can proceed without disregarding the intellectual claims of its competitors. The urgency of practical decision can well, in a case like this, supersede the reasons for indefinite hesitation that can come from the existence of alternatives.

The third case is the one in which the claims of Christianity are seen to be of great importance, and to have a non-negligible degree of probability; but this probability is judged to be less than that of at least one of the possible alternatives to it. Butler would think of this case as analogous to a secular situation in which we judged it prudent to proceed on a less probable assumption rather than a more probable one, because of the magnitude of the risks involved in being mistaken. Butler's prescription here would seem to involve the inquirer in following religious practices whose intent, for him, would have to be the replacement of a belief he has now with a contrary one. For he cannot judge that system S^1 is more probable than system S^2 without being more inclined to believe S^1 than S^2; and in this situation, the adoption of practices intended to reverse this balance represents a deliberate substitution of non-intellectual devices for changing one's beliefs for the intellectual procedures which have (given that he is an honest inquirer) formed them hitherto. In this instance, then, Butler's prescription would represent the sacrifice of the intellectual integrity which he is clearly almost as anxious to substitute for his opponents' heedlessness as he is to direct them towards salvation. This objection vanishes, however, if all that one recommends to a person in this situation is what Butler confines himself to when he is most careful, namely that he bear the importance of Christianity constantly in mind, and continue to *consider* it carefully even when feeling more inclined to believe something else.

In his more positive moods, Butler clearly thinks that the most cautious inquirer can never be worse off than in the second of the situations described above. But he is wrong about this. I think, however, that his prescription is indeed the path of prudence in that situation, and in the first; and that the constant awareness of possible risk is the proper prudential course in the third.

6

I conclude my examination of Butler's religious apologetic with a historical note. I have written throughout as though the task for us in assessing Butler is that of disentangling his arguments from their context in the deistic controversy, since deism itself is long since dead. Although this would be the judgment of most philosophers, I am reminded that in this respect the theological situation is not quite the same. In a book shortly to appear at the time of my writing this,[14] D.W. Brown examines the work of some contemporary Christian theologians who wish, for various reasons, to re-present Christianity without the interventionist view of God, and in consequence without the doctrines of Incarnation and Trinity that presuppose it. He points out that their views are very close to those of the deists whom Butler criticised, and claims that in arguing that interventionist theism is more probable than mere deism, Butler is making a case that applies with undiminished force against them also. He also recognises that the reasons that would prompt anyone to prefer deism to theism should lead them in consistency to atheism or agnosticism. I cannot enter this controversy, and must say that I do not see the neo-deism of such theologians as an option that can exert much appeal to those who begin their reflections outside the Christian tradition altogether. Here also I remain convinced that the intellectual situation I have presupposed is the one in which most potential students of Butler today would find themselves. But it is always pleasing to find one's subject relevant to other debates, even if this means that his influence has been less than it should have been.

Notes

Complete publication information on all works mentioned in these notes will be found in the Bibliography.

Introduction Butler's Life, Personality, and Objectives

1 My main biographical source is Thomas Bartlett, *Memoirs of the Life, Character and Writings of Joseph Butler*. In spite of its gross padding, it contains the fullest information available. The best short biographical sketch is in Austin Duncan-Jones, *Butler's Moral Philosophy*.
2 Letter 7 of the Butler-Clarke correspondence, pp. 331–4 in Bernard's edition of the *Sermons*.
3 The splendid letter to Newcastle is reprinted in Gladstone's edition of the *Sermons*, pp. 364–5.
4 Bartlett, *op. cit.*, p. 76–7.
5 See Sermons II and VI of the 'Six Sermons Preached upon Public Occasions' (pp. 216–29 and 269–83 in Bernard's edition of the *Sermons*).
6 Bartlett, *op. cit.*, p. 231.
7 See the quotation from Sermon xv in Chapter IV, p. 93 below.
8 This is inaccurate, quite apart from its implications for our estimate of Butler. See J. C. A. Gaskin, 'Hume's Attenuated Deism', and D. W. Brown, *The Divine Trinity*.

I Moral Conduct and Human Nature

1 This, and the references to abstract argument in the Preface to the *Sermons*, are allusions primarily to the work of Samuel Clarke. See particularly his *Discourse Concerning the Unchangeable Obligations of Natural Religion*. The point is discussed further in section 4 of Chapter III below.
2 Sermons i,ii,iii, and xi. It cannot be emphasised too much, however, that it is important to augment the key arguments stated there with Butler's many relevant observations in other places.
3 See below, Chapter IV.

4 Note here the choice of text from Romans that Butler preaches from in Sermons ii and iii.

5 See below, Chapter IV, especially section 4.

6 There is a close connection between the argument of the *Sermons* and that of Chapters ii–v of Part I of the *Analogy*; see below, Chapter V.

7 See T. A. Roberts, *The Concept of Benevolence*, p. 33.

8 That is, it is 'adapted to' them more than to anything else.

9 See, for example, *An* I v 18/34.

10 See Diss II 6/8 and *An* I v 13/24 footnote.

11 I leave aside the possibility of a wholly virtuous being living also in an environment that presents no temptations, and being immune to pain. Some interpretations of the Fall doctrine ascribe the ubiquity of temptation, and the fact of physical evil, to the first wrong human choice. But there is no reason to suppose Butler holds either.

12 See below, Chapter III.

13 See below, Chapter V.

14 In *S* i 11/11 he speaks of 'dispositions and principles within', and in *S* ii 2/4 of 'principles, propensions, instincts'.

15 There are good treatments of Butler's psychological terminology in Austin Duncan-Jones, *Butler's Moral Philosophy*, Chapter 2, and in T. A. Roberts, *The Concept of Benevolence*, pp. 34–7.

16 Obviously when the indulgence of a passion is disproportionate, it is unnatural. When we indulge it in a way that is consistent with our nature, this will be innocent. See *S* ix 9/8.

17 Compare *S* Pr 42/37 and *S* xi 5/3.

18 See Duncan-Jones, *op. cit.*, pp. 48–59.

19 See *An* I v.

20 *S* viii 3/4.

21 David Hume, *A Treatise of Human Nature*, p. 417.

22 *S* xi 9/7.

23 Duncan-Jones, *op. cit.*, pp. 48–51.

24 He says there is no such thing as self-hatred, either.

25 Roberts, *op. cit.*, p. 52.

26 On this, see particularly *S* xiii 15/10.

27 See, for example, 9/9 in the same Sermon.

28 See particularly Diss II 2–3/4–5.

29 See Béla Szabados, 'Butler on Corrupt Conscience'.

30 There is one place where he almost does, namely Pr 42/37. He seems clearly to have conscience in mind, although it is not named. But he speaks of 'such principle or affection', and says that virtue, as that which it 'tends towards', is to be pursued for itself, which is 'to say no more of it, than may be said of the object of every natural affection whatever'. I do not think this *quite* adds up to classing conscience as an affection, though it is very near to it.

II   The Reality of Benevolence

1 *An* I vi 12/16 footnote, and *An* II viii 11/24.

2 Thomas Hobbes, *Human Nature*, in *The English Works of Thomas Hobbes*, ed. Molesworth, Vol. IV, p. 49.

3 Butler's keen awareness of how mixed human motives are can be seen from a memorandum on this same theme, where he acknowledges there is 'more of truth in it (Hobbes's theory) than appears at first sight'. See Fragment 8 on p. 306 of Bernard's edition of the *Sermons*, p.,356 of Gladstone's.

4 Hobbes, *op. cit.*, p. 44.

5 Butler's language is not as unambiguously psychological as this. I am paying him the compliment of reading him the way he should have read Hobbes.

6 Austin Duncan-Jones, *Butler's Moral Philosophy*, p. 64.

7 *Ibid.*, p. 106.

8 Hobbes, *op. cit.*, Chapter VII (pp. 31–4).

9 John Stuart Mill, *Utilitarianism*, especially Chapter IV.

10 See above, Chapter I, section 5.

11 Terence Penelhum, 'Pleasure and Falsity', and David L. Perry, *The Concept of Pleasure*.

12 Mill, *op. cit.*, Chapter III.

13 G. E. M. Anscombe, 'On the Grammar of "Enjoy".'

14 See the essay 'Pleasure' in Gilbert Ryle, *Dilemmas*, pp. 54–67. For comments on Ryle's views, see Terence Penelhum, 'The Logic of Pleasure'.

15 David Hume, *A Treatise of Human Nature*, p. 481.

16 *S* xi 20/21. See below, Chapter III, section 4.

17 See Anders Nygren, *Agape and Eros*.

III   The Case for Virtue

1 This interpretation is confirmed by the choice of biblical text that Butler preaches from in Sermons ii and iii, where the doctrines of superior principles, and of the supremacy of conscience, are developed.

2 It has just recently been challenged. See Derek Parfit, *Reasons and Persons*, and 'Rationality and Time'.

3 *S* ii 14/19. Quoted in Chapter I, section 4, above.

4 Nicholas L. Sturgeon, 'Nature and Conscience in Butler's Ethics'.

5 It is interesting here to compare Hume, who speaks of family affection as one of our 'natural obligations', while at the same time holding that moral approval is not the source of it. See *A Treatise of Human Nature*, p. 478.

6 Sturgeon, *op. cit.*, p. 322.

7 *Ibid.*, pp. 324–7.

8 See above, Chapter I, section 6.

9 Sturgeon, *op. cit.*, pp. 322–3.

10 Even this may not be decisive, however, For although Butler says that what conscience does is to approve or disapprove, he nowhere says that *only* conscience does these things. We do not confine these terms to *moral* attitudes, though they are the standard sources of their use.

11 One of Butler's aims is to make us less willing to excuse those numerous

actions which are contrary to duty but supposedly 'natural' for people like us. They are only natural in the sense that beings like us are inclined to want to do them. Naturalness in this sense is not something we should regard as counterbalancing the disapproval of conscience.

12 For comment on the other major passage Sturgeon cites, viz. Diss II 5/7, see below.

13 See the *Oxford English Dictionary* entry on 'conscience'.

14 Sturgeon, *op. cit.*, p. 324.

15 See above, Chapter I, section 3.

16 See C. D. Broad's essay 'Self and Others'.

17 This view is ascribed to the Butler of the *Sermons*, but not to the Butler of the Dissertation, by T. H. McPherson, in 'The Development of Bishop Butler's Ethics'.

18 See C. D. Broad, *Five Types of Ethical Theory*, pp. 79–80, A. E. Taylor, 'Some Features of Butler's Ethics', and Austin Duncan-Jones, *Butler's Moral Philosophy*, pp. 113–15.

19 See above, Chapter I, section 4.

20 Sturgeon, *op. cit.*, pp. 335–44.

21 See above, Chapter I, section 3.

22 Compare here the rather poignant unpublished Fragment no. 9, p. 307 of Bernard's edition of the *Sermons*, p. 357 in Gladstone's: 'Good men surely are not treated in this world as they deserve, yet 'tis seldom, very seldom their goodness which makes them disliked, even in cases where it may seem to be so: but 'tis some behaviour or other, which however excusable, perhaps infinitely overbalanced by their virtues, yet is offensive, possibly wrong; however such, it may be, as would pass off very well in a man of the world.'

23 H. A. Prichard, 'Does Moral Philosophy Rest on a Mistake?', p. 2.

24 See Anthony Kenny, 'Mental Health in Plato's Republic'.

25 Sermon x. See Béla Szabados, 'Butler on Corrupt Conscience'.

26 Unpublished Fragment no. 1, p. 305 in Bernard, p. 355 in Gladstone.

27 See also the note to *An* I vi 12/16.

28 Clarke, *Discourse*, Table of Contents.

29 *Ibid.*, p. 79.

30 Duncan-Jones, *op. cit.*, p. 116.

31 See above, Chapter I, section 2.

32 McPherson, *op. cit.* See also Alan R. White, 'Conscience and Self-Love in Butler's Sermons'.

IV The Nature of Butler's Apologetic

1 E. C. Mossner, *Bishop Butler and the Age of Reason*, p. 231.

2 *Ibid.*, p. 233.

3 See Alban Krailsheimer, *Pascal*. The 'Wager' fragment is no. 418 in the Lafuma ordering, followed by Krailsheimer in his translation of the *Pensées*.

4 This possibility is central to the recent argument of Richard Swinburne's *Faith and Reason*.

5 We should recall again that Butler wants to class prudence as moral obligation (Diss II 6–7/8–11).

6 Samuel Clarke, *A Demonstration of the Being and Attributes of God* (1705).
7 David Hume, *Dialogues Concerning Natural Religion*.
8 E. C. Mossner, 'The Enigma of Hume'.
9 For an extended treatment of fideism, see my *God and Skepticism*.
10 Pascal, *Pensées*, fragment 444.
11 *Ibid.*, fragment 449.
12 See *An* II vi 8/10 and viii 9/19; also below, Chapter VIII.
13 Pascal, *op. cit.*, fragment 691.
14 C. D. Broad, 'Bishop Butler as a Theologian'.
15 On the importance of this in Butler's natural theology, see Anders Jeffner, *Butler and Hume on Religion*.
16 Broad, *op. cit.*, pp. 205–7.
17 The classic statement of this point and its implications in Hume's 'Of a Particular Providence and Of a Future State', which is Section XI of his *Enquiry Concering Human Understanding*.
18 This classification, and Clarke's judgments on each group, are found on pp. 19–45 of the *Discourse*. On Butler's relation to deism, see also Leslie Stephen, *A History of English Thought in the Eighteenth Century*, E. C. Mossner, 'Deism', and S. A. Grave, 'Butler's "Analogy" '.
19 The arguments of Chapter i, which present post-mortem existence as a likely fact of nature, are addressed to all groups, and are even consistent with atheism, as Butler says himself.
20 I have attempted an account of Aquinas's doctrine of faith in 'The Analysis of Faith in St. Thomas Aquinas'.
21 If Mossner were correct in identifying Cleanthes with Butler, then Hume may be accurate in having him present a theistic argument based on observation, even though Butler never himself attempted a proof of God. But he would be mistaken in having Cleanthes, rather than Philo, state the case against Demea's 'cosmological' argument in Part IX.
22 The likeness to Pascal is noticeable again here. Pascal says that deism is 'almost as remote from the Christian religion as atheism, its complete opposite' (*Pensées*, fragment 449). He says this because the deists are unable to accept God's hiddenness, and are forced to sustain their belief in God by underestimating the world's evils.
23 For a defence of the view that this position is Hume's own, see J. C. A. Gaskin, 'Hume's Attenuated Deism'. I have tried to grapple with the vexed question of Hume's intentions in the *Dialogues* in my 'Hume's Skepticism and the *Dialogues*' and 'Natural Belief and Religious Belief in Hume's Philosophy'.
24 David Hume, *Dialogues Concerning Natural Religion*, Parts X and XI.
25 Penelhum, *God and Skepticism*, Chapters 6 and 7.

V *Identity and the Future Life*

1 C. D. Broad, 'Bishop Butler as a Theologian', p. 208.
2 Henry Hughes, *A Critical Examination of Butler's 'Analogy'*, pp. 33f.
3 Terence Penelhum, *Survival and Disembodied Existence*.
4 Broad, *op. cit.*, p. 309.

5 See Oscar Cullmann, *Immortality of the Soul or Resurrection of the Dead?*.

6 For some examples of the literature on self-identity and the puzzle-cases, see John Perry (ed.), *Personal Identity*, and Godfrey Vesey, *Personal Identity*. On the question of what it is for a body to be *my* body, see J. Harrison, 'The Embodiment of Mind, or What Use is Having a Body?', and Richard Swinburne, *The Coherence of Theism*, Chapter 7.

7 See, for example, C. J. Ducasse, *A Critical Examination of the Belief in a Life After Death*, Part V, and I. Stevenson, *Twenty Cases Suggestive of Reincarnation*.

8 See R. T. Herbert, *Paradox and Identity in Theology*, Chapter 6.

9 On the cumulative character of Butler's argument in the *Analogy*, see below, Chapter VII, section 4. For a recent attempt to present a similar cumulative case for religious belief, see Basil Mitchell, *The Justification of Religious Belief*.

10 Thomas Reid, *Essays on the Intellectual Powers of Man*, Essay III, Chapter VI; Antony Flew, 'Locke and the Problem of Personal Identity'; John Locke, *Essay Concerning Human Understanding*, Book II, Chapter 27.

11 H. P. Grice, 'Personal Identity'; David Wiggins, *Sameness and Substance*, Chapter 6; John Perry, 'Personal Identity, Memory and the Problem of Circularity' (in his *Personal Identity*).

12 Sydney Shoemaker, 'Persons and Their Pasts'; Derek Parfit, 'Personal Identity'.

13 Penelhum, *op. cit.*, Chapters 7 and 8.

14 David Wiggins, *Identity and Spatio-Temporal Continuity*, p. 1.

15 Locke, *op. cit.*, p. 443.

16 See Hume, *A Treatise of Human Nature*, Book I, Part IV, Section VI. Actually Hume says that since personal identity is *not* strict, it is 'fictitious'.

17 See Swinburne, *op. cit.*, Chapter 7.

18 David Perry, *Personal Identity*, introduction.

19 John Locke, *Essay Concerning Human Understanding*, Book II, Chapter 23.

20 Swinburne, *op. cit.*, Chapter 7.

21 Richard Swinburne, *The Coherence of Theism*, p. 123.

22 Penelhum, *op. cit.*, Chapter 9.

23 R. T. Herbert, *op. cit.*, Chapter 6.

24 I owe this recognition of the difference between 'concept' and 'conception' to Robert Ware.

VI Divine Government and Human Probation

1 The argument that prudence is a moral virtue is made later, in Diss II 6–7/8–11.

2 See, most importantly, John Hick, *Evil and the God of Love*.

3 Henry Hughes, *A Critical Examination of Butler's 'Analogy'*. Chapter 4.

4 John Hick, *Death and Eternal Life*, p. 206.

VII   Revelation and Miracle

1 Pascal, *Pensées*, fragment 131.
2 Matthew Tindal, *Christianity as Old as the Creation*, pp. 105f.
3 'Of Miracles' is Section X of Hume's *Enquiry Concerning Human Understanding*. It has prompted endless debate. See C. D. Broad, 'Hume's Theory of the Credibility of Miracles'; Antony Flew, *Hume's Philosophy of Belief*, Chapter VII, Richard Swinburne, *The Concept of Miracle*. The views I outline here are developed in more detail in Chapter 19 of my *Religion and Rationality*.
4 But see II ii 5/6 on 'secret' or invisible miracles.
5 Another passage where Butler is reasonably explicit about his understanding of miracles as contrary to natural law is *An* II iv 4/5. Here he makes his suggestion that miracles might be due to 'laws of wisdom', and says that 'there might be wise and good reasons, that miraculous interventions should be by general laws; and that these laws should not be broken in upon; or deviated from, by other miracles'. This seems to mean that miracles deviate from laws of nature, though they conform to *supernatural* laws.
6 John Stuart Mill, *A System of Logic*, Vol. II p. 171.
7 Henry Hughes, *A Critical Examination of Butler's 'Analogy'*, p. 149.
8 See also *An* I vii 8/18–19.
9 See Ninian Smart, *Philosophers and Religious Truth*, Chapter 2.
10 For a highly critical account of the Church's treatment of these testimonies, see D. J. West, *Eleven Lourdes Miracles*.
11 *An* II vii 20–7/22–9.
12 The best discussion of Butler's treatment of this topic is Hughes, *op. cit.*, Chapter 10.

VIII   The Ignorance of Man

1 *An* I vii, II iii, II iv, and II vi.
2 Terence Penelhum, *God and Skepticism*, Chapters 5 and 7.
3 Pascal, *Pensées*, fragment 444.
4 John Hick, *Faith and Knowledge*, p. 127.
5 Pascal is at his most eloquent on this theme. See fragment 427.
6 Penelhum, *op. cit.*, pp. 43–52.
7 *Ibid.*, Chapter 7.
8 Henry Hughes, *A Critical Examination of Butler's 'Analogy'*, Chapter 7.
9 Pascal, *op. cit.*, fragment 449.
10 David Hume, *Dialogues Concerning Natural Religion*, Part X.
11 Pascal, *op. cit.*, fragment 418.
12 See *An* II i, especially 14–25/16–30.
13 *An* I v 19/36; quoted in Chapter I, section 4, above.
14 D.W. Brown, *The Divine Trinity*.

Bibliography

Anonymous, 'Butler's Analogy: its Strength and Weakness', *Westminster Review*, vol. 46, 1874, pp. 1–24.

Anscombe, G. E. M. 'On the Grammar of "Enjoy" ', *Journal of Philosophy*, vol. 64, 1967, pp. 607–14.

Arnold, Matthew. 'Bishop Butler and the Zeit-Geist', in Matthew Arnold, *Essays Religious and Mixed*, ed. R. H. Super, Ann Arbor, University of Michigan Press, 1972, pp. 11–62.

Babolin, Albino. *Joseph Butler*, Padova, Editrice 'La Garangola', 1973.

Baker, Albert E. *Bishop Butler*, London SPCK, 1923.

Bartlett, Thomas. *Memoirs of the Life, Character and Writings of Joseph Butler*, London, John W. Parker, 1839.

Bernard, J. H. 'The Predecessors of Bishop Butler', *Hermathena*, vol. 9, 1896, pp. 75–84.

Broad, C. D. 'Hume's Theory of the Credibility of Miracles', *Proceedings of the Aristotelian Society*, New Series, vol. 17, 1916–17, pp. 77–94.

Broad, C. D. *Five Types of Ethical Theory*, London, Routledge & Kegan Paul, 1930.

Broad, C. D. 'Egoism as a Theory of Human Motives', in C. D. Broad, *Ethics and the History of Philosophy*, London, Routledge & Kegan Paul, 1952, pp. 218–231.

Broad, C. D. 'Bishop Butler as a Theologian', in C. D. Broad, *Religion, Philosophy, and Psychical Research*, London, Routledge & Kegan Paul, 1953, pp. 202–219.

Broad, C. D. 'Self and Others', in D. Cheney (ed.), *Broad's Critical Essays in Moral Philosophy*, London, Allen & Unwin, 1971, pp. 262–82.

Brown, D. W. *The Divine Trinity*, London, Duckworth, 1984.

Butler, Joseph. *The Works of Bishop Butler*, ed. W. E. Gladstone, 2 vols, Oxford, Clarendon Press, 1897.

Butler, Joseph. *The Works of Bishop Butler*, ed. J. H. Bernard, 2 vols, London, Macmillan, 1900.

Clarke, Samuel. *A Demonstration of the Being and Attributes of God* (1705), and *Discourse Concerning the Unchangeable Obligations of Natural Religion*

(1706), Stuttgart-Bad Canstatt, Friedrich Fromman Verlag, 1964 (facsimile reprint).

Cullmann, Oscar. *Immortality of the Soul or Resurrection of the Dead?*, London, Epworth, 1958.

Ducasse, C. J. *A Critical Examination of the Belief in a Life after Death*, Springfield, Charles C. Thomas, 1961.

Duncan-Jones, Austin. *Butler's Moral Philosophy*, Harmondsworth, Penguin, 1952.

Flew, Antony. 'Locke and the Problems of Personal Identity', *Philosophy*, vol. 26, 1951, pp. 53–68.

Flew, Antony. *Hume's Philosophy of Belief*, London, Routledge & Kegan Paul, 1961.

Gaskin, J. C. A. 'Hume's Attenuated Deism', *Archiv für Geschichte der Philosophie*, vol. 63, 1983, pp. 160–73.

Gladstone, W. E. *Studies Subsidiary to the Works of Bishop Butler*, Oxford, Clarendon Press, 1896.

Grave, S. A. 'Butler's "Analogy",' *Cambridge Journal*, vol. 6, 1952–53, pp. 169–80.

Grice, H. P. 'Personal Identity', *Mind*, vol. 50, 1941, pp. 330–50.

Harrison, J. 'The Embodiment of Mind, or What Use is Having a Body?', *Proceedings of the Aristotelian Society*, vol. 74, 1973–74, pp.33–55.

Herbert, R. T. *Paradox and Identity in Theology*, Ithaca, Cornell University Press, 1979.

Hick, John. *Faith and Knowledge*, 2nd edn, Ithaca, Cornell University Press, 1966.

Hick, John. *Evil and the God Of Love*, Macmillan, 1966.

Hick, John. *Death and Eternal Life*, London, Collins, 1976.

Hobbes, Thomas. *The English Works*, vol. 4, ed. Sir William Molesworth, London, Bohn, 1840, repr. Scientia Aalen 1962.

Hudson, W. D. *Ethical Intuitionism*, London, Macmillan, 1967.

Hughes, Henry. *A Critical Examination of Butler's 'Analogy'*, London, Kegan Paul, Trench, Trubner, 1898.

Hume, David. *The Natural History of Religion*, ed. H. E. Root, Stanford University Press, 1957.

Hume, David. *Enquiries*, ed. L. A. Selby-Bigge, 2nd edn, Oxford, Clarendon Press, 1966.

Hume, David. *A Treatise of Human Nature*, ed. L. A. Selby-Bigge, Oxford, Clarendon Press, 1968.

Hume, David. *Dialogues Concerning Natural Religion*, ed. Norman Kemp Smith, Indianapolis, Bobbs Merrill, 1980.

Jeffner, Anders. *Butler and Hume on Religion*, Stockholm, Diakonistyrelsens Bokforlag, 1966.

Kenny, Anthony. 'Mental Health in Plato's Republic', in A. Kenny, *The Anatomy of the Soul*, Oxford, Blackwell, 1973, pp. 1–27.

Kleinig, John. 'Butler in a Cool Hour', *Journal of the History of Philosophy*, vol. 7, 1969, pp. 399–411.

Krailsheimer, Alban. *Pascal*, Oxford University Press, 1980.

Locke, John. *Essay Concerning Human Understanding*, ed. A. C. Fraser, 2 vols, New York, Dover Publications, 1959.

McPherson, T. H. 'The Development of Bishop Butler's Ethics', *Philosophy*, vol. 23, 1948, pp. 317–31, and vol. 24, 1949, pp. 3–22.

Mill, John Stuart, *A System of Logic*, 7th edn, 2 vols, London, Longmans, 1868.

Mill, John Stuart, *Utilitarianism*, 5th edn, London, Longmans, 1874.

Mitchell, Basil. *The Justification of Religious Belief*, London, Macmillan, 1873.

Mossner, E. C. 'The Enigma of Hume', *Mind*, vol. 45, 1936, pp. 334–49.

Mossner, E. C. 'Deism', in Paul Edwards (ed.), *The Encyclopedia of Philosophy*, New York, Macmillan and Free Press, 1967, vol. 2, pp. 326–36.

Mossner, E. C. *Bishop Butler and the Age of Reason*, New York, B. Blom, 1971.

Nygren, Anders. *Agape and Eros*, trans. Philip S. Watson, New York, Harper & Row, 1969.

Parfit, Derek. 'Personal Identity', *Philosophical Review*, vol. 80, 1971, pp. 3–27.

Parfit, Derek. 'Rationality and Time', *Proceedings of the Aristotelian Society*, New Series, vol. 84, 1984, pp. 47–82.

Parfit, Derek. *Reasons and Persons*, Oxford University Press, 1984.

Pascal, Blaise. *Pensées*, trans. A. J. Krailsheimer, Harmondsworth, Penguin, 1979.

Penelhum, Terence. 'The Logic of Pleasure', *Philosophy and Phenomenological Research*, vol. 17, 1955, pp. 488–503.

Penelhum, Terence. 'Pleasure and Falsity', *American Philosophical Quarterly*, vol. 1, 1964, pp. 81–91.

Penelhum, Terence. *Religion and Rationality*, New York, Random House, 1971.

Penelhum, Terence. 'The Analysis of Faith in St. Thomas Aquinas', *Religious Studies*, vol. 13, 1977, pp. 133–54.

Penelhum, Terence. 'Hume's Skepticism and the *Dialogues*', in D. Norton, N. Capaldi, W. Robison (eds), *McGill Hume Studies*, San Diego, Austin Hill Press, 1979, pp. 253–78.

Penelhum, Terence. *Survival and Disembodied Existence*, London, Routledge & Kegan Paul, 1980.

Penelhum, Terence. 'Natural Belief and Religious Belief in Hume's Philosophy', *Philosophical Quarterly*, vol. 33, 1983, pp. 166–81.

Penelhum, Terence. *God and Skepticism*, Dordrecht, Reidel, 1983.

Perry, David L. *The Concept of Pleasure*, The Hague, Mouton, 1967.

Perry, John (ed.), *Personal Identity*, Berkeley, University of California Press, 1975.

Perry, John. 'Personal Identity, Memory, and the Problem of Circularity', in John Perry (ed.), *Personal Identity*, Berkeley, University of California Press, 1975, pp. 135–55.

Prichard, H. A. 'Does Moral Philosophy Rest on a Mistake?', in H. A. Prichard, *Moral Obligation*, Oxford, Clarendon Press, 1949, pp. 1–17.

Ramsey, Ian. 'Joseph Butler, 1692–1752: Some Features of his Life and Thought', Friends of Dr Williams Library 23rd Lecture, 1969, Dr Williams' Trust.

Rashdall, Hastings. 'Bishop Butler', *Modern Churchman*, vol. 16, 1927, pp. 678–94.

Reid, Thomas. *Essays on the Intellectual Powers of Man*, with int. by Baruch Brody, Cambridge, Mass., MIT Press, 1969.

Roberts, T. A. *The Concept of Benevolence*, London, Macmillan, 1973.

Rorty, Amélie Oksenberg. 'Butler on Benevolence and Conscience', *Philosophy*, vol. 53, 1978, pp. 171–84.

Rurak, James. 'Butler's "Analogy": a Still Interesting Synthesis of Reason and Revelation', *Anglican Theological Review*, vol. 62, 1980, pp. 365–81.

Ryle, Gilbert. *Dilemmas*, Cambridge University Press, 1962.

Shiner, Roger. 'Butler's Theory of Moral Judgment' in S. C. Brown (ed.), *Philosophers of the Enlightenment*, Hassocks, Sussex, Harvester Press, 1979, pp. 199–225.

Shoemaker, Sydney. 'Persons and Their Pasts', *American Philosophical Quarterly*, vol. 7, 1970, pp. 269–85.

Smart, Ninian. *Philosophers and Religious Truth*, 2nd edn, London, SCM, 1969.

Spooner, W. A. *Bishop Butler*, London, Methuen, 1901.

Stephen, Leslie. *A History of English Thought in the Eighteenth Century*, 3rd edn, 2 vols, London, Smith & Elder, 1902.

Stevenson, Ian. *Twenty Cases Suggestive of Reincarnation*, New York, American Society for Psychical Research, 1966.

Sturgeon, Nicholas L. 'Nature and Conscience in Butler's Ethics', *Philosophical Review*, vol. 85, 1976, pp. 316–56.

Swinburne, Richard. *The Concept of Miracle*, London, Macmillan, 1970.

Swinburne, Richard. *The Coherence of Theism*, Oxford, Clarendon Press, 1977.

Swinburne, Richard. *Faith and Reason*, Oxford, Clarendon Press, 1981.

Szabados, Béla. 'Butler on Corrupt Conscience', *Journal of the History of Philosophy*, vol. 14, 1976, pp. 462–9.

Taylor, A. E. 'Some Features of Butler's Ethics', *Mind*, vol. 35, 1926, pp. 273–300.

Tindal, Matthew. *Christianity as Old as the Creation* (1730), New York, Garland Publishers, 1978.

Vesey, Godfrey. *Personal Identity*, London, Macmillan, 1974.

West, D. J. *Eleven Lourdes Miracles*, London, Duckworth, 1957.

White, Alan R. 'Conscience and Self-Love in Butler's Sermons', *Philosophy*, vol. 27, 1952, pp. 329–44.

Wiggins, David. *Identity and Spatio-Temporal Continuity*, Oxford, Blackwell, 1967.

Wiggins, David. *Sameness and Substance*. Oxford, Blackwell, 1980.

Index